WARRANT FOR GENOCIDE

WARRANT FOR GENOCIDE

The myth of the Jewish world-conspiracy
and the *Protocols of the Elders of Zion*

NORMAN COHN

HARPER & ROW, PUBLISHERS

NEW YORK AND EVANSTON

FIRST U.S. EDITION

LIBRARY OF CONGRESS CATALOG CARD NUMBER: 67-11324

Contents

Illustrations

between pages 144 and 145

To David Astor

Acknowledgements

THIS book would probably never have been written at all but
for David Astor, who for many years has been deeply concerned about the kind of aberration it describes. By enabling
me to leave university life for a time and devote myself wholly
to research and writing, he reduced to manageable proportions
a task that might otherwise have proved overwhelming.

Boris Nicolaevsky, who was a witness at the Berne trial
in 1934–35, and who died just after this book was completed,
put at my disposal not only valuable documents from his
archives but also his unique knowledge of revolutionary and
counter-revolutionary politics in tsarist Russia. The Rev. Dr
James Parkes and Dr Léon Poliakov gave me the benefit of
their years of research on the history of antisemitism and
offered a number of very useful criticisms and suggestions.
I was much helped, too, by having access to the Parkes
Library and to the fruits of Dr Parkes's own researches on the
Protocols.

Professor Francis Carsten, Professor John Higham, Professor Walter Laqueur, Professor George Mosse, and Professor
Leonard Schapiro brought their powerful equipment to bear
on various chapters, and between them saved me from many
errors. Miss Pearl King applied her rare combination of
psychoanalytical and sociological insight to the Conclusion,
and by her comments not only clarified but modified my own
ideas. If after all the efforts of these critics and guides the
book still shows errors of fact or judgement, the fault is mine
alone.

The staff of the Wiener Library coped with my many
requests with the efficiency and courtesy which users of that
admirable institution soon learn to take for granted; and Mr
C. C. Aronsfeld also guided me to much material that I could
easily have missed.

By appointing me to a fellowship, the Center for Advanced
Study in the Behavioral Sciences, Stanford, California,

provided me with an ideal setting in which to put the finishing touches to the book, including the opportunity of discussing various knotty points with some very stimulating and helpful colleagues.

My wife, having Russian as her native language, read all the Russian works for me. The patience which she brought to this task is appreciated all the more because of the distressing nature of much that she had to read. It was an indispensable contribution, and so was the criticism to which she submitted the entire manuscript.

I am glad of this opportunity of expressing my gratitude to all who have helped me in these various ways.

August 1966 N. C.

... quantum mortalia pectora caecae
noctis habent ...

How much blind night there is in the hearts
of men!

Ovid, *Metamorphoses*

Foreword

ONLY about a third of the civilians killed by the Nazis and their accomplices were Jews, but the Jews nevertheless hold a unique position among the victims of those terrible years. Other peoples were marked out for decimation, subjugation, and enslavement, and the civilian losses of some of these amounted to 11 per cent or 12 per cent of the total population. The Jews were marked out for extermination. They were not simply killed or worked to death – they were humiliated, hunted and tortured with an intensity of hatred which was reserved for them alone; while the killed amounted to well over half, probably to more than two-thirds of all European Jews.[1] Moreover, all this happened to people who did not constitute a belligerent nation or indeed a nation at all but lived scattered across Europe from the English Channel to the Volga, with very little in common to them all save their descent from adherents of the Jewish religion. How can this extraordinary phenomenon be explained?

Like a great many people I constantly asked myself this question while the extermination was taking place, but it was only after the end of the war that I began to feel my way towards what I am now convinced is the correct answer. In the winter of 1945, while awaiting demobilization in central Europe, I happened to have access to a large library of writings by Nazi and proto-Nazi ideologists and propagandists. Several months of reading, reinforced by contact with SS who were undergoing interrogation and investigation, left me with one pretty strong suspicion – that whereas the Russians and Poles and Yugoslavs were decimated in the name of racist theories which were less than a century old, the drive to exterminate the Jews sprang from demonological superstitions inherited from the Middle Ages.

[1] The exact number of Jews killed will never be known, but the best estimates agree in putting it between five and six million, not including those who died of hunger and disease in the ghettos.

The following ten years were spent in investigating popular medieval ideas about Satan and his earthly representatives, the final struggle between the angelic and the demonic hosts, the second coming and the millennium. Although this work was only partly connected with the Jews and their fate, by the time it was finished my original suspicion had turned into a certainty. As I see it, the deadliest kind of antisemitism, the kind that results in massacre and attempted genocide, has little to do with real conflicts of interest between living people, or even with racial prejudice as such. At its heart lies the belief that Jews – all Jews everywhere – form a conspiratorial body set on ruining and then dominating the rest of mankind. And this belief is simply a modernized, secularized version of the popular medieval view of Jews as a league of sorcerers employed by Satan for the spiritual and physical ruination of Christendom.[1]

By the time I returned to the starting-point of my inquiry the scene had changed out of all recognition. The Nazi movement and régime had been exhaustively investigated and the findings filled whole libraries – there were even special institutes devoted to the Nazi persecutions and massacres. Moreover, the history of antisemitism, which before the war had been the preserve of a couple of bold pioneers, was now attracting the attention of many scholars, and detailed studies of this or that aspect of the story were piling up. Yet one conspicuous gap remained: nobody had made a thorough study of the myth[2] of the Jewish world-conspiracy and the part played by that myth in recent history.

It is true that the supreme expression and vehicle of the myth of the Jewish world-conspiracy, the notorious forgery

[1] This is also the argument of J. Trachtenberg, *The Devil and the Jews*, New Haven, 1943.

[2] A couple of years ago a reviewer, I think in *The Times Literary Supplement*, urged that the word 'myth' should be banned for at least a decade, as it was rapidly losing all precise meaning. He had a point, but I can think of no other term so suited to the subject of this book. A myth can mean a false belief; it can mean an imaginative construction by which people try to interpret the world around them; and since Georges Sorel it can also mean a faith which gives people a sense of mission and stimulates them to action. Belief in a Jewish world-conspiracy has shown itself to be a myth in all these senses.

known as the *Protocols of the Elders of Zion,* has received quite a lot of attention. Between 1920, when it made its first appearance in western Europe, and 1942, when it was being exploited to some effect by Goebbels, it was the subject of a dozen critical studies in English, German, French, and Russian. Several of these books were works of scholarship; one, *L'Apocalypse de notre temps* by the late Henri Rollin, was an important piece of original research and would certainly have made its mark if its publication had not been overshadowed by the outbreak of the Second World War, and if the edition had not been seized and destroyed by the Germans the moment they reached Paris. Yet the fact remains that no proper study has ever been made of how, after the French Revolution, the myth of the Jewish world-conspiracy developed out of traditional demonology; how it inspired a whole series of forgeries, culminating in the *Protocols*; how the *Protocols* were used to justify the massacres of Jews during the Russian civil war; how they swept the world after the First World War; how they took possession of Hitler's mind and became the ideology of his most fanatical followers at home and abroad – and so helped to prepare the way for the near-extermination of European Jews.

It is high time that gap was filled. A generation ago Henri Rollin reckoned that the *Protocols of the Elders of Zion* was probably the most widely distributed book in the world after the Bible, and certainly the myth of the Jewish world-conspiracy was a potent factor in the shaping of world history. Very many people who were neither demented nor illiterate were convinced that everything that happened in the political, social, and economic fields – from minor diplomatic appointments to slumps, revolutions, and wars – was ordained by a secret organization of Jews. Today the whole story is already almost forgotten – so much so that it is quite rare, at least in Europe, to meet anyone under the age of forty who has even heard of those strange ideas. One is tempted to say 'a good thing too', but I think the temptation should be resisted. A great madness swept large parts of Europe and a good deal of the world beyond; nothing like it had been seen since the witch-mania which in the course of the sixteenth and seventeenth centuries destroyed perhaps a million women. It seems to me important to study that madness, to analyse the delusional ideas at its core and to understand, so far as possible, the precise nature of its appeal. That is why I decided, with some reluctance, to complete the job I began and abandoned just twenty years ago.

It is perhaps hard to accept that scholarly study, and all the time and energy which that implies, can appropriately be lavished on a ludicrous fantasy such as the *Protocols* or on obscure figures such as the hack novelist Hermann Goedsche, the cheap swindler Osman Bey, the half-crazy pseudo-mystic Sergey Nilus, and the rest. Yet it is a great mistake to suppose that the only writers who matter are those whom the educated in their saner moments can take seriously. There exists a subterranean world where pathological fantasies disguised as ideas are churned out by crooks and half-educated fanatics for the benefit of the ignorant and superstitious. There are times when this underworld emerges from the depths and suddenly fascinates, captures, and dominates multitudes of usually sane and responsible people, who thereupon take leave of sanity and responsibility. And it occasionally happens that this underworld becomes a political power and changes the course of history. It is an incontestable fact that the forgotten eccentrics described in the first half of this book built up the myth which, years later, the masters of a great European nation were to use as a warrant for genocide.

Not, of course, that myths operate in a vacuum. The myth of the Jewish world-conspiracy would have remained the monopoly of right-wing Russians and a few cranks in western Europe, and the *Protocols* would never have emerged from obscurity at all, if it had not been for the First World War and the Russian Revolution and their aftermath. And they would never have become the creed of a powerful government and an international movement if it had not been for the great slump and the utter disorientation it produced. On the other hand all these disasters together could never have produced an Auschwitz without the help of a myth which was designed to appeal to all the paranoid and destructive potentialities in human beings. I have tried to do justice also to those aspects – what one might call the sociological and the psychopathological aspects – of this extraordinary and terrible story.

The book ends in 1945, but that does not mean that the myth died then or that the *Protocols* went out of circulation. Though they are far less prominent than they were and are almost forgotten in the advanced countries of western Europe, they still flourish in other quarters. In his struggle against Israel President Nasser has come out publicly in support of the *Protocols*; large quantities of *Protocols*-type material are produced in Cairo, largely with the help of Nazi émigrés, and distributed in many countries, and notably in South America, also with the help of Nazi émigrés. The debates of the Vatican Council on the attitude to be adopted towards Jews stimulated a spate of antisemitic propaganda from Spain, including a luxurious new edition of the *Protocols* with abundant commentaries.[1] Stalin in his last years produced a new version of the conspiracy-myth, in which Jews figured as agents of an imperialist plot to destroy the Soviet Union and assassinate its leaders; this was used to secure the execution of Rudolf Slansky and his Jewish colleagues on the Central Committee of the Czech Communist party in 1952,[2] and it also formed the basis for the story of the 'doctors' plot' in 1953.

All this would require another volume and someone else to write it. The purpose of this book is to show how between the French Revolution and the Second World War certain ancient and immensely destructive fantasies were reactivated, and with what results. It is a grim story, but one which surely needed to be told.

[1] *Sabios de Sion: Protocolos*, Madrid, 1963. The commentaries are ascribed to a writer with the unusual name of Charles Borough, whom I have been unable to trace in any catalogue or reference book. A companion work is M. Pinay, *Complotto contro la chiesa*, Rome, 1962.

[2] For a German translation of the verbatim record of the Slansky trial see *Prozess gegen die Leitung des staatsfeindlichen Verschwörerzentrums mit Rudolf Slansky an der Spitze*, published by the Ministry of Justice, Prague, 1953. Cf. J. Parkes, *Antisemitism*, London, 1963, p. 152.

CHAPTER I

The Origins of the Myth

1

OVER very large areas of the earth Jews have traditionally been seen as mysterious beings, endowed with uncanny, sinister powers. This attitude goes back to the time, from the second to the fourth centuries after Christ, when the Church and the Synagogue were competing for converts in the Hellenistic world, and when moreover each was still struggling to win adherents from the other. It was to terrorize the judaising Christians of Antioch into a final breach with the parent religion that St John Chrysostom called the Synagogue 'the temple of demons . . . the cavern of devils . . . a gulf and abyss of perdition' and portrayed Jews as habitual murderers and destroyers, people possessed by an evil spirit. And it was to protect his catechumens against Judaism that St Augustine described how those who had been the favourite sons of God were now transformed into sons of Satan. Moreover the Jews were brought into relation with that fearsome figure, Antichrist, 'the son of perdition', whose tyrannical reign, according to St Paul and the Book of Revelation, is to precede the second coming of Christ. Many of the Fathers taught that Antichrist would be a Jew and that the Jews would be his most devoted followers.[1]

Seven or eight centuries later, in the most militant period in the history of the Roman Catholic Church, these ancient

[1] For the demonization of the Jew in Christian teaching see J. Parkes, *The Conflict of the Church and the Synagogue*, London, 1934; J. Trachtenberg, *The Devil and the Jews*, New Haven, 1943; M. Simon, *Verus Israël*, Paris, 1948; L. Poliakov, *Histoire de l'Antisémitisme*, Vol. I: *Du Christ aux Juifs de Cour*, Paris, 1955; J. Isaac, *Genèse de l'Antisémitisme*, Paris, 1956.

fantasies were revived and integrated into a whole new demonology. From the time of the first crusade onwards Jews were
presented as children of the Devil, agents employed by Satan
for the express purpose of combating Christianity and harming
Christians. It was in the twelfth century that they were first
accused of murdering Christian children, of torturing the consecrated wafer, and of poisoning the wells. It is true that popes
and bishops frequently and emphatically condemned these
fabrications; but the lower clergy continued to propagate
them, and in the end they came to be generally believed. But
above all it was said that Jews worshipped the Devil, who
rewarded them collectively by making them masters of black
magic; so that however helpless individual Jews might seem,
Jewry possessed limitless powers for evil. And already then
there was talk of a secret Jewish government – a council of
rabbis, located in Moslem Spain, which was supposed to be
directing an underground war against Christendom and
employing sorcery as its principal weapon.

The propagation of such views by the clergy, century after
century, gradually but decisively influenced the attitude of the
laity. If Judaism, with its profound sense of election and its
elaborate system of tabus, tended in any case to make Jews
into a people apart, Christian teaching and preaching ensured
that they would be treated not simply as strangers but as
most dangerous enemies. During the Middle Ages Jews were
almost wholly without legal rights and were frequently
massacred by the mob. Such experiences in turn greatly encouraged the Jewish tendency to exclusiveness. During the
long centuries of persecution Jews became a wholly alien
people, compulsorily restricted to the most sordid trades, regarding the Gentile world with bitterness. In the eyes of most
Christians these strange creatures were demons in human form
– and some of the demonology that was woven around them
in those centuries has proved extraordinarily durable.

The myth of the Jewish world-conspiracy represents a
modern adaptation of this ancient demonological tradition.
According to this myth there exists a secret Jewish government which, through a world-wide network of camouflaged
agencies and organizations, controls political parties and
governments, the press and public opinion, banks and econo-

mic developments. The secret government is supposed to be doing this in pursuance of an age-old plan and with the single aim of achieving Jewish dominion over the entire world; and it is also supposed to be perilously near to achieving this aim.

In this fantasy the remnants of ancient demonological terrors are blended with anxieties and resentments which are typically modern. The myth of the Jewish world-conspiracy is in fact a particularly degraded and distorted expression of the new social tensions which arose when, with the French Revolution and the coming of the nineteenth century, Europe entered on a period of exceptionally rapid and deep-going change. As everyone knows, it was a time when traditional social relationships were shaken, hereditary privileges ceased to be sacrosanct, age-old values and beliefs were called in question. The slow-moving, conservative life of the countryside was increasingly challenged by an urban civilization which was dynamic, restless, given to innovation. Industrialization brought to the fore a bourgeoisie intent on increasing its wealth and extending its rights; and gradually a new class, the industrial proletariat, began to exert pressure on its own account. Democracy, liberalism, secularism, by the mid-century even socialism, were forces to be reckoned with. But all over Continental Europe there were large numbers of people who abominated all these things. A long, bitter struggle began between those who accepted the new, mobile society and the opportunities it offered, and those who hoped to retain or restore the vanishing traditional order. These changes, which affected European society as a whole, brought both new opportunities and new perils to Europe's Jews.

In one country after another in western and central Europe Jews were relieved of their legal disabilities. Most Jews wanted nothing so much as to live by the same routines as other people, and they quietly adapted themselves to their new freedom. Nevertheless in the eyes of many people 'the Jew' still had a highly symbolic significance, and for two quite different reasons. On the one hand Jews remained an identifiable and – though to a rapidly diminishing extent – an exclusive community; and this meant that they retained something of the mysterious quality which they had possessed in earlier centuries. On the other hand they came to be seen as symbolic of the modern world by those who most detested that world. Various circumstances were responsible for this. For centuries Jews had of necessity been town-dwellers, and they still remained concentrated to an overwhelming extent in the cities, especially the capital cities. In politics Jews naturally tended to side with the liberal and democratic forces which alone could guarantee and increase their liberties. Being still denied access to many traditional occupations, they were encouraged to pioneer new ways of making a living; and in doing so, a few became extremely rich. And in general it can be said that a feeling of suddenly liberated energies made many Jews exceptionally enterprising, exceptionally given to experiment and innovation. In industry and commerce, politics and journalism, Jews became identified with everything that was most wholeheartedly modern. As a result, by about 1870 it was possible to see in 'the Jews' the supreme incarnation of modernity, even while continuing to see them as uncanny, semi-demonic beings.

Of course other, quite different types of antisemitism also existed. There was, for instance, a left-wing antisemitism, compounded of contempt for Jewish religion – which was blamed for Christianity – and of resentment at the power of Jewish bankers, notably the Rothschilds. The socialist movements of France and Germany were full of this kind of antisemitism, and they finally rid themselves of it only at the very end of the century. The demonological type of antisemitism, on the other hand, flourished among those who were most thoroughly disconcerted by the civilization of the nineteenth century. It was above all the landed aristocracy and the clergy who saw in 'the Jews' a symbol of all that most threatened their world – and not only their material interests but the values that gave meaning to their lives. These people were only too happy to believe that such alarming changes must spring not from any defects in the old order, nor from impersonal historic processes, but from the machinations of a handful of devils in human form. Moreover by putting this idea about they could hope to achieve certain highly practical aims. To portray democracy, liberalism, and secularism as the work of the Jews was a way of making these things suspect in the eyes of a growing but ill-educated electorate.

So the new political form of antisemitism came into being. From now on antisemitism was to be deliberately whipped up by ultra-conservative politicians and publicists in their struggle against the progressives. And although Jews were still sometimes accused of such things as ritual murder, these age-old superstitions gradually yielded in importance to the new political superstition concerning a secret Jewish government. This new fantasy was of course just as remote from reality as the old, but it was also just as effective. What Jews really were or did or wanted, or what Jews possibly could be or do or want, had nothing whatsoever to do with the matter. To understand how the fantasy arose and spread it is much less important to know about Jews than to know what persecution-mania means and how, given a suitable situation, it can be deliberately exploited in multitudes of ordinary human beings. This had happened before, during the witch-mania that gripped Europe in the sixteenth and seventeenth centuries. It was to happen again as the myth of the Jewish world-conspiracy began its deadly work.

2

Today when people think of the myth of the Jewish world-conspiracy they think of the forgery known as the *Protocols of the Elders of Zion,* which circulated through the world in millions of copies in the 1920s and 1930s. But the *Protocols* are only the most celebrated and influential in a long series of fabrications and forgeries reaching back almost to the French Revolution.

In its modern form the myth of the Jewish world-conspiracy can be traced back to a French Jesuit, the Abbé Barruel. As early as 1797 Barruel, in his five-volume *Mémoire pour servir à l'histoire du Jacobinisme,* argued that the French Revolution represented the culmination of an age-old conspiracy of the most secret of secret societies. As he saw it, the trouble began with the medieval Order of Templars, which had not really been exterminated in 1314 but had survived as a secret society, pledged to abolish all monarchies, to overthrow the papacy, to preach unrestricted liberty to all peoples and to found a world-republic under its own control. Down the centuries this secret society had poisoned a number of monarchs; and in the eighteenth century it had captured the Order of Freemasons, which now stood entirely under its control. In 1763 it had created a secret literary academy, consisting of Voltaire, Turgot, Condorcet, Diderot, and d'Alembert, and meeting regularly in the house of the Baron d'Holbach; by its publications this body had undermined all morality and true religion among the French. From 1776 onwards Condorcet and the Abbé Sièyes had built up a vast revolutionary organization of half a million Frenchmen, who were the Jacobins of the revolution. But the heart of the conspiracy, the true leaders of the revolution, were the Bavarian *Illuminati* under Adam Weishaupt – 'enemies of the human race, sons of Satan'. To this handful of Germans all the Freemasons and Jacobins of France already owed blind allegiance; and it was Barruel's view that unless it was stopped, this handful would soon dominate the world.

One need waste no time on the claim that the French Revolution was produced by a conspiracy reaching back to the fourteenth century. As for the obscure German group known as the *Illuminati*, they were not Freemasons at all but rivals of the Freemasons and had in any case been dissolved in 1786. And the role of the Freemasons was also fantastically over-simplified and exaggerated. It is of course true that the Free-masons shared that concern with humanitarian reform which is commonly associated with the Enlightenment – for instance, they contributed to the abolition of judicial torture and of witchcraft trials, and to the improvement of schools. On the other hand at the time of the revolution most Freemasons were Catholic and monarchist – indeed King Louis XVI and his brothers were all Freemasons; while during the Terror Freemasons were guillotined by the hundred and their organization, the *Grand Orient*, was suppressed.

The fact is that Barruel himself never noticed any Masonic influence at work while the revolution was in progress. The idea was presented to him some years later, in London, by the Scottish mathematician John Robison, who was himself preparing a book called *Proofs of a Conspiracy against all the Religions and Governments of Europe, carried on in the secret*

meetings of Freemasons, Illuminati and Reading Societies.
Barruel felt inspired to produce a book on the very same subject, if possible before the imprudent Robison. And he succeeded – his *Mémoire* forestalled Robison's by a year, it was
translated into English, French, Italian, Spanish, and Russian,
and it made its author a rich man.

Nevertheless at the time when he wrote his five volumes
Barruel still imposed certain limits on his imagination.
Though he was more than willing to blame the revolution on
the Freemasons, he scarcely mentioned the Jews – understandably enough, since no Jew played any significant part
either in the revolution itself or in the philosophical revolution
that preceded it. Others, however, were less inhibited than
Barruel. In 1806 he received a document which seems to be the
earliest in the series of antisemitic forgeries that was to cul-
minate in the *Protocols*. This was a letter from Florence
ostensibly written by an army officer called J. B. Simonini, of
whom nothing else is known and with whom Barruel himself
failed to establish contact.[1] After congratulating Barruel on
having 'unmasked the hellish sects which are preparing the
way for Antichrist' he draws his attention to 'the Judaic sect'
– surely 'the most formidable power, if one considers its great
wealth and the protection it enjoys in almost all European
countries'. The mysterious Simonini goes on to reveal some
extraordinary information which he claims to have obtained
by a ruse. He once pretended to some Piedmontese Jews that
he himself had been born a Jew and, though separated from
the Jewish community in early childhood, had always retained
his love of his 'nation'. Thereupon the Jews showed him 'sums
of gold and silver for distribution to those who embraced their
cause'; promised to make him a general if only he would

[1] The Simonini letter will be found in *Le Contemporain*, Paris, issue of
July 1878, pp. 58–61. It has been reprinted in many antisemitic works,
e.g. N. Deschamps, *Les sociétés secrètes et la Société*, Avignon–Paris, n.d.,
Vol. III, pp. 658–61, and A. Netchvolodov, *L'Empereur Nicolas II et les
Juifs*, Paris, 1924, pp. 231–4. Internal evidence shows that it does indeed
date from around 1806. M. Léon Poliakov, in a private communication
to the author, has argued convincingly that it was fabricated by the
French political police under Fouché with the object of influencing
Napoleon against the Jews at the time of 'the Great Sanhedrin'; see
below, pp. 29–30.

become a Freemason; presented him with three weapons bearing Masonic symbols; and revealed their greatest secrets.

These were indeed surprising. Simonini learned, for instance, that Mani and the Old Man of the Mountain were both Jews (though in reality neither of them was);[1] and that the Order of Freemasons and the *Illuminati* were both founded by Jews (though their founders are known, and were not Jews). More surprising still, he discovered that in Italy alone more than 800 ecclesiastics were Jews; these included bishops and cardinals and would shortly, it was hoped, include a pope. In Spain much the same state of affairs obtained; and indeed everywhere Jews were disguising themselves as Christians. Equally menacing were their political and economic stratagems. Already certain countries had granted full civil rights to the Jews and soon the remaining countries, harassed by plots and seduced by money, would do likewise. That accomplished, the Jews would buy up all lands and houses, until the Christians were completely dispossessed. And then the last stage of the plot would be carried out: the Jews 'promised themselves that in less than a century they would be masters of the world, that they would abolish all other sects and establish the rule of their own sect, that they would turn Christian churches into so many synagogues and reduce the remaining Christians to a state of absolute slavery'. Only one serious obstacle remained – the House of Bourbon, which was the Jews' worst enemy; and the Jews would annihilate that.

Barruel once remarked that if the Simonini letter were published it might provoke a massacre of Jews, and on that occasion he was talking sense; for in embryo the letter does indeed contain the whole myth of the Judeo-Masonic conspiracy. But the letter also points very clearly to the circum-

---

[1] In the third century of the Christian era the Persian Mani founded the religion of Manicheeism, which in one form or another competed with Christianity for a thousand years.

The Old Man of the Mountain: the supreme ruler of the Moslem sect known as the Assassins, which was active from the eleventh to the thirteenth centuries and had its headquarters in the mountain fortress of Alamut in Persia. The sect employed secret assassination against all enemies. Those required to kill were made obedient by means of hashish – whence the word 'assassin'. Crusaders from France came across the Assassins in Syria.

stances which gave birth to that myth. Needless to say it had
nothing to do with the real relationship between Jewry and
Freemasonry, which was tenuous. In the eighteenth century
the Freemasons were on the whole hostile to the Jews (and so,
incidentally, were the Bavarian *Illuminati*). At the time of the
Simonini letter many lodges were still reluctant to accept
Jewish members. At no time have Jews, or persons of Jewish
descent, played a disproportionate part in Freemasonry. These
are the sober facts. But facts such as these have never deterred
anyone who wished to believe in a Judeo-Masonic conspiracy.
Had not Barruel shown that the French Revolution was the
work of a conspiracy of Freemasons? And had not the Jews
benefited from the revolution? No more was required to
establish that Freemasons and Jews were closely associated,
in fact practically identical.

It is of course true that the French Revolution, like the
American Revolution before it, really did help the Jews. Since
it proclaimed 'the rights of man' and championed the principles
of liberty, equality, and fraternity, it was logically bound to
grant civil rights to French Jews. And not only this – where-
ever Napoleon's power extended the Jews were emancipated;
in the Simonini letter one can hear the crash of the Italian
ghettos as they fell before the French armies. This was quite
enough to convince reactionaries that Napoleon was the ally
of Jewry, if not a Jew himself. Those who identified themselves
with the *ancien régime* had to account somehow for the collapse
of a social order which they regarded as ordained by God.
The myth of the Judeo-Masonic conspiracy supplied the
explanation they craved.

Then, in 1806, Napoleon summoned an assembly of prominent French Jews – mostly rabbis and scholars – at Paris.
The Emperor's motives were of course purely political and
administrative; he was interested in stamping out the money-
lending which, as a legacy from pre-emancipation days, was
still practised by Jews in Alsace, and he also wanted to satisfy
himself that the Jewish population was as submissive as the
rest of France. But he called the assembly 'the Great Sanhedrin', after the supreme Jewish court of antiquity – and this
automatically suggested that a Jewish government had been
secretly in existence down the centuries. Above all, in the eyes

of many of Napoleon's enemies the calling of this 'Sanhedrin'
established him once and for all as that Antichrist who, in the
last days of this earth, is to appear as the Messiah of the Jews.
The journal of the French *émigrés* in London, *L'Ambigu*,
commented: 'Does he hope to form, from these children of
Jacob, a legion of tyrannicides? . . . Time will show. It remains
for us only to watch this Antichrist fight against the eternal
decrees of God; that must be the last act of his diabolic
existence.'[1] In Moscow the Holy Synod of the Orthodox
Church thundered: 'Today he proposes to reunite the Jews
whom God's wrath had scattered over the face of the earth,
to urge them on to overthrow the Church of Christ and to
proclaim a false messiah in his person.'[2] The Simonini letter,
with its mention of Antichrist and its prophetic tone, fitted
perfectly into such an atmosphere. Barruel duly passed it
around in influential circles in France, with the express object
'of forestalling the effect which might be produced by the
"Sanhedrin" '.[3]

The Simonini letter seems in fact to have given a new direction to Barruel's own thinking. Just before his death in 1820,
at the age of seventy-nine, Barruel opened his mind to a fellow-
Jesuit, Father Grivel – and what emerged was the myth of the
Judeo-Masonic conspiracy, elaborated far beyond the hints in
the Simonini letter.[4] He had written a vast manuscript, which
he destroyed two days before his death, to show how a revolutionary conspiracy has existed down the ages, from Mani
to the medieval Templars and thence to the Freemasons.
As for the Jews, he believed them to have made common cause
with the Templars and to have occupied commanding positions
in the conspiracy ever since. At that moment Europe was
covered by a network of Masonic lodges, penetrating into
every village in France, Spain, Italy, and Germany; and the

[1] *L'Ambigu*, London, issue for 20 October 1806, pp. 101–17: 'Grand
Sanhédrin des Juifs à Paris'.

[2] Quoted in S. Doubnov, *Histoire moderne du peuple juif*, Paris, 1933,
Vol. I, p. 376. Cf. R. Anchel, *Napoléon et les Juifs*, Paris, 1928, Chapter
VI, and P. Vulliaud, *Joseph de Maistre, franc-maçon*, Paris, 1926,
Chapter IX.

[3] 'Souvenirs du P. Grivel sur les PP. Barruel et Feller', in *Le Contemporain*, issue of July 1878, p. 62.

[4] Ibid., pp. 67–70.

whole organization was rigidly controlled by a supreme
council of twenty-one, which included no less than nine Jews.
This council had no fixed residence, but wherever the statesmen of the great powers met in congress it was to be found
somewhere in the background; in addition, its individual
members travelled a great deal, under the pretext of pursuing
business interests or attending learned conferences but in
reality to direct the activities of the organization. The supreme
council was not, however, the ultimate authority in Freemasonry; it appointed an inner council of three, which in turn
elected a Grand Master, who was the secret head of this secret
International.

Around the figure of the Grand Master, Barruel weaves a
truly lurid tale. The Grand Master takes all decisions, and he
takes them 'as despotically, as irrevocably, as the Old Man of
the Mountain'. Disobedience to his orders is punished by death;
every Freemason is bound by oath to assassinate any member
of the order, even up to the members of the inner council, if
the Grand Master so ordains. This is in fact the explanation of
almost every apparently inexplicable assassination. And of
course the sole true aim of Freemasonry is to produce revolutions. Orders to this end are sent out by the Grand Master in
code, and are carried across Europe by relays of Freemasons,
all of them on foot. 'And so,' concludes Barruel, 'from neighbour to neighbour and from hand to hand the orders are
transmitted with incomparable speed, for these pedestrians
are delayed neither by bad weather, nor by the mishaps that
normally befall horsemen or carriages; a man on foot can
always get along when he knows the country, and that is the
case here. They stop neither to eat nor to sleep, for each one
covers only two leagues. The mail-coach takes ten hours from
Paris to Orleans, stopping for an hour; the distance is thirty
leagues. Fifteen or twenty pedestrians, replacing one another,
can reach Orleans from Paris in nine hours, using short-cuts
and above all never stopping.' Clearly the supreme council,
even though only partly Jewish, already possessed that super-
human capacity for organizing vast and invisible manoeuvres
that later generations were to attribute to the Elders of Zion.

3

Barruel's fantasies and the Simonini letter found little echo in
the first half of the nineteenth century. Antisemitic propaganda, though it existed, was neither abundant nor influential
at that time, and the myth of the Judeo-Masonic conspiracy in
particular passed into oblivion even among antisemites. Indeed
the first important reference to the idea appears not in antisemitic propaganda but, in the form of a rather naughty joke, in
Disraeli's novel *Coningsby*, which appeared in 1844. In Chapter
XV of Book III there is a passage where the rich and aristocratic Jew Sidonia describes how, when raising a loan for the
Russian Government, he travelled from country to country –
Russia, Spain, France, Prussia – and in each capital found that
the minister concerned was a Jew. And he ends his tale with
the comment: 'So you see, my dear Coningsby, that the world is
governed by very different personages from what is imagined
by those who are not behind the scenes.' It is a passage which
was later to be quoted by innumerable antisemitic writers –
for did it not after all come from a famous Jew who was later
himself to be prime minister? What was not mentioned, and
was perhaps seldom realized, is that the various ministers
named – who include Napoleon's marshal, Soult, and the
Prussian Count Arnim – were not in fact Jews.

It was around 1850 that the myth of the Judeo-Masonic
conspiracy reappeared – this time in Germany – as a weapon
of the extreme right in its struggle against the growing forces
of nationalism, liberalism, democracy, and secularism. Writing
under the immediate impact of the risings of 1848, the publicist
E. E. Eckert describes how the Freemasons are organizing
not only all revolutionary movements but also the situations
that produce revolutionary movements – how they deliberately plunge the masses into moral barbarism and religious despair and finally into economic desperation. This points forward
unmistakably to the *Protocols*, save that Eckert makes no
mention of Jews. The gap was filled by the Catholic periodical
Historisch-politische Blätter, of Munich, which in 1862 published a protest signed 'A Berlin Freemason' but which was
manifestly not written by a Freemason at all.

THE ORIGINS OF THE MYTH

After complaining of the growing influence of Jews in public and political life in Prussia, the anonymous correspondent describes an (entirely imaginary) association in Germany which, while employing the symbols and rituals of Freemasonry, in reality pursues secret aims – aims that have nothing to do with Freemasonry and that threaten the security of all states. This association is governed by 'unknown superiors' and consists mostly of Jews. Nor are such machinations confined to Germany. In London 'the Grand Master' Palmerston presides over the forces of revolution in Europe – but behind Palmerston are two pseudo-Masonic lodges consisting entirely of Jews, and whose threshold no Gentile can ever cross. Another such Jewish centre is in Rome – the struggle for the national unity of Italy is in fact nothing but a Jewish plot in which Mazzini and his colleagues are puppets in the hands of 'unknown superiors'. And during the annual fair at Leipzig an exclusively Jewish lodge functions uninterruptedly, though in deadly secret. German Freemasons feel themselves being impelled hither and thither by unknown forces, although the oath of secrecy prevents them from comparing notes and thus penetrating the fearsome secret.[1]

A few years after this extravaganza there appeared, also in Germany, a document which in due course was to become the model for the *Protocols* themselves. The author of this prototype of the most famous of all antisemitic forgeries was one Hermann Goedsche, who had formerly been a minor official in the Prussian postal service. In the reaction following the revolutionary upheavals of 1848 this man had made an unfortunate miscalculation. In order to incriminate the democratic leader Benedic Waldeck, whose politics were proving inconvenient to the King of Prussia, Goedsche produced letters which if they had been genuine would have unmasked Waldeck as conspiring to overthrow the constitution and assassinate the King. In the event it was quickly proved not only that the letters were forgeries but that Goedsche knew them to be so. His career in the postal service being at an end, Goedsche joined the staff of the newspaper *Die Preussische Kreuzzeitung*, which was much favoured by conservative landowners; and he also began to write novels, the more

[1] *Historisch-politische Blätter*, Munich, Vol. V (1862), pp. 432–4.

sensational under the pseudonym of Sir John Retcliffe. One of these novels, *Biarritz*, contained a chapter called 'In the Jewish Cemetery in Prague'. It is a piece of straight fiction of the most romantically sensational kind, but it was nevertheless to become the basis for a very influential antisemitic forgery.[1]

The chapter describes a secret nocturnal meeting which is supposed to have been held in the cemetery during the Feast of Tabernacles. At eleven o'clock the gates of the cemetery creak softly and the rustling of long coats is heard, as they touch against the stones and shrubbery. A vague white figure passes like a shadow through the cemetery until it reaches a certain tombstone; here it kneels down, touches the tombstone three times with its forehead and whispers a prayer. Another figure approaches; it is that of an old man, bent and limping; he coughs and sighs as he moves. The figure takes its place next to its predecessor and it too kneels down and whispers a prayer. A third figure appears – a tall, impressive figure, clad in a white mantle; as though unwillingly, he too kneels down at the tombstone. Thirteen times this procedure is repeated. When the thirteenth and last figure has taken its place a clock strikes midnight. From the grave there comes a sharp, metallic sound. A blue flame appears and lights up the thirteen kneeling figures. A hollow voice says, 'I greet you, heads of the twelve tribes of Israel.' It is the Devil speaking; and the figures dutifully reply: 'We greet you, son of the accursed.'

The assembled figures are in fact meant to represent the twelve tribes of Israel, including the lost tribes, although the author has omitted two of the Biblical list and invented others to take their place. The additional member of the party represents 'the unfortunates and the exiles'. Under the chairmanship of the representative of the house of Aaron, these various personages report on their activities during the century which has elapsed since the last meeting. The Levite announces that after centuries of oppression and striving, Israel is rising again, thanks to the gold which has fallen into her hands. The Jews can now look forward to a future, not far off, when the whole earth will belong to them. The representative of

[1] Sir John Retcliffe (pseudonym of Hermann Goedsche), *Biarritz*, Vol. I, Berlin, 1868, pp. 162–93.

Reuben reports that through the stock exchanges the Jews have managed to get all the princes and governments of Europe into their debt and are thereby able to control them. Simeon outlines a scheme for breaking up the great estates and getting all land into Jewish hands, so that the workers on the land will become workers for the Jews. Judah shows how independent artisans are being reduced by Jewish machinations to the status of factory-workers, who can then be controlled and directed for political purposes. The Aaronic Levite is concerned with undermining the Christian Church, by fostering free thought, scepticism, and anti-clericalism. Issachar thinks that the military class, being the defender of the throne and the exponent of patriotism, has to be discredited in the eyes of the masses. Zebulon maintains that, though the Jewish people is by nature intensely conservative, Jews must now appear to side with forces of progress; for unrest and revolutions can be so directed that they bring no real benefits to the poor but merely increase the power of the Jews. Dan, 'a Jew of the lower order', has more modest ambitions; he is concerned that Jews should monopolize the trade in liquor, butter, wool, and bread. Naphtali demands that governmental positions should be thrown open to Jews, particularly those which carry great influence, such as Justice and Education. Benjamin makes a similar demand with respect to the liberal professions. Asher considers that marriage with Christian women can only serve the purpose of the Jews, and that a Jew desiring the pleasures of fornication or adultery should always seek them with Christian and not with Jewish women. Manasseh concludes the series of speeches with an impassioned plea for capturing and controlling the press; in this way Jews will be able to decide what the masses shall believe, what they shall desire, what they shall reject.

After the assembled representatives have all had their say the presiding Levite gives his message of encouragement. What has been said will be as a sword with which Israel will strike down its enemies. If these prescriptions are faithfully followed, future generations of Jews will suffer no more oppression but, on the contrary, will enjoy happiness, wealth, and power. When the next meeting is held, a hundred years hence, the grand-children of those now present will be able to

announce at that graveside that they have indeed become
princes of the world and that all other nations are their slaves.
The Levite concludes with the command: 'Let us renew our
oath, sons of the golden calf, and go out to all the lands of the
earth!' Thereupon a blue flame appears above the tomb, while
each of the thirteen throws a stone upon the tomb; and in the
midst of the flame there appears a monstrous golden calf. So
the meeting ends; but what none of the participants knows is
that these clandestine proceedings have been observed throughout by two men, a German scholar and a baptized Jew, who
now swear to spend all their strength in fighting this devilish
Jewish plot.

The relevant volume of *Biarritz* was published in 1868, and
the date is significant. In Germany the partial emancipation of
the Jews during the years of Napoleon's sway had been
followed by a violent antisemitic reaction. With the slow
growth of a middle class which was at least partly liberal,
Jews again enjoyed greater freedom and acceptance, until this
tiny fraction of the population – 1·2 per cent, to be precise –
was granted approximately the same civil rights as were enjoyed by the remaining 98·8 per cent. This came about in the
North German states in 1869, and was extended to the whole
of the new German Reich in 1871. Nevertheless in a country
which never accepted with any real conviction the ideals of
liberalism and democracy, antisemitism remained a powerful
factor. Moreover, precisely because German national unity
was achieved extremely late, Germans became quite abnor-
mally emphatic in their nationalism; and this too fostered
antisemitism. It is therefore not surprising that the first
comprehensive formulation of the modern myth of the Jewish
conspiracy should have appeared in Germany at the very
moment when the Jews were about to be granted full emancipation.

But this was only the beginning of the story – for soon this
frankly fictional episode began to turn into a forged document!
It was Russian antisemites who first thought of treating the
story as an authentic record; in 1872 the relevant chapter was
published in St Petersburg as a pamphlet, with the sinister
comment that, although the story was a piece of fiction, it had
a basis in fact. In 1876 a similar pamphlet appeared in

Moscow, with the title *In The Jewish Cemetery in Czech Prague (the Jews sovereigns of the world)*. In 1880 a second edition of this pamphlet was published; and similar pamphlets appeared in Odessa and Prague. Some years later the story appeared in France, in *Le Contemporain* for July 1881. Now it was no longer presented as a piece of fiction. All the various speeches made by the fictional Jews at Prague were consolidated into a single speech, which was supposed to have been made by a chief rabbi to a secret meeting of Jews. The authenticity of this speech was vouched for – in fact it was supposed to be extracted from a forthcoming work by an English diplomat, *Annals of the Political and Historical Events of the Last Ten Years.*

Goedsche, as we know, had written his novel under the *nom de plume* of Sir John Retcliffe; so it was only appropriate that the English diplomat should be called the same – or rather, carelessly, Sir John Readclif. This gentleman was to have a most adventurous career. When François Bournand printed the 'speech' in *Les Juifs et nos contemporains* (1896) he prefaced it with a startling revelation: 'We find the programme of Jewry, the real programme of the Jews expressed by . . . the Chief Rabbi John Readclif. . . . It is a speech made in 1880.' Mercifully Sir John quickly recovered himself. Later editions of the 'speech' were often accompanied by touching tributes to that heroic antisemite, Sir John Readclif. The tributes were by no means unmerited, for when in 1933 the 'speech' appeared for the first time in Sweden, it was prefaced by a melancholy statement: Sir John Readclif had paid with his life for exposing the great Jewish conspiracy. It was a sad end for a man who, if he had been a German novelist, had also been an English diplomat and historian, and who if he had been a heroic antisemite had also been a chief rabbi.

This, then, is the origin of what came to be known as *The Rabbi's Speech*.[1] But the ludicrousness of its origin did not prevent this 'speech' from having a most successful career. In 1887 Theodor Fritsch published it in his 'catechism' for antisemitic agitators; in the same year, and again in 1891, it appeared in the famous antisemitic anthology *La Russie juive*. In 1893 it was printed in an Austrian newspaper, the *Deutsch-*

[1] The text of *The Rabbi's Speech* is given in Appendix I.

soziale Blätter. In 1896, as already indicated, it figured in Bournand's book *Les Juifs et nos contemporains*. In 1901 a paraphrase of the speech in Czech was printed in Prague, under the title *Speech of a Rabbi about the Goyim*. The pamphlet was confiscated by the authorities; but this measure was circumvented by a Czech deputy, Břzenovskí, who in a question in the Reichstag in Vienna quoted the entire pamphlet verbatim; whereupon it was promptly printed in two newspapers, *Michel wach auf* and the *Wiener Deutsche Zeitung*, and so re-entered circulation.

In Russia, where the 'speech' had taken the first steps towards fame in the 1870s, it continued on its triumphant way. In 1891 it appeared in Russian translation in the Odessa newspaper, *Novorossiysky Telegraf*. Now it was established that the 'speech' had been made by a rabbi to a 'secret Sanhedrin' in 1869 (presumably the reference is to the First Congress of Reform Judaism held in that year at Leipzig); and again its authenticity is guaranteed by the well-known English aristocrat, Sir John Readclif. Early in the new century the fabrication was used in Russia for the purpose of instigating pogroms. And at this stage its history became intertwined with that of the *Protocols of the Elders of Zion*. The professional antisemite P. A. Krushevan seems to have used a pamphlet containing *The Rabbi's Speech* as a help in provoking the pogrom at Kishinev in Bessarabia in 1903. A few months later, as we shall see, he published the *Protocols* in his newspaper *Znamya* (*The Banner*); and on 22 January 1904 he published the 'speech' in the same newspaper. In 1906 Krushevan's friend Butmi included it in his edition of the *Protocols*; and in the same year it was published as a pamphlet in Kharkov. The *Deutsch-soziale Blätter* rejoiced that this powerful weapon from the ideological arsenal of German antisemitism was helping the Russian people to liberate itself from its 'mortal enemy', the Jews.

Shortly afterwards the hitherto nameless rabbi who was supposed to have delivered the 'speech' was given a name, or rather two names: sometimes he is Rabbi Eichhorn and sometimes Rabbi Reichhorn. As such he figured at the non-existent congress at Lemberg in 1912. After the First World War the pronouncements of this imaginary gentleman, refurbished to suit the new conditions, shared in the triumphs of the *Protocols*; many editions include both works. By this time there were naturally several variants of the 'speech' in circulation, and these different versions were used to bolster up one another's authenticity. Indeed their resemblance was taken as proving not only that they were all genuine but that they were successive expressions of a long-established Jewish plot. *The Rabbi's Speech* was also, inevitably, constantly invoked as proof of the authenticity of the *Protocols*.

It was in post-war Germany that this fabrication, like the *Protocols*, enjoyed the greatest vogue. Already in 1919 it made up the contents of two different pamphlets. One of these, entitled *What is the Jewish Spirit?* and published in Württemberg, announces in its preface that 'John Retcliffe's warning cry, addressed to the whole non-Jewish world (it must be forty or fifty years old) is today, in 1919, when Jewry has attained the greater part of its appointed aim, still sufficiently interesting to be presented anew to the German people'. The other edition, published in Berlin, bears the melodramatic title: *The Secret of Jewish World-Domination, from a work of the last century, which was bought up by the Jews and so disappeared from circulation.* In the early 1920s the 'speech' was also reprinted in several popular antisemitic books; and when the Nazis came to power Johann von Leers, of whom we shall be hearing more, produced yet another edition. Moreover by this time it had become a commonplace that 'the great knower and warner' Hermann Goedsche, alias Sir John Retcliffe, had himself witnessed the meeting in the cemetery in Prague – having been led there by the Jewish socialist, Ferdinand Lassalle!

Goedsche's fantasy was by no means the only German contribution to the myth of the Jewish world-conspiracy. When, in the 1880s, antisemitism became an important political movement, Germany emerged as the leading producer of antisemitic propaganda of every kind. Both French and Russian antisemites borrowed heavily from German authors and journalists. Conversely, no antisemitic idea or fable or slogan could appear anywhere in Europe without being promptly snapped up by some German writer. In the vast mass of German antisemitic writing the myth of the Jewish world-conspiracy and the secret Jewish government became one of the more important themes. If, for instance, one examines Theodor Fritsch's 'antisemitic catechism',[1] one finds a whole section devoted to 'Jewish secret societies'. Here all the fantasies which had been elaborated in Germany or France or Russia are refurbished for the benefit of the German public. And the book proved very popular. First published in 1887, later enlarged and dignified with the title *Handbook of the Jewish Question*, it had sold 100,000 copies by 1933. It eventually sold far more than that, for in the Third Reich it became – along with the *Protocols* themselves – one of the texts prescribed for compulsory study in schools.

[1] *Antisemiten-Katechismus: Eine Zusammenstellung des wichtigsten Materials zum Verständnis der Judenfrage*, written under the pseudonym Thomas Frey (1887).

CHAPTER II

Against Satan and the Alliance Israélite Universelle

1

In the Middle Ages Jews had been seen as agents of Satan, devil-worshippers, demons in human form. It is one of the achievements of the modern antisemitic movement that in the late nineteenth century it was able to revive this archaic superstition. As we have seen, Goedsche closed the Prague meeting with a supernatural apparition: in the form of a golden calf Satan offers himself to the adoration of the assembled Jews. Within a year of the publication of Goedsche's fantasy there appeared in France the book which was to become the Bible of modern antisemitism: *Le Juif, le judaïsme et la judaïsation des peuples chrétiens,* by Gougenot des Mousseaux. Here Satan bulks large indeed, for the author is convinced that the world is falling into the grip of a mysterious body of Satan-worshippers, whom he calls 'kabbalistic Jews'.

In reality the kabbalah is nothing but a body of Jewish mystical and theosophical doctrine, dating in the main from the later Middle Ages. It is fully expounded in such works as the *Zohar* and there is nothing secret about it. During the Renaissance it was made available to Christendom by humanists such as Pico di Mirandola and Johann Reuchlin, and it charmed a number of thoughtful men, including Pope Leo X. Des Mousseaux, however, imagined the kabbalah as something quite different: a secret demonic religion, a systematic cult of evil, established by the Devil at the very beginning of the world. According to him the first adepts of this cult were the sons of Cain, who after the Flood were succeeded by the sons of Ham; these are the same as the Chaldeans, and in due course they passed on their secret to the Jews. In later days the cult was to be practised also by the Gnostics, the Manichees, and the Moslem sect of the Assassins; these last transmitted the diabolic lore to the Templars, who handed it on to the Freemasons. But at all times the Jews, as 'the representatives on earth of the spirit of darkness' have supplied the grand masters. And if one asks in what precisely the cult consists, the answer is that it centres on the worship of Satan. The chief symbols are the serpent and the phallus, and the ritual includes erotic orgies of the wildest kind. But that is not all: by murdering Christian children the Jews in particular are able to acquire magical powers; and this too is part of 'the kabbalah'.

The extraordinary fact is that even these weird extravagances found believers. It is certain that many twentieth-century devotees of the *Protocols* really have imagined the secret Jewish government as composed of oriental sorcerers – one has only to look at the commentary on the *Protocols* published in Madrid in 1963 to find pages upon pages about 'the kabbalah'. Nor is this the only respect in which des Mousseaux provides the link between the *Protocols* and archaic, half-forgotten religious beliefs. One of the most unexpected features of the *Protocols* is that Jewish world-domination is to be exercised through a Jewish king, whom all nations will accept as their saviour. This figure is taken straight from the end of the last chapter of Gougenot des Mousseaux. As he nears his 500th page the industrious author allows himself a flight of prophetic frenzy in which he foretells how, in the midst of a great European war, the Jews will raise up 'a man with a genius for political imposture, a sinister bewitcher, around whom fanatical multitudes will cluster'. The Jews will hail this man as the Messiah, but he will be more than that. After destroying the authority of Christianity he will unite mankind in one great brotherhood and bestow on it a superabundance of material goods. For these great services the Gentile nations too will accept him, exalt him, worship him as a god – but in reality, for all his apparent benevolence, he will be Satan's instrument for the perdition of mankind.[1]

[1] Gougenot des Mousseaux, *Le Juif, le Judaïsme et la judaïsation des peuples chrétiens*, Paris, 1869, pp. 485–98.

Gougenot des Mousseaux states repeatedly that what inspired him to write this passage was the prophecy of Antichrist. According to the prophecy in the second chapter of the Second Epistle to the Thessalonians, the second coming of Christ and the Last Judgement will be immediately preceded by the appearance of Antichrist, 'the man of sin, the son of perdition'. He will demand to be worshipped as God; and by the miracles which he will perform with the Devil's help he will deceive all who are willing to be deceived. He will establish his rule over the whole world until the returning Christ destroys him with the breath of his mouth. So far the New Testament – but in the second and third centuries after Christ, as the Church and the Synagogue came more and more sharply into competition and conflict with one another, Christian theologians began to give a new interpretation to this prophecy. They foretold that Antichrist would be a Jew and would love the Jews above all peoples; while the Jews for their part would be the most faithful followers of Antichrist, accepting him as the Messiah. As to what would happen next, the theologians were divided. If some expected the Jews to be miraculously converted to Christianity, others expected that they would follow Antichrist to the end and on the return of Christ would be sent, along with Antichrist, to endure the torments of hell for all eternity.

It has been argued elsewhere that the Nazi belief in a Jewish world-conspiracy represents a revival, in a secularized form, of certain apocalyptic beliefs which once formed part of the Christian world-view.[1] In this instance one can trace the precise way in which an apocalyptic belief – in the coming of Antichrist – contributed to the making of the *Protocols*, which were to become part of the Nazi scriptures. And indeed the connexion between the *Protocols* and the Antichrist prophecy does not stop there. In later chapters we shall see how the first important edition of the *Protocols* appeared in a Russian book about the imminent coming of Antichrist; and how something of the same apocalyptic atmosphere appears even in the thinking and writing of Hitler and Rosenberg as soon as they touch on the *Protocols* and the Jewish world-conspiracy.

[1] N. Cohn, *The Pursuit of the Millennium*, revised editions, London and New York, 1961–62, pp. 62–3, 310.

But if Gougenot des Mousseaux revived archaic fantasies, he also modernized them. The long chapters on 'Gold' and on 'The Press' belong entirely to the world of modern, political antisemitism (indeed certain phrases in the *Protocols* seem to have been lifted straight from these pages). Above all the world-state which is to be established by Antichrist is astonishingly modern. It is an international order, in which all peoples are united in allegiance to a single unity, mankind, and in which material goods abound and are enjoyed by all with a good conscience. Reading these descriptions, one may well wonder why the Judeo-Masonic conspirators should not be regarded as the benefactors rather than as the exploiters of mankind. One has to remind oneself that if nowadays almost all political parties in the advanced countries subscribe to some extent to the ideals of international co-operation and material well-being, such notions were frankly abominated by the extreme Right so long as an extreme Right existed. Hitler and Gougenot des Mousseaux would have been at one in regarding such a world-order as quite intolerable.

Le Juif, le judaïsme et la judaïsation des peuples chrétiens was written at a time of bitter conflict between Freemasonry and the Roman Catholic Church. For, although the French Revolution was certainly not engineered by a Masonic conspiracy, in the course of the nineteenth century the Freemasons of France and Italy did indeed identify themselves more and more completely with the principles of that revolution. Staunchly republican and anti-clerical, the French Freemasons felt not insulted but flattered when reactionaries blamed them for the overthrow of the *ancien régime*. In Italy the Masonic lodges took a very active part in the struggle for national unity and therefore in attacking the temporal power of the Pope. But in the eyes of many Catholics the end of the Papal State meant the end of the Church; and to these people Freemasons seemed quite literally agents of Satan. It is in the years immediately before the Vatican Council of 1870 that Freemasons are first portrayed as devil-worshippers: in 1867, in his book *Les Francs-Maçons*, Mgr Ségur declared that black masses were celebrated in the 'inner lodges'. Gougenot des Mousseaux belonged to the same world of extreme right-wing, ultramontane Catholicism, and with his talk of 'the kabbalah' he was at least as much concerned to discredit Freemasonry and the progressive forces in general as to attack the Jews. His book, armed with an enthusiastic foreword from the head of the Foreign Mission Seminary in Paris, was explicitly directed to the Fathers at the Council – and not wholly in vain, for des Mousseaux was blessed by Pope Pius IX for his courage.

In France Gougenot des Mousseaux found a worthy successor in the Abbé Chabauty, *curé* of Saint-André at Mirebeau in Poitou, honorary canon of Poitiers and Angoulême. In 1881 this man published a 600-page volume called *Les Francs-Maçons et les Juifs: Sixième Age de l'Eglise d'après l'Apocalypse*, in which he argued that Satan, through the Judeo-Masonic conspiracy, was preparing the way for the Jewish Antichrist and the world-dominion of the Jews. In his most influential book, *Les Juifs nos maîtres* (1882), Chabauty did more than re-hash his predecessor's arguments, he added an important discovery of his own. He had found, in the *Revue des études juives* for 1880, two letters which seemed to him to be full of the most sinister significance, and which were indeed later to acquire a sinister significance in the history of antisemitism. They are known as *The Letter of the Jews of Arles* (or, in some versions, of Spain) and *The Reply of the Jews of Constantinople*; and they read as follows:

Honourable Jews, greetings and blessings!

This is to tell you that the King of France, who is again master of Provence, has ordained by public proclamation that we must become Christians or leave his territory. And the people of Arles, Aix and Marseilles want to take away our belongings, they threaten our lives, they wreck our synagogues, they cause us much vexation; and all this makes us uncertain about what we ought to do to keep the Law of Moses. This is why we ask you to be so good as to let us know, in your wisdom, what we ought to do.

CHAMOR
Rabbi of the Jews of Arles
the 13th of Sabath, 1489

Well-beloved Brethren in Moses, we have received the letter in which you tell us of the anxieties and adversities you are suffering.

The advice of the grand satraps and rabbis is as follows:

You say that the King of France demands that you become

Christians: do so, since you cannot do otherwise, but keep the Law of Moses in your hearts.

You say that you are forced to surrender your belongings: then make your children merchants, so that, little by little, they may strip the Christians of their belongings.

You say that attempts are made against your lives: then make your children doctors and apothecaries, so that they may deprive Christians of their lives.

You say that they are destroying your synagogues: then make your children canons and clerics, so that they may destroy their churches.

You say that people are vexing you in many other ways: then see to it that your children become advocates and notaries, so that you will get the Christians under your yoke, you will dominate the world, and you will be able to take your revenge.

Do not depart from this order that we give you, for you will see by experience that, from the abasement in which you now find yourselves, you will attain the summit of power.

> V.S.S.V.F.F.
> Prince of the Jews of Constantinople
> the 21st of Casleu, 1489[1]

From the point of view of the literary historian these 'letters', which date at least from the sixteenth century, are not without interest. Probably they were originally written in Spain, as a satirical comment on the Marranos – the Spanish Jews who claimed to have been converted to Catholicism but who were suspected, often rightly, of remaining Jews at heart. What is certain is that they were meant as a joke – the signature Chamor, for instance, is simply the Hebrew for donkey! For Chabauty, however, there was no possible doubt as to their authenticity – after all, as he pointed out, was not the *Revue des études juives*, which reprinted them, founded by the Baron de Rothschild?

And indeed thanks to these 'letters' the enterprising *curé* stumbled on an idea which had not occurred to any of his predecessors. He convinced himself that a single, secret Jewish government had existed throughout the Dispersion, that it was pursuing an unchanging plan for world-domination, and that all Jews owed it absolute obedience. And he was also

---

[1] The 'letters' are reprinted in E. A. Chabauty, *Les Juifs nos maîtres*, Paris–Brussels–Geneva, 1882, Chapter I.

concerned that 'Bismarck, William II and the other ministers and sovereigns of Europe and America are only the docile and often the blind instruments' of the hidden Jewish government. By such imaginings he not only prepared the way for the *Protocols of the Elders of Zion* but established the *Letter of the Jews of Constantinople* as an important 'document' in its own right. When, half a century later, the *Protocols* became a world-famous work, this 'letter' was republished again and again, often in the same volume as the *Protocols*, as confirmatory evidence. And not one editor realized that the signature V.S.S.V.F.F., which looks so cryptic and sinister, is simply the name Ussuff, i.e. Joseph!

Chabauty found his first imitators in Italy. In the mid-1880s Pope Leo XIII embarked on a fresh struggle against Italian Freemasonry; and although he himself never stooped to antisemitic propaganda, he permitted others to do so. The Jesuits associated with *La civiltà cattolica*, in particular, considered it perfectly legitimate to discredit Freemasonry by presenting it as part of the Jewish world-conspiracy. Two of these reverend gentlemen, Father R. Ballerini and Father F. S. Rondina, waged a campaign which lasted right through the 1890s. According to them all the afflictions in the modern world, from the French Revolution to the latest Italian bankruptcies, were simply fruits of two thousand years of Jewish conspiracy. *La civiltà cattolica* portrayed Italy as in the grip of violence, immorality, and general chaos – all thanks to the Jews; it described Jewry in terms that Hitler was to use – as a giant octopus squeezing the world; it even printed the tales of ritual murder which were later to grace the pages of *Der Stürmer*. It is not surprising that, with such an illustrious example before their eyes, provincial Catholic newspapers demanded a repeal of Jewish emancipation and the confiscation of all Jewish property.

It is true that the campaign failed to undermine the tolerant outlook of most Italian Catholics – how could they, after all, forget that the whole of Italian Jewry numbered barely 30,000? – but that does not mean it had no influence at all. The time was to come, after the First World War, when two successive popes were to honour the Frenchman Mgr Jouin for his life-long struggle against that mythical entity, the Judeo-

Masonic conspiracy; in one case, when he was already celebrated as an editor of the *Protocols*. *La civiltà cattolica* can
certainly take some credit for the outlook that made that
possible.[1]

In France, too, the theme of a Satanic world-conspiracy of
Freemasons, or of Jews, or of both together, continued to
inspire a prodigious amount of nonsensical propaganda
throughout the 1890s.[2] There it appealed above all to the
country clergy – nearly all of them sons of peasants or of
village artisans, poorly educated, infinitely credulous. What
they were prepared to believe beggars description. In 1893
that great hoaxer, Léo Taxil, had no difficulty at all in persuading them that the head of American Freemasonry had a
telephone system invented and manned (if that is the word)
by devils, and so was kept in constant touch with the seven
major capitals of the world; or that beneath the Rock of
Gibraltar squads of devils were at work, concocting epidemics
to destroy the Catholic world. And if Taxil confines his attention to Freemasons and makes no mention of Jews, others were
less restrained. *La Franc-Maçonnerie, Synagogue de Satan*, by
Mgr Meurin, Archbishop of Port-Louis, Mauritius – which also
appeared in 1893 – insists on the contrary that 'everything in
Freemasonry is fundamentally Jewish, exclusively Jewish,
passionately Jewish, from the beginning to the end'.[3]

This extraordinary work seems indeed to have been one of
the most immediate sources of the *Protocols* which, as we shall
see, were fabricated just about that time. And like so many of
the devotees of the *Protocols* after him, the Archbishop was
convinced that the whole of human history could be interpreted in terms of a Jewish conspiracy which was now within
sight of its goal. He also knew the means by which this plan
was being carried out: 'Some day history will tell how all the
revolutions of recent centuries originated in the Masonic sect
under the supreme command of the Jews.'[4] And not only that –

[1] On the campaign of *La civiltà cattolica*, see R. De Felice, *Storia degli
ebrei italiani sotto il fascismo*, Turin, 1961, pp. 37 seq.

[2] Cf. R. F. Byrnes, *Antisemitism in Modern France*, New Brunswick,
1950, notably pp. 256–313.

[3] L. Meurin, *La Franc-Maçonnerie, Synagogue de Satan*, Paris, 1893,
p. 260.

[4] Ibid., p. 196.

whatever the appearances, it is the governments themselves that foment the revolutions, because they too are controlled by Jews: 'The fact that all revolutions are made in the depths of the Masonic back-lodges would be inexplicable, if we did not know that the ministries of all countries . . . are in the hands of Freemasons who in the last analysis are controlled by Jews.'[1]

And the Archbishop has something else to tell about these mysterious 'back-lodges': they consist of Freemasons and Jews 'of the 33rd degree' – just as the *Protocols* themselves end with the words 'Signed by the Representatives of Zion of the 33rd degree'. It is quite clear where this idea came from. There really is one particular Masonic system which has thirty-three grades: 'the old and accepted Scottish rite', which was instituted in the United States at the beginning of the nineteenth century and spread to many countries. So far from concerning itself with political and economic strategies, this branch of Freemasonry has specialized in symbolism and in philanthropy; and in no sense does it control the whole of Freemasonry. But these facts were of no interest to the worthy Archbishop, or to the fabricator of the *Protocols*; for them, the Freemasons of the 33rd degree are the heart of the conspiracy to set up a Jewish king as ruler of the world. And the Archbishop goes further: these Freemasons of the 33rd degree are agents of the Devil in the most literal sense of the term. Assembled in their 'back-lodges', they worship Satan in the form of a serpent or a phallus, and on occasion Satan even honours them with a visit in person.

Once more, at the end of this fantastic book, one finds oneself plunged into the familiar apocalyptic atmosphere. The struggle against the imaginary Judeo-Masonic conspiracy is equated with the battle between the heavenly and the Satanic hosts foretold in the Book of Revelation:

As we write these lines, a hurricane, sighing and roaring, passes over our little island. . . . It is the image of our century! Science explains the origin and nature of the hurricane. This book explains our tormented century. . . . Paganism, Judaism, the vices and the passions, under the supreme command of Lucifer, are rising up

[1] Ibid., p. 202.

together to assault the Heavenly Jerusalem, in the hope that, united, their batallions may achieve the victory which they have never, to this day, gained by attacking separately.[1]

The Archbishop calls on the rulers of Europe to league themselves against the Jewish conspiracy before it destroys them. And although he declares that he will be satisfied if Jews are excluded from banking, commerce, journalism, teaching, and medicine, his final outburst is dramatic indeed:

Do not hope, O Jews, to be able to escape the calamity that once more threatens you. . . . The day when you are crushed will see the Church, your victim, enjoying a vital expansion such as has never been seen.

We do not wish to be slaves of the Jews, and we will not be such. . . . We shall forget our political differences to stand united and firm against the impudence and insolence of the enemies of God and of his Christ. Victory is assured. The future belongs to us. Lucifer and his emissaries will be forced to haul down their Masonic flag; Satan and the evil spirits who tour the world for the purpose of ruining souls will be cast back into Hell, from which they have audaciously climbed to assault the City of God.[2]

When one reflects that France had been the first country to emancipate its Jews (in 1791) and that by 1890 French Jews were still a mere handful (less than 80,000), one can only marvel at the intensity of such hatred. And the antisemitic fever that gripped France in the 1880s and 1890s had in fact practically nothing to do with contacts between individual non-Jewish Frenchmen and individual Jews. Talk of the Judeo-Masonic conspiracy found most belief in provinces such as Normandy, Brittany, Maine, Anjou, and Poitou, where there were very few Jews; in Montdidier, where Chabauty published his newspaper *L'Anti-Sémitique*, there lived not a single Jew. What the Jew symbolized for this public was the mysterious and sinister power of Paris, where most Jews lived. Here again one sees how the latter-day revival of antisemitism expressed above all the protest of traditional, rural society against the forces of modernity.

There was also the example of Germany. Militant antisemitism appeared in Germany at the very moment when German

[1] Ibid., p. 462.
[2] Ibid., pp. 466–8.

power and prestige were increasing; and there were Frenchmen who argued that France's salvation lay in imitating her
formidable neighbour. Chief among these was that talented
demagogue Edouard Drumont. Moreover, in his extremely
influential book *La France juive* (1886), Drumont popularized
the arguments of the little-known Gougenot des Mousseaux –
admittedly by the curious method of incorporating large sections of his book without acknowledgement. He also reprinted
Chabauty's find, the *Letter from the Jews of Constantinople*;
and altogether he did far more than anyone else to turn the
myth of the Judeo-Masonic conspiracy into a political force in
France.

As we shall see, the fabricator of the *Protocols of the Elders of
Zion* wrote in French and lived in France. There can be no
doubt that he drew heavily on the tradition of French political
antisemitism as it had developed in the last third of the nineteenth century, and particularly on the writings of des
Mousseaux, Chabauty, Meurin, and Drumont.

2

In the late nineteenth century antisemitism was a very much
more serious business in Russia than in any of the countries of
western or central Europe. Various circumstances combined
to make it so. Russia was in outlook still largely a medieval
country, where Jews were traditionally exposed to the same
kind of religiously motivated hatred as they had had to endure
in medieval Europe. Russia was also the last absolute
monarchy in Europe, and as such the greatest stronghold of
opposition to the liberalizing, democratizing tendencies
associated with the French Revolution. And as it happened,
Russia was also the country which had the largest Jewish
population, both absolutely and relatively: some 5,000,000
Jews, or about a third of all the Jews in the world, lived in the
Pale of Jewish Settlement, a group of provinces extending
from the Baltic to the Black Sea and embracing much of what
is now Poland. They represented about 5 per cent of the total
population of the Russian Empire, but a much larger proportion of the population in the areas to which they were restricted.

These Russian Jews were by no means newcomers. Mostly they were descended from Jews who had been driven out of Germany and France in the later Middle Ages and had settled in Poland; in the Crimea Jews had been settled since Roman times. But compared with the Jews of western Europe, Russian Jews did form a very closed, distinctive, unassimilated minority. They lived separate from the Russians, dressed differently, spoke and wrote Yiddish in preference to Russian. Many were passionately attached to the Jewish religion in its strictest form. They were on the whole miserably poor, but they included enough traders and moneylenders to incur the resentment of their Russian rivals in the towns and sometimes the hatred of the down-trodden Russian peasantry.

Russian Jews were subject to severe economic, residential, and educational restrictions. Throughout the nineteenth century they were harried and persecuted by the Government – not however as members of an alien race but as adherents of a detested religion. Any Jew who claimed to have been converted to Orthodoxy was at once relieved of the disabilities which afflicted his fellows. Conversions of convenience therefore represented a constant temptation to ambitious young men, and it is astonishing how few yielded to it.

Persecution was much intensified when the relatively liberal Tsar Alexander II was assassinated in 1881 and succeeded by his son, the ruthless and ultra-reactionary Alexander III. Both Alexander III and his son Nicholas II, the last tsar, were fanatical antisemites; and during their reigns everything possible was done, with every official encouragement, to clear Russia of Jews. The persecution was carried out partly by administrative measures – for instance, by expelling the Jews from the rural areas while preventing them from finding employment in the towns – and partly by officially sponsored pogroms. These methods were so successful that at some periods Russian Jews were emigrating at the rate of 100,000 a year, mostly to the United States of America.[1]

These developments had however been preceded by some

[1] For a good contemporary account of the situation of the Jews under Alexander III, by a non-Jewish Russian, see Stepniak (pseudonym of S. M. Kravchinsky), *King Stork and King Log, a study of modern Russia*, London, 1896, Vol. I, pp. 142–94.

years of antisemitic propaganda. As in France and Germany, the idea of the Jewish world-conspiracy was developed and elaborated from 1868 onwards, and began to take its full effect in the 1880s. Around 1868 the Jews of central Europe – in the German states and in Austria-Hungary – were being granted full citizenship; and one object of the propaganda was certainly to counter any pressure for similar reforms within the Russian Empire. Once instituted, the propaganda proved to have many uses. This was a time when the Russian autocracy was beginning to encounter active political opposition, notably from clandestine terroristic groups. The authorities were determined at all costs to mask the fact that there were real Russians – and educated ones at that – who so hated the autocracy that they were prepared to assassinate its representatives. They accordingly pretended that all opposition to the régime, and particularly all terrorism, was the work of the Jewish world-conspiracy.

This was not because Jews had any real part in the terroristic movement of the 1860s and 1870s. On the contrary, it was largely because of the intensified persecution which began in the 1880s that a small minority of Jews eventually joined the revolutionary movement, and particularly the Social-Democratic party which later split into the rival factions of Mensheviks and Bolsheviks; and even this small minority consisted, of course, not of Jews in the religious sense but of people of Jewish descent who had broken with Judaism and with the traditional Jewish community. Such distinctions were however ignored by the police. For them the whole revolutionary movement was from the start a tool in the hands of – incredible as it may seem – adherents of the Jewish religion. This was the story which they put out in their propaganda; and many of them certainly came to believe it themselves.

In Russia, then, in contrast with France and Germany, propaganda about the Jewish world-conspiracy was officially sponsored; it was a regular activity of the political police. Foreign contributions, such as *The Rabbi's Speech*, were eagerly snatched up; but there were also inventive spirits at work in Russia itself. The first of these in date was Jacob Brafmann, a Jew who not only underwent a tactical conversion to Orthodoxy but went on to become a police spy. In 1866 this man laid before certain high-ranking officials strange evidence concerning what he called 'the Kahal'. The Hebrew word 'kahal' means simply 'community-organization'. As Jews in medieval Europe were normally allowed a certain degree of local self-government, each Jewish settlement was automatically a kahal. In Russia a similar state of affairs existed until 1844, when the kahals, and with them all traces of Jewish autonomy, were abolished. But according to Brafmann 'the Kahal' was something quite different and far more menacing.

By way of proof Brafmann published a work which he called *The Book of the Kahal* (1869). In reality this was based on some minutes of routine business kept by the officially recognized kahal of Minsk from 1789 to 1828, supplemented by some similar material from other towns. But to this material Brafmann added a commentary which made it look as if the kahal in each town aimed at enabling Jewish traders to oust their Christian competitors and in the end to acquire possession of all the property of the Christians. *The Book of the Kahal* was issued at public expense and distributed to government officials to guide them in their dealings with the Jewish population. It had a great effect, particularly on the political police, and it was frequently reprinted. The word 'kahal' passed into the international vocabulary of antisemitic propaganda as an immensely sinister term – often described as 'a name which few Gentiles are ever allowed to hear.'[1]

Still more noxious was another book by Brafmann, first published in 1868 and later (1888) reprinted in the same volume as *The Book of the Kahal*. This work, called *Jewish Fraternities, local and universal*, can be regarded as the Russian counterpart to the fantasies of Goedsche and des Mousseaux. In it the existence of certain international Jewish organizations is 'unmasked', as though it were a great secret. The organizations in question are a society for the reprinting of basic Jewish texts; the Alliance Israélite Universelle; the Society for the Dissemination of Education among the Jews in Russia; the Society for the Promotion of Colonization in

---

[1] One of the American editors of the *Protocols*, who calls himself 'Earnest Sincere', even knows that the membership of 'the Kahal' numbers precisely 1,921,601!

Palestine; and the Association for the Support of Jewish Refugees in London. These were all well-known philanthropic organizations, with nothing secret about them; but that did not prevent Brafmann from treating them as branches of a secret, world-wide Jewish conspiracy. The Alliance Israélite Universelle, which was shown as the hub of the conspiracy, had been founded at Paris in 1860 and quickly became hated by all antisemites. In reality it was a purely French institution and not at all international. It was however concerned to help the persecuted Jews of Russia and Rumania, both by providing educational facilities and by succouring refugees; and this was quite enough to prompt Brafmann to the comment that 'the net of the Jewish world-alliance is spread over the whole globe'. Like *The Book of the Kahal*, the book on Jewish fraternities attracted much attention in the antisemitic bureaucracy. Thanks to it the Alliance Israélite Universelle was forbidden to operate in Russia and the work of the Society for the Dissemination of Education among the Jews in Russia was much restricted.

A decade later, when in France the Abbé Chabauty was constructing his fantasies around the *Letter from the Jews of Constantinople*, a former Roman Catholic priest of Polish extraction, Hippolytus Lutostansky, was engaged in a similar exercise in Russia. Having been unfrocked for a variety of offences ranging from embezzlement to rape, Lutostansky joined the Orthodox Church and became a student at a religious academy. The first result of his studies was a book on the use of Christian blood in Jewish religious ritual (1876). Some years later he made an interesting proposal to leading representatives of Russian Jewry: at a price, he would be prepared to publish a refutation of this book and to denounce it in lectures in the principal cities; if the price was not forthcoming he would publish further antisemitic writings. This attempt at bribery having failed, Lutostansky continued his career as an antisemitic propagandist until 1905; then, when it looked as though a more democratic régime might expose him to prosecution for forgery, he changed tack once again. In an open letter he assured the Jews that he had never really been their enemy; and signed it 'a repentant sinner'. This did not of course prevent the Black Hundreds from invoking his writings at the time of the Beiliss ritual murder trial.[1]

Lutostansky's most important book was a three-volume work called *The Talmud and the Jews* (1879–80). Totally ignorant of Hebrew, Lutostansky confined his researches to collecting every scurrilous rumour and forgery that had ever been concocted concerning the Talmud. The horrifying account which he gave of the principles of Judaism undoubtedly helped and encouraged the political police in their new task of provoking pogroms. But the book also contains a chapter on 'the Jewish Freemasons', based on the ideas of Gougenot des Mousseaux; and for Russia this was a novelty. As every reader of *War and Peace* knows, Freemasonry had once flourished among the more enlightened of the Russian nobles; already in the eighteenth century Russian Freemasons had in fact rendered great services in organizing famine relief and disseminating education. But that was a long time ago; in 1822 Freemasonry was banned in Russia and it never revived. Lutostansky can claim the honour of having introduced the myth of the Judeo-Masonic conspiracy into a country where there were probably no Freemasons at all.

Ingeniously, he combined this myth with Brafmann's attacks on the Alliance Israélite Universelle: Freemasonry is a Jewish secret society governed by the Alliance Israélite Universelle. The philanthropic aims of the Alliance are camouflage: 'This noble aim serves the Jews simply as a cloak for their grandiose political machinations. In this shape the society commands the services of journalists, secret agents and politicians, who day and night carry on their work of undermining the Christian states, by destroying their foundation, which is morality, and by weakening religious faith, so that all the inhabitants can easily be changed into freethinkers, atheists, nihilists, and anarchists.' 'Indeed, what government can rely on such a great number of agents, representing all the governments of the world?' The Alliance is in fact 'only the official public organ of the real centre of the Jewish state, a

---

[1] In 1913 Mendel Beiliss, a Jewish clerk of Kiev, was tried for the ritual murder of a Christian boy. The case caused great excitement and indignation far beyond the borders of Russia. Despite the most strenuous efforts by the prosecution Beiliss was acquitted. See M. Samuel, *Blood Accusation, the strange history of the Beiliss case*, New York, 1966.

centre which is wrapped in deepest darkness'. Like Brafmann, Lutostansky singles out for special attention the Society for the Dissemination of Education among the Jews in Russia; and he calls on the Russian government to suppress it. As justification for his whole argument he reprints – *The Rabbi's Speech*!

But the most extraordinary of these figures was surely an international crook of Jewish origin whose real name was Millinger but who preferred the names of Osman-Bey or Kibridli-Zade. Expelled from Venice in 1870 and from a whole series of countries during the following decade, this man turned to antisemitism as a way of making a living. Arrested in Milan, he solemnly withdrew all his antisemitic inventions – which did not prevent him later from producing new antisemitic pamphlets and selling them from door to door, from Athens to Constantinople and Alexandria. Constantly on the move, frequently arrested and imprisoned for swindles of every kind, he continued his picturesque and nefarious career until his death around 1898.

Though Osman-Bey came, apparently, from Serbia, and wrote in German, and published his major work in Switzerland, it was in Russia, and through the Russian antisemitic movement, that he tried to make his career. He wrote old-style stories of ritual murder – but he also wrote a book called *World Conquest by the Jews*. Like Brafmann and Lutostansky, he claimed that the source of all evil was the Alliance Israélite Universelle – which, in a fine flight of metaphor, he describes as an invisible and intangible power, casting an unnoticeable net of gold and steel around the world, while creeping in darkness with a dagger in one hand and dynamite in the other. As he portrayed it, the Alliance was no creation of nineteenth-century philanthropy but as old as the Jewish people itself. It had caused the French Revolution, through the instrumentality of William Pitt and his Jewish agitators, and was now dominating France through the Jews [*sic*] Thiers and Renan. At the moment it was mobilizing the whole of Jewry against Holy Russia. The Russian terrorists were its creatures and the assassination of Alexander II was its masterpiece – had it not smuggled the assassin out of Russia and brought him to (of all people) Karl Marx in (of all places) Berlin? The next step would be for 'nihilists and Jews' to rise in their masses, set up barricades and proclaim a constitution.

Fortunately the hour found the man, in Osman-Bey. 'It was our duty to delay no longer,' writes Osman-Bey, 'but to save Russia by seizing the helm.' Armed with 400 roubles from the political police he left St Petersburg for Paris on 3 September 1881; 'Russia,' he remarks, 'should note the date as a memorable one, for on that day began my mission, which was to be crowned with the uncovering of the universal conspiracy and the restoring of peace.' In Paris he visited the headquarters of the Alliance and at once noticed 'a strong nihilistic smell'. His aim was however a more concrete one – to capture documents which should reveal the part of the Alliance in the world-conspiracy. And sure enough he made a discovery which in his view 'saved Russia and will help to open the eyes of the rest of mankind'.[1]

Osman-Bey describes how he bribed a young Jew to smuggle out of the offices of the Alliance letters which had been received from various Jewish committees in countries bordering on Russia. He admits that he never met the young Jew and remarks that the whole affair was arranged through French friends of his, whom he does not name. Once in possession of the letters, he sat up all night copying them out; then he marked on a map the location of the committees. The result astonished and appalled him: the committees stretched along the Russian frontier; clearly they represented a Jewish force massed against Russia, under the command of the rabbis of Königsberg and Liegnitz, with the Russian terrorists as their vanguard. In reality the only Jewish committees were those responsible for succouring the thousands of Jewish refugees as they left Russian territory, hungry and penniless; but Osman-Bey saw things in a different light. In phrases worthy of the Abbé Barruel he describes how, while the Russian police watched the main roads, agents passed to and fro between these committees and the terrorists inside Russia, all travelling cross-country or by water, without ever being spotted.

'In the Ministries of the Interior, of Foreign Affairs and of

---

[1] Osman-Bey (pseudonym of Millinger), *Enthüllungen über die Ermordung Alexanders II*, Bern, 1886, pp. 116–29. On Osman-Bey see W. Laqueur, *Russia and Germany*, London, 1965, p. 96.

War,' remarks this adventurous traveller, 'they fought one another to get at my reports, and universal horror reigned.' This need not be taken too seriously – he also claimed that in the Russian–Turkish war he had captured the town of Kars single-handed. Osman-Bey was a near-paranoiac, who believed that but for a conspiracy of hack politicians he would be recognized as Russia's saviour and appointed minister and dictator. But he has a real claim to be remembered, nevertheless – as a truly sinister prophet and portent.

In *World Conquest by the Jews* – which had already reached its seventh edition in 1875, that is to say before Hermann Goedsche's fantasy had turned into *The Rabbi's Speech* – and in his *Revelations concerning the assassination of Alexander II* (1886), Osman-Bey expounds the whole delusional system which, fifty or sixty years later, was to work itself out in the greatest of all massacres. In a world without Jews, he says, wars will be less frequent, because nobody will stir one nation up against another; class-hatred and revolutions will cease, because the only capitalists will be 'national' ones, who never exploit anyone; socialists and suchlike will realize the folly of their ways. 'The Golden Age would lie before us all, it would be the ideal of progress itself.' But first there must be a great purge: 'Drive out the Jews with an enthusiastic shout: "Long live the principle of nationalities and races! Out with the intruders...."' And if one asks where the Jews are to go, sometimes he replies 'to Africa', just as Hitler was to talk of Madagascar. At other times, however, he is franker: 'The Alliance Israélite Universelle can be destroyed only through the complete extermination of the Jewish race.'[1]

[1] Osman-Bey, *Enthüllungen über die Ermordung Alexanders II*, pp. 189–92.

CHAPTER III

The *Protocols* and the *Dialogue aux Enfers*

1

THE nineteenth-century transmitters of the myth of the Jewish world-conspiracy, then, are a varied crew. They include Barruel and the 'Simonini letter' at the beginning of the century; and much later, in the last third of the century, Goedsche in Germany, and *The Rabbi's Speech*; the Frenchmen Gougenot des Mousseaux, Mgr Meurin, the Abbé Chabauty, Edouard Drumont; the Russian Brafmann, the Pole Lutostansky, and the Serb Osman-Bey. Together these people prepared the way for the famous forgery which was to survive long after their own writings had faded into obscurity.

'Around 1840,' wrote Osman-Bey in his *World Conquest by the Jews*, 'a Jewish parliament was summoned at Cracow. It was a sort of Ecumenical Council, where the most eminent leaders of the Chosen People met to confer. The purpose of summoning them was, to determine the most suitable means to ensure that Judaism should spread safely from the North Pole to the South . . .

'Suddenly a clear voice rang out and automatically imposed silence. It was the voice of a recognised authority, a man of overwhelming intelligence, whose name we unfortunately do not know. . . .

'His words had a startling effect on the assembly; people saw that an oracle had spoken, that a new illumination had dawned upon their minds, to give a firm direction to their efforts . . .'[1]

This fantasy provides the framework for the *Protocols of the*

[1] Osman-Bey, *Die Eroberung der Welt durch die Juden*, Wiesbaden, 1875, p. 48.

Elders of Zion. For the *Protocols* consists of lectures, or notes for lectures, in which a member of the secret Jewish government – the Elders of Zion – expounds a plot to achieve world-domination.

In the standard version the 'protocols', or lectures, or chapters, are twenty-four in number; together they fill a booklet – about a hundred small pages in both British editions. They are not easy to summarize, for the style is turgid and diffuse, the argument tortuous and illogical. With perseverance one can however distinguish three main themes: a critique of liberalism; an analysis of the methods by which world-domination is to be achieved by the Jews; and a description of the world-state which is to be established. These themes are interwoven in a most confusing manner, but on the whole it can be said that the first two themes predominate in the first nine 'protocols', while the remaining fifteen 'protocols' are devoted mainly to a prophecy of the coming kingdom. And if one insists on reducing the argument to some sort of order, it comes out roughly as follows.

The Elders base their calculations on a particular view of politics. As they see it, political liberty is only an idea – admittedly an idea which has great attraction for the masses, but one which can never be translated into reality. Liberalism, which attempts this impossible task, results merely in chaos; for the people are incapable of governing themselves, they do not know their own mind, they are easily deceived by appearances, they cannot choose rationally between conflicting counsels. When the aristocracy ruled it was right that aristocrats should have liberty, for they used it for the general good; it was in their own interest, for instance, to care for the workers from whose labour they lived. But aristocracy is a thing of the past, and the liberal order which has succeeded it cannot last but must inevitably lead to despotism. Only a despot can ensure order in society. Moreover, since there are more evil men than good in the world, force is the only appropriate means of government. Might is right; and in the modern world the basis of might is the possession and control of capital. Today it is gold that rules the world.

Over a period of many centuries a plot has been in operation to place all political power firmly in the hands of those who alone are qualified to use it properly – that is to say, in the hands of the Elders of Zion. Much has been achieved but the plot has not yet reached fruition. Before the Elders can establish their rule over the whole world the existing Gentile states, already seriously undermined, must be finally abolished; and the Elders have very precise ideas as to how this is to be accomplished.

In the first place everything possible must be done, in each existing state, to foster discontent and unrest. Fortunately the means for this are provided by the very nature of liberalism. Already, by encouraging the incessant proclamation of liberal ideas and the incessant chatter with which parliaments fill their days, the Elders will be helping to produce complete mental confusion in the populace. This confusion will be increased by the multiplicity of political parties; the Elders will foster it by secretly supporting them all. Again, they will exert themselves to alienate the people from their rulers. In particular they will keep the workers in perpetual unrest by pretending to sympathize with their grievances while secretly contriving to raise the cost of living.

Within each state authority must be discredited. The aristocracy is to be finally eliminated by heavy taxation on land; as aristocrats will not easily abandon their luxurious way of life this should plunge them deep in debt. Presidential régimes will be instituted, and this will enable the Elders to make their own puppets into presidents – preferably men with some discreditable episode in their past lives, for this will make them easier to control. Freemasonry and secret societies must be penetrated and turned into mere tools of the Elders; any Freemasons who show signs of resistance must be secretly executed. Industry must be concentrated into giant monopolies, so that all Gentile fortunes can be destroyed together when it suits the Elders.

Relations between states, too, are to be bedevilled. National differences are to be emphasized until international understanding becomes impossible. Armaments must be perpetually increased and there must be frequent wars. These wars must, however, lead to no gains on any side but only to ever greater economic chaos. And meanwhile there will be a steady undermining of Gentile morality. Gentiles are to be encouraged to become atheists and to indulge in every kind of luxury, licence, and depravity; for this purpose the Elders are already placing chosen tutors and governesses as their agents in Gentile homes. Drunkenness and prostitution must be vigorously fostered.

The Elders recognize that their plot may yet be obstructed by the Gentiles but are confident of their ability to overcome all resistance. They can use the common people to overthrow the rulers; by reducing the masses to starvation level they can bring them to a point where they will rise up, simultaneously in all countries and all under the complete control of the Elders, to destroy all private property – except of course that owned by Jews. They can use governments against governments; after years of carefully fostered intrigue and hostility it will be easy for them to organize a war against any nation which resists their will. Even if by any chance the whole of Europe should unite against them, they will still be able to call on the cannon of America, China, or Japan. And then there are the underground railways: these have been devised with the sole purpose of ensuring that the Elders will be able to meet any serious opposition by blowing whole capital cities sky high. After which any surviving remnants of opposition can always be inoculated with frightful diseases. Even the possibility that the Jews themselves might become refractory has been foreseen; this is to be coped with by stimulating outbreaks of antisemitism.

Surveying the contemporary scene the Elders see grounds for confidence. Already they can claim to have destroyed religious faith, and especially Christian faith. Now that the Jesuits have been brought low the Papacy remains defenceless and can be destroyed at a convenient moment. The prestige of secular rulers, too, is on the decline; assassinations and threats of assassination have made them afraid to appear in public except with a guard, while the assassins have been glorified as martyrs. Neither rulers nor aristocrats can now command the allegiance of the common people. Economic disorder is already far advanced. Cunning financial manipulations have produced depressions and enormous national debts, public finances have been reduced to hopeless confusion, the gold standard has everywhere produced national ruin.

The time must soon come when the Gentile states, reduced

to desperation, will be only too glad to hand over all control to the Elders, who indeed have already been able to establish the foundations for their future rule. In the place of aristocracy they have set up plutocracy or the rule of gold; and the gold is controlled by them. They have established their control over the law and have brought it into utter confusion; the invention of arbitration is an example of their devilish subtlety. Education too is firmly in their hands, and here their baleful influence is shown in the invention of teaching by visual media; the purpose of this technique is simply to turn the Gentiles into 'unthinking submissive beasts, waiting for things to be presented before their eyes in order to form an idea of them'. Above all, the Elders already control politics and the politicians; all parties, from the most conservative to the most radical, are in reality simply their tools. Hiding behind Freemasonry, the Elders have already penetrated all state secrets; and as governments well know, they have the power to create political order or disorder as they wish. After centuries of struggle, and at the cost of thousands of Gentile and even of many Jewish lives, the Elders are perhaps within a century of the final attainment of their goal.

That goal is the Messianic Age, when the whole world will be united in a single religion, Judaism, and will be ruled over by a Jewish sovereign of the House of David. This age is divinely ordained, for God has chosen the Jews to dominate the world; but it will also be characterized by a very definite political structure. Society will be organized to take full account of the reality of human inequality. The masses will be kept well away from politics; both their education and their press will be designed to prevent them from developing any political interests whatever. All publications will be strictly censored and freedom of speech and association will be stringently curtailed. These restraints will be imposed in the guise of temporary measures, to be ended when the enemies of the people have been subdued; but they will be maintained permanently. History will be taught only as a way of stressing the difference between past chaos and present order; the successes of the new world-empire will be perpetually contrasted with the political weaknesses and failures of the old Gentile governments. Everyone will be spied upon. A vast secret police will be recruited from all strata of the population, and it will be an absolute obligation for every citizen to report any criticism of the régime. Seditious agitation will be treated as a shameful crime, comparable with theft or murder. Liberalism will be utterly extirpated and unquestioning obedience demanded from all. Liberty will, admittedly, be promised for some future time but it will never be granted.

On the other hand everything will be done to ensure the efficient functioning of society. Unemployment will be abolished and taxation will be proportionate to wealth. The interests of the small man will be furthered by the stimulation of small-scale industry. Education will be designed to train the young for the particular station in life for which each is destined. Drunkenness will be severely discouraged; and so will independence of thought.

All this will tend to keep the masses quiet and contented, and the example set by their rulers will help in this. The laws will be clear and unalterable; judges will be incorruptible and infallible. All the Jewish leaders will show themselves able, efficient, and benevolent. Above all, the sovereign will be a man of exemplary character; unsuitable heirs will be ruthlessly set aside. This Jewish ruler of the world will be seen to go freely among the people, accepting their petitions; nobody will realize that those who surround him are security police. His private life will be above reproach, he will bestow no favours on his relatives, he will possess no property. He will work constantly at the task of government. The result will be a world without violence or injustice, in which true well-being will be enjoyed by all. The peoples of the earth will rejoice in being so well governed; and so the kingdom of Zion will endure.

Such, then, is the plot attributed to those mysterious gentlemen, the Elders of Zion. It was first revealed to the public when a number of editions were published in Russia, between 1903 and 1907. The earliest is a version, slightly shortened at the end, which appeared in the St Petersburg newspaper *Znamya* (*The Banner*) from 26 August to 7 September 1903. *Znamya* was edited by P. A. Krushevan, the noted and militant antisemite. A few months before publishing the *Protocols* he had instigated the pogrom at Kishinev in Bessarabia, in which forty-five Jews were killed and more than 400 injured and 1,300 Jewish houses and shops destroyed.

Krushevan does not reveal who sent or gave him the manuscript – only that it was a translation of a document originally written down in France and that the translator had entitled it *Minutes of the Meeting of the World Union of Freemasons and Elders of Zion*; for his part he called it *Programme for World Conquest by the Jews*. Some two years later the same version, but no longer truncated, appeared in the form of a booklet with the title *The Root of our Troubles* and the sub-title: 'Where the root is of the present disorder of society in Europe and especially in Russia. Extracts from the ancient and modern Protocols of the World Union of Freemasons'. This work was handed to the St Petersburg Censorship Committee on 9 December 1905; permission to print was given at once and the book was published the same month, in St Petersburg, under the imprint of the Imperial Guard. No editor's name was given but it is very likely that the editor was in fact a retired officer called G. V. Butmi, who was a close associate of Krushevan and like him a Bessarabian.

At that time – from October 1905 onwards – Butmi and Krushevan were busily helping to build up an extreme right-wing organization, the Union of the Russian People, commonly known as the Black Hundreds, with armed squads of toughs to assassinate radicals and liberals and to massacre Jews. In January 1906 this organization published a new edition of the pamphlet *The Root of our Troubles*, but this time bearing the name of Butmi and the title *The Enemies of the Human Race*, with the sub-title: 'Protocols extracted from the secret archives of the Central Chancellery of Zion (where the root is of the present disorder of society in Europe in general and of Russia in particular).' This edition appeared under the imprint no longer of the Imperial Guard but of a society of the deaf and dumb. Three further editions of this version appeared in 1906 and another in 1907, all in St Petersburg; another appeared at Kazan in 1906, with the title *Extracts from the Protocol of the Freemasons*.

The Root of our Troubles and *The Enemies of the Human Race* are cheap pamphlets meant for mass distribution. Quite different is the edition of the *Protocols* that appeared as part of a book called *The Great in the Small*. *Antichrist considered as an imminent political possibility*, by a mystical writer, Sergey Nilus. The first two editions of this work, published in 1901 and 1903, did not contain the *Protocols*, but they were inserted in the third edition, published in December 1905 under the imprint of the local Red Cross at the imperial residence outside St Petersburg, Tsarskoe Selo. As we shall see, this edition was produced to influence Tsar Nicholas II, and it bears all the signs of its origin. It is elegantly printed, it forms part of a mystical work such as the Tsar loved to read; above all it abounds in reference to French events and personalities, whereas the Krushevan-Butmi version refers more to purely Russian affairs.

Nilus's book was passed by the Moscow Censorship Committee on 28 September 1905, but it was still in manuscript; even so it appeared in print about the same time as *The Root of our Troubles*. And it had made its mark before that. At that time Sergey Nilus was much in favour at the imperial court; as a result, the Metropolitan of Moscow ordered a sermon quoting his version of the *Protocols* to be read in all the 368 churches of Moscow. This was duly done on 16 October 1905, and the sermon was promptly reprinted in the right-wing newspaper *Moscovskia Vedomosti* – yet another edition of the *Protocols*, of a sort.

It was Nilus's version, not Butmi's, that was to become a force in world history. That did not even begin to happen in 1905, nor when further editions of *The Great in the Small* were published in 1911 and 1912. It happened only when the book reappeared, somewhat revised and enlarged, under the title *He is Near, At the Door . . . Here comes Antichrist and the reign of the Devil on earth*. And then it happened because of the moment: 1917.

2

When one is confronted with a highly secret document ostensibly recording a series of lectures one naturally wonders who delivered the lectures to whom and on what occasion, and also how the document came to be seen by eyes for which it was obviously not intended. The various editors of the *Protocols* have done their best to satisfy such curiosity, but unfortunately their answers are anything but clear or unanimous.

Even the earliest edition, that in *Znamya*, plunges us into confusion. While the translator tells us that the document was taken from 'the Central Chancellery of Zion, in France', the editor admits that 'we do not know how, where or by what means the minutes of these meetings, which took place in France, could be copied down, nor above all who copied them . . .'. And that is not all. The translator, in a postscript, warns us sharply against confusing the Elders of Zion with the representatives of the Zionist movement – but that does not prevent the editor from claiming that the *Protocols* reveal the menace of Zionism 'which has the task of uniting all the Jews in the whole world in one union – a union which is more closely knit and more dangerous than the Jesuits'.[1]

For Butmi too the *Protocols* are 'extracted from the secret archives of the Central Chancellery of Zion'; but he has a more colourful tale to tell: 'These minutes or "protocols", being secret documents, were extracted with great effort, in the form of detached pages, and translated into Russian on 9 December 1901. It is almost impossible to penetrate a second time into the secret archives where they are kept; that is why they cannot be confirmed by precise indications as to the place, day, month and year, that is to say as to where and when they were drawn up. The reader who is at all familiar with the Masonic mysteries will be convinced of their authenticity when he learns of the criminal plan exposed in these "protocols".'[2]

Nilus is still more communicative – so much so, in fact, that he ends by contradicting not only Butmi but also himself. In the 1905 edition the *Protocols* are followed by a note: 'These "protocols" were removed from a whole book of "protocols." All this was obtained by my correspondent from the secret archives of the Central Chancellery of Zion, which is at present situated in France.'[3] This tallies well enough with Butmi; but

---

[1] *Znamya*, St Petersburg, issue of 26 August 1903.

[2] Mgr Jouin, *Le Péril Judéo-maçonnique*, Vol. IV: *Les 'Protocols' de 1901 de G. Butmi*, Paris, 1922, p. 4.

[3] S. Nilus, *Velikoe v Malom*, Tsarskoe Selo, 1905, p. 394.

unfortunately in the same edition the *Protocols* are also preceded by a note, saying that they were 'stolen by a woman from
one of the most influential and most highly initiated leaders of
Freemasonry, after one of the secret meetings of the "initiated" in France, that nest of Masonic conspiracy'.[1] And in the
1917 edition Nilus confuses the issue still further:

. . . only now have I learned authoritatively from Jewish sources
that these *Protocols* are nothing else than a strategic plan for the
conquest of the world, putting it under the yoke of Israel, the
struggle against God, a plan worked out by the leaders of the
Jewish people during the many centuries of dispersion, and finally
presented to the Council of Elders by 'the Prince of the Exile',
Theodor Herzl, at the time of the first Zionist congress, summoned
by him at Basel in August 1897.[2]

There could hardly have been a worse choice. The original
manuscript of the *Protocols* was in French, but at the first
Zionist congress there was not a single French delegate and
the official language was German; Herzl, the founder of
modern Zionism, was an Austrian; and the entire proceedings
of the congress were held in public, while the town of Basel
overflowed with journalists who would hardly have overlooked
so extraordinary a meeting. But in any case Nilus himself, in
his edition of 1905, had categorically stated that the lectures
were delivered not in 1897 but in 1902–3.

As though the confusion was not already sufficient, the
editors of various later translations of the *Protocols* invented
still further stories. The editor of the first German edition
(1919), who passed under the name of Gottfried zur Beek,
maintains that the Elders of Zion were simply the members of
the Basel congress; and he explains, too, just how their
machinations were unmasked. According to him the Russian
government, always anxious about Jewish activities, sent a
spy to observe the congress. A Jew who was entrusted with
taking the minutes of the (non-existent) secret meetings from
Basel to the 'Jewish Masonic lodge' at Frankfort-on-Main
was bribed by this spy to lend them for a night at an unnamed
town on the way. Fortunately the spy had with him a whole
squad of copyists. Writing frantically, these men managed

[1] S. Nilus, *Velikoe v Malom*, Tsarskoe Selo, 1905, p. 322.
[2] S. Nilus, *Bliz est, pri dverekh*, 1917, p. 88.

during that night to copy many of the minutes, which were then sent to Nilus for translation into Russian.

Thus Gottfried zur Beek; but Theodor Fritsch, 'the Nestor of German antisemitism', took an entirely different view of the matter in his edition of the *Protocols* (1921). For him too the document was a Zionist production – indeed he called it *The Zionist Protocols* – but it was stolen not from the Basel congress but from an unspecified Jewish house by the Russian police. Moreover it was not in French but in Hebrew – so the police passed it for translation to 'the orientalist Professor Nilus' (who in reality was neither a professor nor an orientalist – nor, as we shall see, a translator of the *Protocols*). Different again is the tale told by Roger Lambelin, the editor of the most popular French edition: according to him the *Protocols* were stolen from a cupboard in a town in Alsace, by the wife or fiancée of the leader of the Freemasons. After such picturesque stories it is a sad anticlimax to learn from a Polish edition that the *Protocols* were simply taken from the flat of Theodor Herzl in Vienna.

A Russian-American lady, sometimes known by her maiden name of Lesley Fry and sometimes by her married name of Mrs Shishmarev, wrote much about the *Protocols* from 1922 onwards. Her major contribution was to argue that the author of the *Protocols* was none other than Ascher Ginzberg, who wrote under the name of Achad Ha-am (i.e. 'One of the People') – in reality as unpolitical and unworldly an author as one can imagine. According to Miss Fry the *Protocols* were written by Ginzberg in Hebrew, read by him to a secret gathering of initiates at Odessa in 1890 and then sent, in a French translation, to the Alliance Israélite Universelle at Paris and thence to the congress at Basel in 1897 – where, one must assume, it would have had to be translated into German for the benefit of the delegates. A complicated hypothesis, but one which found influential adherents nevertheless.

Between the various writers on the *Protocols* there is, then, almost no agreement. Even the conviction that the Elders of Zion are the same as the leaders of Zionism is not shared by them all. As we have seen, the unknown Russian translator of the original French manuscript, as quoted by Krushevan and Butmi, explicitly states that the Elders are not to be confused with the representatives of the Zionist movement. For Nilus, until his belated discovery, the 'Central Chancellery of Zion' was the headquarters of the Alliance Israélite Universelle in Paris; and Urbain Gohier, one of the first editors of the *Protocols* in France, was equally convinced that the Elders were members of the Alliance. Others, following in the footsteps of Miss Fry, have attempted to combine the two beliefs – no easy feat, since the Alliance, a purely philanthropic and unpolitical organization which set all its hopes on the assimilation of the Jews to their Gentile compatriots, was as hostile to Zionism as could be. And then of course there were the Freemasons, so frequently named in connexion with the *Protocols*. . . . And meanwhile in 1921 something came to light which conclusively proved the *Protocols* to be a forgery.

The *Protocols* are such a transparent and ludicrous forgery that one may well wonder why it was ever necessary to prove the point. The fact remains that in the years immediately after the First World War, when the *Protocols* were emerging from obscurity and becoming a world-famous document, multitudes of people who were by no means insane took them perfectly seriously. To realize this one has only to consider what *The Times* had to say on the matter in its issue of 8 May 1920: 'What are these "Protocols"? Are they authentic? If so, what malevolent assembly concocted these plans, and gloated over their exposition? . . . Have we, by straining every fibre of our national body, escaped a "Pax Germanica" only to fall into a "Pax Judæica"?'[1]

A year later, on 18 August 1921, *The Times* devoted a resounding editorial to admitting its error. It had just published, in its issues of 16, 17, and 18 August, a lengthy despatch from its correspondent in Constantinople, Philip Graves, revealing that the *Protocols* were largely copied from a pamphlet directed against Napoleon III and dated 1865. Philip Graves wrote as follows:

I must confess that when the discovery was communicated to me I was at first incredulous. Mr X, who brought me the evidence, was convinced. 'Read this book through,' he said, 'and you will find

[1] The text is given more fully below, pp. 152-3.

irrefutable proof that the *Protocols of the Learned Elders of Zion* is a plagiarism.'

Mr X, who does not wish his real name to be known, is a Russian landowner with English connections. Orthodox by religion, he is in political opinion a Constitutional Monarchist. He came here as a refugee after the final failure of the White cause in South Russia. He had long been interested in the Jewish question as far as it concerned Russia, had studied the *Protocols*, and during the period of Denikin's[1] ascendancy had made investigations with the object of discovering whether any occult 'Masonic' organization, such as the *Protocols* speak of, existed in Southern Russia. The only such organization was a Monarchist one. The discovery of the key to the problems of the *Protocols* came to him by chance.

A few months ago he bought a number of old books from a former officer of the Okhrana[2] who had fled to Constantinople. Among these books was a small volume in French, lacking the title-page, with dimensions $5\frac{1}{2}$ by $3\frac{1}{2}$ inches. It had been cheaply re-bound. On the leather back is printed in Latin capitals the word Joli. The preface, entitled 'Simple Avertissement', is dated Geneva, 15 October 1864. . . . Both the paper and the type are characteristic of the sixties and seventies of the last century. These details are given in the hope that they may lead to the discovery of the title of the book. . . .

Mr X believes it must be rare, since, had it not been so, the 'Protocols' would have speedily been recognized as plagiarism by anyone who had read the original.

That the latter is a 'fake' could not be maintained for an instant by anyone who had seen it. Its original possessor, the old Okhrana officer, did not remember where he obtained it, and attached no importance to it. Mr X, glancing at it one day, was struck by a resemblance between a passage which had caught his eye and a phrase in the French edition of the *Protocols*. He followed up the clue, and soon realized that the *Protocols* were to a very large extent . . . a paraphrase of the Geneva original. . . .

Before receiving the book from Mr X I was, as I have said, in-credulous. I did not believe that Serge Nilus' *Protocols* were authentic. . . . But I could not have believed, had I not seen, that the writer who supplied Nilus with his originals was a careless and shameless plagiarist.

The Geneva book is a very thinly veiled attack on the despotism

[1] General Anton Denikin, Commander-in-Chief of the 'White' armies in southern Russia during the civil war, 1918–20.

[2] Okhrana: the secret police in tsarist Russia.

of Napoleon III in the form of a series of 25 dialogues. . . . The
speakers are Montesquieu and Machiavelli. . . .[1]

Before publishing the dispatch from its Constantinople
correspondent *The Times* carried out some research at the
British Museum. The name 'Joli' on the book's cover provided
the clue. The mysterious volume was quickly identified as the
Dialogue aux Enfers entre Montesquieu et Machiavel, by a
French lawyer called Maurice Joly; it was first published at
Brussels (though with the imprint Geneva) in 1864.

In the autobiography which he wrote in 1870 Maurice Joly
has described how, strolling one evening by the Seine in Paris,
he suddenly conceived the idea of writing a dialogue between
Montesquieu and Machiavelli. Montesquieu would present the
case for liberalism, Machiavelli the case for a cynical despotism.
It was forbidden to criticize openly the régime of Napoleon
III; but in this way it should be possible, through the mouth
of Machiavelli, to present the Emperor's motives and methods
stripped of their usual camouflage of humbug. So thought Joly,
but he underestimated his adversary. The *Dialogue aux Enfers*
was printed in Belgium and smuggled into France for distribution, but the moment it crossed the border it was seized by
the police and its author was quickly traced and arrested. On
25 April 1865 Joly was tried and sentenced to fifteen months'
imprisonment; his book was banned and confiscated.

Joly's later career was equally unfortunate. Witty, aggressive, no respecter of persons, he proceeded from disappointment to disappointment until, in 1879, he committed suicide.
He deserved a better fate. He was not only a brilliant stylist,
he had a fine intuition for the forces which, gathering strength
after his death, were to produce the political cataclysms of the
present century. In his novel *Les Affamés* he showed a rare
understanding of those tensions in the modern world which
foster revolutionary movements, whether of the right or the
left. Above all, in his reflections on the amateurish despotism
of Napoleon III he arrived at insights which remain valid
when applied to various authoritarian régimes of our own
time. Moreover, something of Joly's insights even survived
when the *Dialogue aux Enfers* was transformed into the

[1] *The Times*, issues of 16, 17, and 18 August 1921.

Protocols of the Elders of Zion; that is one reason – though, as we shall see, not the only reason – why the *Protocols* often seem to forecast twentieth-century authoritarianism. But that after all is a poor kind of immortality; and there is a cruel irony in the fact that a brilliant but long-forgotten defence of liberalism should have provided the basis for an atrociously written piece of reactionary balderdash which has swept the world.

Joly's pamphlet is indeed an admirable work, incisive, ruthlessly logical, beautifully constructed. The debate is opened by Montesquieu, who argues that in the present age the enlightened ideas of liberalism have made despotism, which was always immoral, impracticable as well. Machiavelli replies with such eloquence and at such length that he dominates the rest of the pamphlet. The mass of the people, he insists, are simply incapable of governing themselves. Normally they are inert and are only too happy to be ruled by a strong man; while if something happens to arouse them they show unlimited capacity for senseless violence – and then they need a strong man to control them. Politics have never had anything to do with morality; and as for practicability, it has never been so easy as now to impose despotic rule. A modern ruler need only pretend to observe the forms of legality, he need allow his people only the merest semblance of self-government – and he will have not the slightest difficulty in attaining and exercising absolute power. People readily acquiesce in any decision which they imagine to have been their own; therefore the ruler has only to refer all questions to a popular assembly —having first, of course, arranged that the assembly shall give the decision he requires. The forces that might oppose his will can be dealt with easily enough: the press can be censored, political opponents can be watched by the police. Neither the power of the Church nor financial problems need be feared. So long as the prince dazzles the people with his prestige and by winning military victories he can be sure of their support.

Such is the book that inspired the forger of the *Protocols*. He plagiarized it shamelessly – just how shamelessly can be seen by skimming the selection of parallel passages at the end of this book.[1] In all, over 160 passages in the *Protocols*, totalling

[1] See pp. 275–9.

two-fifths of the entire text, are clearly based on passages in Joly; in nine of the chapters the borrowings amount to more than half of the text, in some they amount to three-quarters, in one (Protocol VII) to almost the entire text. Moreover with less than a dozen exceptions the order of the borrowed passages remains the same as it was in Joly, as though the adaptor had worked through the *Dialogue* mechanically, page by page, copying straight into his 'protocols' as he proceeded. Even the arrangement in chapters is much the same – the twenty-four chapters of the *Protocols* corresponding roughly with the twenty-five of the *Dialogue*. Only towards the end, where the prophecy of the Messianic Age predominates, does the adaptor allow himself any real independence of his model. It is in fact as clear a case of plagiarism – and of faking – as one could well desire.

The forger constructed his argument out of the two con-flicting arguments in the *Dialogue*: that of 'Machiavelli', in favour of despotism, and that of 'Montesquieu', in favour of liberalism. His borrowings are mostly from 'Machiavelli'. What Joly put into the mouth of Machiavelli, the forger put into the mouth of the mysterious lecturer, the nameless Elder of Zion – but with certain important differences. Whereas 'Machiavelli', representing Napoleon III, is describing a state of affairs which already exists, in the *Protocols* this description is recast in the form of a prophecy for the future. Again, 'Machiavelli' argues that a despot may find in democratic forms a useful cover for his tyranny; in the *Protocols* the argu-ment is reversed, so that all democratic forms of government are shown as being simply masks for tyranny. But the forger also borrows certain passages from 'Montesquieu'; and here he makes it seem that the ideals of liberalism were invented by Jews, and are being propagated by them, for the sole pur-pose of disorganizing and demoralizing the Gentiles.

Given sufficient leisure, it might be possible to construct a coherent argument out of such materials, but the *Protocols* give the impression of having been concocted in a hurry. The *Dialogue aux Enfers*, for instance, distinguishes perfectly clearly between the policy of Napoleon III striving for power and his policy once power is firmly in his hands. The *Protocols* knows nothing of such distinctions. At one moment the lecturer talks as though the Elders already hold absolute control and at the next moment as though they have still a century to wait. Sometimes he boasts that the Gentile governments are utterly intimidated by the Elders, and sometimes that they have not discovered what the Elders are plotting or even that they exist. Other illogicalities arise from the fact that whereas the despot portrayed by Joly was concerned to dominate France, the Elders are supposed to be trying to dominate the world. The forger takes no steps to eliminate the resulting discrepancies – any more than he minds interrupting the argument by irrelevancies of his own, such as the threat to blow up recalcitrant cities from their underground railways.

More strangely still, the forger introduces whole passages which are devoted simply to attacking liberal ideas and to extolling the landed aristocracy as an indispensable bulwark of monarchy. These passages are so conspicuously un-Jewish in spirit that they have caused real embarrassment to the editors of the *Protocols*. Some editors have simply suppressed them, others have added comments to the effect that that fervent Russian conservative, Sergey Nilus, must have interpolated certain reflections of his own. Their uneasiness is understandable. Nilus was not himself the forger but, as we shall see, the invective against liberalism and the eulogy of the aristocratic and monarchical order do point to the real nature and motives of the forgery.

CHAPTER IV

Secret Police and Occultists

1

AFTER Hitler came to power in Germany the *Protocols* were promoted and distributed throughout the world both by German Nazi associations and by Nazi sympathizers in other countries. A vigorous response to this provocation came from the Jewish communities of Switzerland, which brought an action against the leadership of the Nazi organization in Switzerland and against certain individual Nazis. The charge was of publishing and distributing improper literature; but the case, which was heard in Berne partly in October 1934 and partly in May 1935, became in effect an inquiry into the authenticity or spuriousness of the *Protocols*. Incredible as it may seem nowadays, this inquiry attracted world-wide attention and was covered by journalists from all parts of the world.

Much of the interest of the proceedings at Berne lies in the light which they threw upon the activities of the tsarist secret police – the Okhrana – and their possible connexion with the *Protocols*.[1] The plaintiffs called as witnesses several Russian émigrés of liberal views. One of these was Professor Sergey Svatikov, a former Social-Democrat of the Menshevik wing. Under the Provisional Government which ruled Russia during the six months between the Tsar's abdication and the Bolshevik

---

[1] The Okhrana was founded by imperial decree after the assassination of Alexander II in 1881, for the 'protection of public security and order'. ('Okhrana' means 'protection' in Russian.) Previously the chief organ of the secret police had been the Third Section of the Imperial Chancellery, which was founded after the Decembrist revolt of 1825. The Okhrana had branches in all the principal towns of Russia, as well as a foreign service centred on Paris. Like the rest of the police forces, the Okhrana was subordinate to the Minister of the Interior.

revolution in 1917, Svatikov was sent to Paris to dissolve the foreign branch of the Russian secret police, which had its headquarters there. One of the agents he interviewed was Henri Bint, a Frenchman of Alsatian origin who had been in the service of the Russians ever since 1880. According to Bint, the *Protocols* had been concocted on instructions from the head of his organization, Pyotr Ivanovich Rachkovsky. Another witness, the celebrated journalist Vladimir Burtsev, gave evidence pointing in the same direction. He claimed to have been told by two former directors of the Department of Police, Lopukhin and Beletsky, that Rachkovsky was involved in the fabrication of the *Protocols*.[1]

A great deal is in fact known about Rachkovsky, the sinister and gifted head of the Okhrana outside Russia. 'If ever you meet him in society,' wrote a Frenchman who knew him, 'I very much doubt whether you will feel the slightest misgivings about him, for nothing in his appearance reveals his sinister function. Fat, restless, always with a smile on his lips . . . he looks more like some genial, jolly fellow on a spree. . . . He has one rather noticeable weakness – that he is passionately fond of our little Parisiennes – but he is the most skilful operator to be found in the ten capitals of Europe.'[2] A Russian compatriot gave his impression in equally striking terms: 'His slightly too ingratiating manner and his suave way of speaking – which made one think of a great feline carefully concealing its claws – only dimmed for a moment my clear perception of what was fundamental in this man – his subtle intelligence, his firm will, his profound devotion . . . to the interests of imperial Russia.'[3]

Rachkovsky started life as a minor civil servant, and he even cultivated relations with students of more or less revolu-

---

[1] Mimeographed copies were made of the verbatim report of the proceedings at Berne, under the title *Stenographisches Protokoll der Verhandlungen . . . vor Richteramt V von Bern in Sachen Schweizerischer Israelitischer Gemeindebund und Israelitische Kultusgemeinde Bern gegen die Gauleitung des Bundes National-Sozialistischer Eidgenossen sowie gegen Unbekannte*. A copy is available in the Wiener Library, London. Svatikov's and Burtsev's evidence are items iii and iv.

[2] Papus, in *Echo de Paris*, issue of 27 October 1901.

[3] de Taube, *La Politique russe d'avant-guerre et la fin de l'Empire des sars (1904–1917)*, Paris, 1928, p. 26.

tionary leanings. The turning-point in his career came in 1879, when he was arrested by the secret police and charged with activities prejudicial to the safety of the state. An attempt had been made on the life of the Adjutant-General Drentel; and although Rachkovsky was merely a friend of a man who was accused of sheltering the would-be assassin, this was sufficient to land him in the hands of the Third Section of the Imperial Chancellery – the future Okhrana. As so often happened in such circumstances, Rachkovsky found himself faced with the alternative of banishment to Siberia or else of a lucrative career in the secret police itself. He chose the latter course, and it led him to a position of great power.

By 1881 Rachkovsky was active in the right-wing organization, the Holy Druzhina, an early attempt at what was later to become the Union of the Russian People. In 1883 he was adjutant to the head of the security services at St Petersburg. The following year he was in Paris, in charge of the operations of the entire secret police outside Russia. In this position he was brilliantly successful, and he retained it for eighteen years (1884–1902). He organized a network of agencies in France and Switzerland, London and Berlin; as a result he was able to keep a close check on the activities of Russian revolutionaries and terrorists, not only abroad but in Russia itself. Soon he was revealing an extraordinary talent for intrigue. In 1886 his agents – Henri Bint among them – blew up the printing works of the Russian revolutionary group Narodnaya Volya (The People's Will) in Geneva – and at the same time made it look as if this was the work of traitors among the revolutionaries themselves. In 1890 he 'unmasked' an organization which was supposed to be manufacturing in Paris, bombs to be used for assassinations in Russia. In Russia itself the Okhrana was able, as a result of this *coup*, to arrest no less than sixty-three terrorists. It was only nineteen years later that the journalist Burtsev – the same who was to give evidence before the court at Berne – discovered and revealed the truth about this affair: that the bombs had been planted by Rachkovsky's men, acting on Rachkovsky's instructions.

The 1890s were the time when bombs were being made – and thrown – in western Europe as well as in Russia; it was the golden age of the anarchists and 'nihilists'. In 1893 Vaillant threw his rather harmless bomb, full of nails, into the French Chamber of Deputies; in 1894 a whole series of much more dangerous bombs were thrown at Liége. It is certain that Rachkovsky deliberately provoked and organized the latter outrage, and highly probable that he was behind the former also. In all this the wily Russian was playing at high politics. Never satisfied with his job as a security chief, he tried to influence the course of international affairs. His motive in arranging outrages in France and Belgium was to force a *rapprochement* between the French and Russian police as a first step towards the Franco-Russian military alliance on which he had set his heart – and which indeed he did much to bring about.

Rachkovsky also built up a fortune by speculation on the stock exchange, and this enabled him to live in great style. He cultivated personal relationships with leading French politicians, including President Loubet himself, and with Russian dignitaries, including some who stood close to the Tsar. But he was ruthlessly ambitious, and it is remarkable how many of those who in any way obstructed his ambition – from General Seliverstov, who was sent to inquire into his activities in Paris in 1890, to the Minister of the Interior Plehve, who recalled him from Paris in 1903 – were assassinated by his subordinates in the secret police.

This born intriguer delighted in forging documents. As head of the Okhrana outside Russia his main concern was to cope with Russian revolutionaries who had taken refuge abroad. One of his favourite methods was to produce a letter or pamphlet in which a supposed revolutionary attacked the revolutionary leadership. In 1887 there appeared in the French press a letter by a certain 'P. Ivanov', who claimed to be a disillusioned revolutionary, asserting – quite falsely – that the majority of the terrorists were Jews. In 1890 there appeared a pamphlet entitled *Une confession par un vieillard ancien révolutionnaire (A confession by an old man who was once a revolutionary)*, accusing the revolutionaries who had taken refuge in London of being British agents. In 1892 a letter appeared over the famous name of Plekhanov, accusing the leadership of Narodnaya Volya of having published this 'confession'. A few weeks later came a further letter, in which

Plekhanov in turn was attacked by other supposed revolutionaries. In reality all these documents were written by the same man, Rachkovsky.

Rachkovsky also did much to develop a technique which, half a century later, was to be employed on a massive scale by the Nazis. This was, to present the whole progressive movement, from the most moderate liberals to the most extreme revolutionaries, as being a mere tool in the hands of the Jews. His object here was simultaneously to discredit the progressive movement in the eyes of the Russian bourgeoisie and proletariat and to direct against the Jews the widespread discontent engendered by the tsarist régime. Among the materials presented by the plaintiffs at the Berne trial was a letter sent in 1891 by Rachkovsky in Paris to the Director of the Department of Police in Russia, announcing his intention of launching a campaign against the Russian Jews.

And then there is the book *Anarchie et Nihilisme*, published in Paris in 1892 over the pseudonym of Jehan-Préval. *Anarchie et Nihilisme* was quite certainly inspired by Rachkovsky – it even contains one of his own notorious forgeries – and in places it reads like a sketch for the *Protocols*. It tells how, as a result of the French Revolution, the Jew has become 'the absolute master of the situation in Europe . . . governing by discreet means both monarchies and republics'. The one remaining obstacle to Jewish world-dominion is presented by 'the Muscovite fortress'; to overthrow it, an international syndicate of extremely rich and powerful Jews, bestriding Paris, Vienna, Berlin, and London, is preparing to hurl a coalition of nations against Russia. And it is with a shock of recognition that we come across a phrase that appears in innumerable apologies for the *Protocols*: 'The whole truth is to be found in this formula, which provides the key to a host of disturbing and seemingly insoluble riddles'. From all this a practical lesson is to be drawn: that a Franco-Russian league must be formed forthwith to combat the 'mysterious, occult, irresponsible power'[1] of the Jews.

In 1902 Rachkovsky actually tried to bring such a league into being, and nothing could be more typical of the man than the method he adopted. He distributed in Paris an appeal to

[1] Jehan-Préval, *Anarchie et Nihilisme*, Paris, 1892, pp. 202–7.

the French to support a 'Russian Patriotic League' which was supposed to have its headquarters in Kharkov. The appeal was a forgery, for it was worded as though it came from the league itself – and in reality there was no league. And this is not all: the appeal contains bitter complaints about Rachkovsky, whom it accuses of misrepresenting the league's aims and activities and even of pretending that it does not exist at all – but what, it adds, could one expect of a security chief who employs as his agents a former revolutionary, a literary adventurer, and a blackmailer 'whose cheeks still bear marks of the slaps he received, for attempted extortion, in 1889'?[1] The appeal ends with a hope – that Rachkovsky may yet discover his error and come to value the league as it deserves. The whole weird concoction was composed by Rachkovsky himself, and so skilfully that it deceived not only many eminent Frenchmen but the Russian Foreign Minister himself![2]

This time Rachkovsky had overreached himself, however, and when the hoax was unmasked he was recalled from Paris. It proved only a temporary setback. When revolutionary activities were intensified in 1905 and General Trepov was given near-dictatorial powers to crush them, he appointed Rachkovsky Assistant Director of the Department of Police. In this capacity he was able to resume his activities as a forger of documents, and on a far more dangerous scale. Vast numbers of pamphlets were printed on behalf of non-existent organizations, calling on the populace and even on the soldiers to kill Jews. And now at last he was able to help found an antisemitic league: it was that Union of the Russian People whose members, from Butmi in 1906 to Vinberg and Shabelsky-Bork in the 1920s, were to play so large a part in the dissemination of the *Protocols*. The armed bands organized and paid by this Union of the Russian People established a pattern in political terrorism and in the massacre of Jews which – as we shall see – was to have a direct influence upon

[1] See below, p. 88.
[2] A photostat of this document, which is in French, was sent by the Soviet authorities to Berne at the time of the trial, and a typed copy of this is in the Wiener Library, London (file 'Russische Urkunden des Berner Prozesses').

the Nazis. All in all, it is not surprising that Gottfried zur
Beek, the editor of the first foreign translation of the *Protocols*,
should have asserted that Rachkovsky, who died in 1911, was
murdered on orders from the Elders of Zion.

There are, then, very good grounds for suspecting Rachkovsky of instigating the forgery that resulted in the *Protocols*.
The evidence of Svatikov and Burtsev, the book *Anarchie et
Nihilisme*, Rachkovsky's activities as a militant antisemite
and organizer of pogroms, his taste for forgery and for immensely complicated deceptions – all this seems to point to
him. That being so, it is worth noting that at the very time
when he was trying to create his antisemitic 'Russian Patriotic
League', in 1902, Rachkovsky became involved in a court
intrigue in St Petersburg which also involved the future editor
of the *Protocols*, Sergey Nilus. It was an intrigue against a
Frenchman called Philippe who, like Rasputin after him,
established himself at the imperial court as a faith-healer and
became the idol and guide of the Tsar and Tsaritsa.[1] Rachkovsky and Nilus both took part in the intrigue against him, and
on the same side.

The man always called himself Philippe, though his full
name was Philippe-Nizier-Anthelme Vachod. He was born in
1850 into a family of poor peasants in Savoy. When he was six
the local priest regarded him as possessed by devils; at thirteen
he began to practise faith-healing; later he set up at Lyons as
a 'mesmerizer'. As he possessed no medical qualifications he
was forbidden to practise as a doctor and was three times
prosecuted for doing so; but he managed to go on treating
patients nevertheless. It seems certain that he really had
exceptional intuitive gifts and was able, by means of suggestion, to perform some remarkable cures.

When the Tsar and Tsaritsa visited France in 1901 Philippe
was presented to them by the two 'Montenegrin princesses'
Militsa and Anastasia – daughters of Prince Nicholas of
Montenegro, but married to Russian dukes and wholly intent
on ingratiating themselves with the imperial couple. Now the
Tsar, a weak and timid mediocrity who suffered a good deal

[1] It is a mystery how the form Tsarina, which is a cross between the
Russian *Tsaritsa* and the German *Tsarin*, ever came into the English
language, and there seems no good reason for perpetuating it.

under the burden of autocratic power, yearned for some holy man who could act as intermediary between him and the God whose indubitable but woefully inadequate representative he felt himself to be. And the Tsaritsa was a hysteric whose instability was constantly aggravated by the conspiracies which surrounded her and her husband at court as well as by the terrorists with their bombs; she too was quite ready to submit to any quack who could offer her solace and at least some semblance of security. Above all Tsar and Tsaritsa, though they had four daughters, had no son, and they desperately needed one. Any medicine-man who claimed to know the answer to this problem could hope to dominate them – just as, later, Rasputin was able to build his career on their need to keep their haemophilic son alive.

No wonder that Philippe was invited to Tsarskoe Selo and loaded with honours. Already in France the Tsar had addressed a personal request to the French Government that this un-qualified practitioner should be awarded a medical diploma. This of course was unthinkable for the French – but in Russia, where he was master, the Tsar made the St Petersburg Military Medical Academy appoint Philippe doctor to the army. He also appointed him a Counsellor of State with the rank of general. But if Philippe was cherished and flattered and almost worshipped by the imperial couple and by the 'Montenegrin princesses' and their husbands, he also had powerful enemies – in fact he found himself in much the same controversial and dangerous position as came to be occupied by Rasputin. In the circles around two formidable ladies – the Dowager Empress Maria Feodorovna and the Grand Duchess Elizaveta Feodorovna – he was resented and hated. To break Philippe these people turned to Rachkovsky.

Rachkovsky was asked for information about Philippe's past. Thanks to the relations he had cultivated with the French police he was able to draw up a detailed and, no doubt, suitably distorted report, which he brought with him when he visited St Petersburg early in 1902. The first person to whom he showed it, the Minister of the Interior, Sipyagin, advised him to throw it on the fire which was burning in the hearth. But Rachkovsky persisted: he took his report to the commandant of the imperial palace and it seems he even wrote the Dowager

Empress a personal letter denouncing Philippe as an instrument of the Freemasons. But Sipyagin's misgivings proved justified. Although the Tsar did in the end yield to pressure and refrain from inviting Philippe to take up permanent residence in Russia, he was furious. In October 1902 Rachkovsky was recalled from France, the following year he was dismissed, retired without a pension, forbidden to return to France – and there is no doubt that if this was partly due to his manoeuvres with his imaginary Patriotic League, it was also due to his campaign against Philippe. Even later, when Philippe had returned to France for good and he himself was living in Russia as a private person, Rachkovsky used his connexions with the French police to persecute the unfortunate faith-healer. Vindictive and merciless as ever, he pursued the unwitting cause of his downfall until in the end he harried him to death. Watched day and night by police spies, his letters opened, slandered in the press, Philippe died in August 1905 – just one week before Rachkovsky, restored to favour, reached the height of his career with his appointment as Assistant Director of the Department of Police.

The intrigue against Philippe also involved Sergey Alexandrovich Nilus. A Frenchman, Alexandre du Chayla, who lived many years in Russia and who saw quite a lot of Nilus in 1909, gave an account of these developments in an article in *La Tribune Juive* in May 1921. He tells how Nilus, a landowner who lost his entire fortune while living in France, returned to Russia and adopted the life of a perpetual pilgrim, wandering from monastery to monastery. Around 1900 he wrote a book describing how he had been converted from an atheistic intellectual into a fervent believer in Orthodox Christianity and a mystic. The book – it was the first edition of *The Great in the Small*, without the *Protocols* – received favourable reviews in conservative and religious newspapers and so came to the attention of the Grand Duchess Elizaveta Feodorovna. The Grand Duchess was a woman of deep piety (she later became a nun), but she was deeply suspicious of the mystical adventurers and faith-healers whom the Tsar collected around him. She blamed this state of affairs on the Archpriest Yanishev, who was confessor to the Tsar and Tsaritsa, and set out to replace him by a man whom she regarded as a genuine mystic and unshakably orthodox: Sergey Nilus.

Nilus was accordingly brought to Tsarskoe Selo. It was the end of 1901 or the beginning of 1902, and the immediate task was to oust Philippe. The clique of Philippe's enemies hit on the following plan: Nilus was to be ordained priest and he was also to be married off to one of the Tsaritsa's ladies-in-waiting, Yelena Alexandrovna Ozerova.[1] Then a concerted effort would be made to impose him on the Tsar and Tsaritsa as their confessor; if it succeeded, there would be no more room for Philippe or for any similar 'holy men'. It was an ingenious stratagem, but Philippe's supporters were able to counter it. They drew the attention of the ecclesiastical authorities to certain facts concerning Nilus's life that precluded ordination (presumably these concerned his love-life, which was always colourful). Nilus fell into disgrace and had to leave court. Some years later he did indeed marry Ozerova, but his chance of becoming the Tsar's confessor had gone for ever.

Were the *Protocols* used in the intrigue against Philippe, and if so, were they used at Rachkovsky's instigation? According to du Chayla the answer to both questions is yes. Nilus, he tells us, was convinced that the original 'discoverer' of the *Protocols* was Rachkovsky – 'a fine man, very active, one who in his time has done much to deprive Christ's enemies of their sting' and who 'had fought with much self-sacrifice against Freemasonry and the Satanic sects', as Nilus put it.[2]

And du Chayla goes on to explain what Rachkovsky could have hoped to achieve by sending the *Protocols* to Nilus. The *Protocols* claims to reveal a devilish plot by Freemasons as well as by Jews – or rather by Freemasons identified with Jews. Philippe was a Martinist, i.e. a member of an association which claimed to follow the teachings of the eighteenth-century occultist Claude de Saint-Martin, 'the unknown philosopher'. The Martinists were not really Freemasons, but the Tsar could hardly be expected to realize that. If the Tsar could be persuaded that Philippe was the agent of a conspiracy such as

[1] Priests in the Russian Orthodox Church are required to be married.
[2] A. du Chayla, 'Serge Alexandrovitch Nilus et les Protocols des Sages de Sion (1909–1920)', in *La Tribune Juive*, Paris, issue of 14 May 1921, pp. 3–4.

that portrayed in the *Protocols*, he would certainly send him packing. By the peculiar standards of the Okhrana the calculation was a perfectly sound one, and it was just the kind of calculation that fascinated Rachkovsky.

How reliable is du Chayla? He makes occasional slips, as when he says that Nilus published a first edition of the *Protocols* in 1902, but on the whole he shows himself very well informed. In his article of 1921 he states, for instance, that in 1905 Nilus published an edition of the *Protocols* at Tsarskoe Selo, under the imprint of the local Red Cross organization. That is perfectly accurate: the book in question is the second edition of *The Great in the Small*, which contains the *Protocols*. What is more, he remarks that it was Yelena Ozerova who made this edition possible – and years later, when the Soviet authorities sent photostats of documents to the court at Berne, this proved to be accurate also. Among these documents are several letters to and from the Moscow Censorship Committee, which show quite clearly how Ozerova used her position as lady-in-waiting to secure publication for the book of her fiancé and future husband.

These documents reveal something else as well – and something of which du Chayla cannot possibly have been aware. They contain an item, so elusive that it has hitherto escaped notice, which suggests that Rachkovsky had had some contact either with Nilus or with the manuscript copy of the *Protocols* in Nilus's possession. The Moscow Censorship Committee, at its session of 28 September 1905, received a report from State Counsellor and Censor Sokolov which quotes the following phrase as being attached by Nilus to his manuscript of the *Protocols*: 'Naturally the head of the Russian Agency,[1] the Jew Efron, and his agents, who are also Jews, have not reported on these matters to the Russian Government.'[2] The committee, in authorizing publication, stipulated that all proper names must be removed from the manuscript – that of Efron among them. The name was duly removed before the book was printed, but one can identify the passage where it was to have

[1] In Paris.

[2] A photostat of the report of the Censorship Committee was sent by the Soviet authorities to Berne. German translation in the Wiener Library (file 'Russische Urkunden des Berner Prozesses').

appeared – it is in the epilogue to the *Protocols*. This epilogue
also appears in all the other early Russian editions of the *Protocols*, that in *Znamya* and those of Butmi. None of these
editions was subjected to the stipulation concerning proper
names – indeed the *Znamya* version had appeared two years
before the Moscow Censorship Committee made the stipulation – and yet none of them contains any reference to Efron.
We can only assume, therefore, that the reference to Efron
was specially inserted into Nilus's manuscript. And it can only
have been done or prompted by some enemy of Efron.

Who then was Efron, and who can his enemy have been?
Akim Efron, or Effront, was the secret agent in Paris of the
Russian Ministry of Finance. When he died in 1909 the French
press referred to him as the director of the political agency
attached to the Russian embassy. He certainly did not belong
to Rachkovsky's organization but employed his own agents
and sent his own reports back to St Petersburg. One could
assume that this would suffice to earn Rachkovsky's hatred,
but as it happens there is no need to assume, for we have
proof. One thing that is known about Efron is that during the
International Exhibition in Paris in 1889 his face was publicly
slapped in the Russian pavilion for attempted blackmail. In
other words, Efron must have been the person whom Rachkovsky described, in his forged appeal for the 'Russian Patriotic League', as bearing on his cheeks the marks of the slaps
which he received in 1889 for attempted blackmail.[1] As for the
statement in the same appeal that Efron was one of Rachkovsky's own men, it was a deliberate lie, and just the tortuous and malicious kind of lie that most delighted Rachkovsky. So the mention of Efron in Nilus's manuscript does
suggest that some link, direct or indirect, existed between the
persecutor and the rival of Philippe.

2

We have seen what kind of man Rachkovsky was and it seems
worth while to take a look at Nilus too. We possess a good deal
of information about him, some of it very odd indeed. Again

[1] See above, p. 82.

it is Alexandre du Chayla who has left the fullest account.[1]
He tells how, wishing to study the inner life of the Orthodox
Church, he made his way in January 1909 to the famous
monastery of Optina Pustyn, a couple of miles from the town
of Kozelsk in what was then the government of Kaluga. In the
nineteenth century Optina Pustyn had played an important
part in Russian intellectual life; the figure of Father Zosima in
The Brothers Karamazov is modelled on one of its leading
personalities; Tolstoy also often visited the monastery and at
one time even lived there. Near the monastery were a number
of villas occupied by laymen who wished to withdraw to some
extent from the world. Du Chayla set up house in one of these
villas. The day after his arrival the Father Superior, the
Archimandrite Xenophon, introduced him to one of his neighbours, who was Sergey Nilus.

Nilus, who was then aged forty-seven, is described by du
Chayla as 'a man of truly Russian type, big and strong, with a
grey beard and deep eyes – blue, but with a veiled, somewhat
troubled look. He wore boots, and a Russian shirt with a belt
which had a prayer embroidered on it.' He and his dependents
occupied four rooms in a large villa; and rest of the villa was
employed as a home for cripples, idiots, and mentally sick
people, who lived there in hope of a miraculous cure. The whole
establishment was supported by the pension which the
imperial court paid to Ozerova as a former lady-in-waiting.
Ozerova, otherwise Mme Nilus, struck du Chayla as being
absolutely submissive to her husband. She even had the most
amiable relations with Nilus's former mistress, who lived in the
same villa and, having lost her own fortune, also on Mme
Nilus's pension.

During the nine months he passed at Optina Pustyn, du
Chayla learned a lot about Nilus. A former landowner in the
government of Orel, he was an educated man who had
graduated in Law at the University of Moscow; he spoke
excellent French, German, and English and had a good grasp
of contemporary European literature. But in character he was
capricious, unruly, and despotic – so much so in fact that he
had been obliged to resign from the position of magistrate
which he had held in Transcaucasia. He had also tried his

[1] In *La Tribune Juive*, loc. cit.

hand at managing his estate in Orel, but had had no success with that either. Finally he had gone abroad with his mistress and had lived at Biarritz – until one day he heard from his steward that he was ruined.

This news produced a major emotional crisis in Nilus and altogether changed his outlook on life. So far he had been a theoretical anarchist with a cult of Nietzsche. Now he became a convert to Orthodox Christianity and an ardent champion of the tsarist autocracy, he fancied himself a mystic and also a heaven-sent defender of Holy Russia. He had always repudiated modern civilization; now he saw it as a conspiracy of the powers of darkness. He became a systematic anti-rationalist. Science, technological progress, democracy, even the application of reason to religious and philosophical questions – all these features of modern civilization, says du Chayla, were rejected by Nilus as 'the abomination of desolation in the holy places' and as portents of the coming of Antichrist. It is an attitude which, in one form or another, we shall meet again and again among the devotees of the *Protocols*.

In a couple of pages which deserve a place in any anthology of religious eccentricity du Chayla has shown just what the *Protocols* meant to their most celebrated editor:

Nilus took his book from the shelves and began to translate into French the most remarkable passages of the text and of his own commentaries. At the same time he watched the expression on my face, for he assumed that I would be dumbfounded by this revelation. He was rather upset himself when I told him that there was nothing new for me in all this and that the document must be closely related to the pamphlets of Edouard Drumont. . . .

Nilus was shaken and disappointed by this. He retorted that I took this view because my knowledge of the *Protocols* was superficial and fragmentary, and because their effect was weakened by the oral translation. It was absolutely necessary that I should feel the full impact. And it would be easy for me to get to know the *Protocols*, because the original was in French.

Nilus did not keep the manuscript of the *Protocols* in his house for fear lest it should be stolen by the Jews. I recall how amused I was by his perturbation when a Jewish chemist of Kozelsk, taking a walk with a friend in the monastery forest and trying to find the quickest route to the ferry, happened to stray into Nilus's garden.

Poor Sergey Alexandrovich was convinced for a long time that the chemist had come to carry out a reconnaissance.

Later I learned that the note-book containing the *Protocols* was deposited until January 1909 with the priest and monk Daniel Bolotov (a portrait-painter who was quite well known at St Petersburg).[1] After his death it was deposited at the hermitage of St John the Baptist, a third of a mile from the monastery, in the keeping of the monk Alexis, a former engineer.

Some time after our first conversation about the *Protocols*, one afternoon about four o'clock, one of the patients from Nilus's home for the sick brought me a letter: Nilus was asking me to come and see him on an urgent matter.

I found Sergey Alexandrovich in his study. He was alone, his wife and Mme K. having gone to vespers. Dusk was falling but it was light, for the earth was covered in snow. I noticed on his writing-table something like a rather large envelope, made of black material and decorated with a big triple cross and the inscription: 'In this sign you shall conquer'. A little picture of St Michael, in paper, was also stuck on to the envelope. Quite clearly all this was intended as an exorcism.

Sergey Alexandrovich crossed himself three times before the great icon of the Mother of God . . . and opened the envelope, from which he took a leather-bound note-book. I learned later that the envelope and the binding had been prepared in the monastery workshop under the personal supervision of Nilus, who carried the manuscript to and fro himself, for fear of its being stolen. The cross and the other symbols had been drawn by Yelena Alexandrovna,[2] according to her husband's instructions.

'Here it is,' said Nilus, 'the charter of the Kingdom of Antichrist.'

He opened the note-book. . . . The text was written in French by various hands and, it seemed to me, with different inks.

'You see,' said Nilus, 'during the sessions of the secret Jewish government, at different times, various people filled the office of secretary. Hence the different handwritings.'

Clearly Sergey Alexandrovich regarded this peculiarity as proving that the manuscript was an original document. Yet he had no fixed views on this matter, for on another occasion I heard him say the manuscript was only a copy.

After showing me the manuscript, Sergey Alexandrovich placed

[1] The same monk figures, in a somewhat dubious role, in Mme Kashkina's account. See below p. 95.
[2] Ozerova.

it on the table, opened it at the first page and, settling me in his armchair, said: 'Well, now read!'

While reading the manuscript I was struck by certain peculiarities in the text. There were some spelling mistakes and above all some expressions which were not French. It is too long ago for me to be able to say that the text contained 'Russianisms', but one thing is beyond doubt: the manuscript was written by a foreigner.

It took me two and a half hours to read the document. When I had finished Nilus took the note-book, replaced it in its envelope and locked it up in the drawer of his writing-table. . . .

Sergey Alexandrovich wanted to know what impression my reading had produced on me. I told him straight out that I stood by my previous judgment; I didn't believe in the 'Elders of Zion' . . .

Nilus's face clouded. 'You really are under the Devil's influence,' he said. 'Satan's greatest ruse is to make people deny not simply his influence on the things of this world but even his very existence. What will you say now if I show you how what is said in the *Protocols* is being fulfilled, how the mysterious sign of the coming of Antichrist appears on all sides, how the imminent advent of his kingdom can be felt everywhere?'

Sergey Alexandrovich got up and we all went into his study. He took his book and a file, and he also brought from his bedroom a small chest, which I came later to call 'the Museum of Antichrist'. He began to read bits from his book and from material he had prepared for publication. He read everything that in any way expressed the eschatological expectations of contemporary Christianity: the dream of the Metropolitan Philaret, quotations from an encyclical of Pius X, the sermons of St Seraphim of Sarov and of Roman Catholic saints, fragments of Ibsen, Solovyev, Merezhkovsky.

He read for a long time. Then he proceeded to the 'exhibits in the case'. He opened his chest. Inside there were, in an indescribable state of disorder, detachable collars, india-rubbers, household utensils, insignia of various technical colleges, even the cipher of the Empress Alexandra Feodorovna and the cross of the Légion d'honneur. On all these objects he detected, in his hallucination, the 'seal of Antichrist', in the form of a triangle or of two superimposed triangles. . . . If an object bore a trade-mark even vaguely suggesting a triangle, that was enough to secure it entry to his museum. And nearly all these examples were included in his 1911 edition of the *Protocols*.

With increasing excitement and anxiety, in the grip of a sort of mystical terror, Nilus explained to me that the sign of 'the son of perdition' is now contaminating all things, that it shines even from the designs of church ornaments and from the scrolls of the great icon behind the altar in the church of the hermitage.

I felt a sort of fear. It was nearly midnight. The gaze, the voice, the reflex-like gestures – everything about Nilus gave me the feeling that we were walking on the edge of an abyss and that at any moment his reason might disintegrate in madness.[1]

Later du Chayla tells how, when the 1911 edition of his book was published, Nilus sent to the eastern patriarchs, to the Holy Synod, and to the Pope an epistle urging that an ecumenical council be summoned, with the task of working out common measures for the defence of Christendom in view of the imminent coming of Antichrist. And he began to preach on the same subject to the monks of Optina Pustyn – and so effectively that he was asked to leave the monastery for good.

Clearly, then, Nilus really believed in the Jewish world-conspiracy. Yet, with that curious capacity for double-think so characteristic of fanatics, he was sometimes prepared to admit that the *Protocols* themselves might be spurious. One day in 1909 du Chayla asked him whether Rachkovsky might not have been deceived and whether Nilus might not be working with a forgery. Nilus replied: 'You know my favourite quotation from St Paul? – "The power of God works through human weakness." Let us admit that the *Protocols* are spurious. But can't God use them to unmask the iniquity that is being prepared? Didn't Balaam's ass prophesy? Can't God, for the sake of our faith, change dog's bones into miracle-working relics? So he can put the announcement of truth into a lying mouth!'[2]

Another neighbour of Nilus has also recorded her recollections. On 1 June 1934, when preparations for the Berne trial were under way, Maria Dmitrievna Kashkina, *née* Countess Buturlin, made a statement which has not previously been published, but which certainly deserves publication, and not only for the light it throws upon the personality of Sergey Nilus. Anyone who probes into the world of the *Protocols* must at times feel suffocated by the miasma of superstition, gullibility, and quackery which it exudes. It is good to be reminded, for once, that even in tsarist Russia there were people – and

---

[1] A. du Chayla in *La Tribune Juive*, pp. 3–4.   [2] Ibid., p. 4.

not urban intellectuals either, but country folk, landowners
and peasants – who were capable of healthy scepticism and
knew craziness and roguery when they saw them. The most
relevant parts of the statement read as follows:

In 1905 I married Kashkin, who owned an estate in the Kozelsk
district in the government of Kaluga. . . . Our estate was about 2½
miles from Optina Pustyn – the monastery was built on land
donated by my husband's ancestors. . . . I met Nilus soon after
my arrival on the estate and knew him throughout the years I lived
there. . . . All those years he lived at the monastery . . . He was
known to be a writer; he gave his book *The Great in the Small* to
everyone he met. The Abbot was the Archimandrite Xenophon, a
good and honest man but quite uneducated. He was impressed by
Nilus and was still more impressed when Nilus promised to dedicate
to him his forthcoming history of the monastery; from then on
Xenophon quite melted and opened all his archives to Nilus. And
he didn't only allow him to use the archives, often he simply gave
him the documents. . . . My husband got to know about it and was
indignant. 'Nilus will loot the whole archive,' he used to say. . . .
Altogether, my husband regarded Nilus as a very tricky and shady
character, who ought to be very carefully watched. Of course this
opinion was based not on Nilus's love for documents from the
archives but on much worse things.

It should be said here that in those years Optina Pustyn was a
centre for all sorts of 'holy idiots'. Outstanding among them was
'the barefooted Mitya Kozelsky'. . . . A butcher by trade, he came
from the town of Kozelsk. . . . He was a big, strong fellow but he
could hardly utter recognizable words, he was a real idiot. It was
impossible to understand him. Nevertheless he had the reputation of
being able to cast out devils. . . . His methods . . . were more than
peculiar: he hit his patients with his fists, mainly in the stomach,
he pushed them into barrels, and so on. People said that his cures
sometimes worked. He became famous after curing the widow of a
rich merchant – I seem to remember her name was Ivanova and
she came from Moscow. Mitya diagnosed that there were seven
devils in her – and he drove them all out by his methods. The
grateful widow married him. Her fortune was substantial. Now
Mitya was washed and clothed and kept his own horses – I remember
vividly seeing him, sitting well back in his carriage, stretching his
legs, every inch a conqueror. . . .

Nilus frequented these circles. . . . His own private life gave rise
to many misgivings. In a little house adjoining and belonging to

the monastery there lived with him, apart from his wife, *née* Ozerova, his first wife, who was not officially divorced, and also part of the time yet another woman, always ailing, with a girl of eleven or twelve. The girl was said to be Nilus's daughter. In the circle around Nilus she was used as a medium in spiritualist séances. She stayed with Nilus, when her mother left. . . . They could be seen going for walks, all of them together. Nilus walked in the middle, with his long white beard and usually dressed in a white peasant's shirt, with a monk's cord as a belt. On either side of him walked his wives, the first and the second, as a supporting audience, gazing into his eyes, hanging on his every word. The little girl and her mother walked a little way behind. When they reached the wood they would settle down under the trees. Ozerova would begin to sketch something – she had a little artistic ability. The first wife . . . might do some needlework. Nilus himself would lie down – and it was rare for him to say anything.

I was told that the peace that reigned in Nilus's family had not been achieved at once – that at first, at the beginning of her marriage, Ozerova had tried to rebel. There were scenes – something, in particular, concerning the little girl. I don't know the details. But Ozerova soon gave in. . . . Nilus could control her easily enough. . . . The whole family lived on her pension. . . .

Nilus circulated amongst the odd beings who clustered around the monastery. . . . In particular, he took a lot of trouble to cultivate Mitya Kozelsky, whom he tried to introduce into the higher spheres of society. As Ozerova's husband Nilus had connections with the imperial court . . . and he used these to advance Mitya. One of Nilus's friends at the monastery was a monk called Daniel – a rather dubious personality but a fair painter. Certainly with Nilus's knowledge and possibly at his instigation, this Daniel painted a picture. It showed the Tsar, the Tsaritsa and their son enveloped and supported by clouds. . . . These clouds were full of devils with horns, tails and hoofs, who were all trying to get at the Tsarevich, reaching for him, sticking out their tongues at him. But through this throng of devils there strides, with sure step, Mitya Kalyada,[1] the fearless fighter against the Satanic powers, coming to save the Tsar's son . . . With Nilus's help this canvas was sent to St Petersburg. One can guess at the kind of publicity that Nilus must have made there for Mitya. Anyway, Mitya was summoned to St Petersburg and presented to the Tsar and Tsaritsa. Nilus went with him, as interpreter of the incomprehensible sounds he uttered;

[1] Kalyada was the real surname of 'Mitya Kozelsky', or Mitya of Kozelsk.

already before that he had established himself in this capacity. Mitya travelled first class.

You can imagine what sort of impression this journey of Mitya's made on our local population. There was no great esteem for the monks there, particularly not among the peasants. Those who saw the monks at close quarters knew that there was little place for holiness in their lives – not far from the monastery there was a whole hamlet populated with 'the monks' sins'. The local population distrusted especially all those 'holy beggars' and 'fools of God' – they considered them, with rare exceptions, a lot of loafers and charlatans. And then suddenly it turned out that the Tsar had extended an invitation to that charlatan Mitya. I myself heard some of the steadiest and most thoughtful peasants express their bewilderment. 'What can this mean?' they said. 'Doesn't the Tsar understand? Or is he making fun of us?'

The local landowners and civil servants were also shocked. I remember a talk I had with our local police chief, Rakhmaninov. . . . He showed me telegrams from the Minister, asking him to give Mitya every assistance, to provide him with a special compartment on the train, first class, and so on. Of course he did what he was told, but he made no secret of his embarrassment. My husband put the blame for Mitya's journey squarely on Nilus. He didn't hesitate to call him an adventurer and a charlatan. This business was a blow to the Tsar's prestige, and my husband regarded Nilus as wholly responsible for that.[1]

The rather cool accounts supplied by du Chayla and Mme Kashkina can be set alongside a biography of Nilus published in Yugoslavia in 1936. The author of this book, Prince N. D. Zhevakhov, was a fervent admirer of Nilus; in his eyes the *Protocols* were incontestably 'produced by a Jew writing to the dictation of the Devil, who revealed to him the methods for destroying Christian states and the secret of how to conquer the whole world'.[2] It is all the more significant that the biographical data he gives should tally almost exactly with those given by du Chayla. Moreover we discover from him what Nilus had in mind when he was delving among monastic

[1] This statement was taken down by the late Boris Nicolaevsky in Russian in Mme Kashkina's presence and was then read back to her; she approved it in every detail. The Russian transcript is in the B.I. Nicolaevsky Collection at the Hoover Institution, Stanford University, California.

[2] N. D. Zhevakhov, *Sergey Alexandrovich Nilus*, Novi Sad, 1936, p. 11.

archives. One of Nilus's achievements was to edit the diary of a hermit who, according to Zhevakhov, 'described the after-life with extraordinary realism. Thus he tells of a youth who was cursed by his mother and was thereupon lifted up by unknown powers into the airless space above the earth, where for forty days he lived the life of the spirits, mingling with them and being subject to their laws. . . . In short, this diary was a book of exceptional value, a veritable manual of holiness'.[1]

Zhevakhov also tells of the last years of Nilus, at a time when he had quite passed out of the ken of du Chayla and Mme Kashkina and when, all unknown to him, his edition of the *Protocols* was sweeping the world. It seems that after leaving Optina Pustyn Nilus lived on the estates of various friends. It is curious to note that for some six years after the Bolshevik coup d'état, while Russia was convulsed by re-volution and civil war, terror, counter-terror, and famine, Nilus and Ozerova lived peacefully somewhere in south Russia, in a house which they shared with a former hermit called Seraphim and which had a chapel constantly overflowing with dozens of pilgrims. It is true that, according to Nilus's letters, some time in 1921 a squad of Red Army soldiers, led by a local bandit, arrived with the intention of murdering the two holy men – but even then, we are told, they were preserved by a mysterious and miraculous night-watchman who disappeared into thin air as soon as he was hit. The leader of the squad was paralysed on the spot and could be cured only by the hermit Seraphim himself.

The Bolshevik authorities, however, having defeated the 'White' armies and liquidated their political opponents, were not to be permanently deterred by a vanishing night-watch-man. In the end Nilus and his companions were all evicted. After some years of wandering and two short periods of imprisonment, in 1924 and 1927, Nilus died of heart failure, at the age of sixty-eight, on New Year's Day, 1930.

From the Freyenwald documents at the Wiener Library, London, we learn the fate of some of those who were closest to Nilus. According to a manuscript note by the right-wing Russian known as Markov II, Ozerova was arrested during

[1] Ibid., p. 20.

the great purges of 1937 and deported to the Kola peninsula on the Arctic sea, where she died of hunger and cold the following year. There is also a good deal of correspondence from and concerning a son of Nilus, presumably by his first wife. Sergey Sergeyevich Nilus, who was a Polish citizen, put himself at the disposal of the Nazis when they were preparing their appeal against the judgement of the Berne court in 1935. A letter which he wrote to Alfred Rosenberg from Poland in March 1940 deserves to be quoted:

> I am the only son of the discoverer of the *Protocols of the Elders of Zion*, S. A. Nilus. . . . I can and must not remain indifferent in these times when the fate of the whole Aryan world hangs in the balance. I feel that the victory of the Führer, that man of genius, will liberate my poor country also, and I believe that I could contribute to this in any position. After the brilliant victory of the mighty German army I . . . have done everything to earn the right to take part actively in liquidating the Jewish poison. . . .[1]

This seems an appropriate note on which to close our examination of Sergey Alexandrovich Nilus.

3

It is certain that Rachkovsky and Nilus were both involved in the intrigue against Philippe, it is even possible that they conspired to use the *Protocols* for their common purpose. This has led to the assumption, which is to be found in several works on the *Protocols*, that the forgery was carried out for the express purpose of influencing the Tsar against Philippe. Yet this theory is implausible. Philippe was a Martinist and a faith-healer – surely then, if the *Protocols* were forged to help Nilus in his struggle with Philippe, they should contain at least some suggestion that Martinism and/or faith-healing form part of the Jewish plot? As it is, they contain almost everything else, from banking and the press to international wars and underground railways. It is one thing to use a forgery which is already available – and Rachkovsky was certainly not fastidious in his choice of weapons. It is quite another thing to fabricate a whole book which is almost wholly irre-

[1] The letter is in the Freyenwald Collection at the Wiener Library.

levant to the task on hand. Could even Rachkovsky's tor-
tuousness really have gone so far?

It is, then, worth looking at any evidence there may be for
the existence of the *Protocols* before 1902. There is in fact a
good deal of evidence, some of it from 'White' Russian refugees, but not necessarily worthless on that account. In the
first place there is an affidavit sworn by Filip Petrovich
Stepanov, formerly procurator of the ecclesiastical synod of
Moscow, court chamberlain, and privy councillor, at Stary
Futog, Yugoslavia, on 17 April 1927. It reads as follows:

> In 1895 my neighbour in the government of Tula, the retired
> major Alexey Sukhotin, gave me a manuscript copy of the *Protocols
> of the Elders of Zion*. He told me that a lady of his acquaintance,
> whom he did not name, when residing in Paris had found this copy
> at the home of a Jewish friend; and that before leaving Paris she
> had secretly translated the manuscript and had brought it with her
> to Russia, where she gave it to Sukhotin.
> First of all I reproduced this translation in hectograph jelly,
> but finding it difficult to read, I decided to have it printed without
> any mention of date, place or publisher. In all this I was assisted
> by Arkady Ippolitovich Kelepovsky, who was at that time head
> of the household of the Grand Duke Sergey. He had the document
> printed on the press of the district. This took place in 1897. Sergey
> Nilus inserted these *Protocols* in his work and added his own
> commentaries.[1]

Save for the passing reference to the lady's 'Jewish friend'
this document seems quite useless as propaganda; so Stepanov
was probably trying to tell the truth as he remembered it,
admittedly after a lapse of thirty years. As it happens there is,
or was, very solid evidence to confirm his statement. Although
no copy of Stepanov's printed book is known, a copy of the
hectograph was still extant at the time of the Berne trial in
1934. At that time it was to be found in the Pashukanis Collection in the Lenin Library, Moscow; and the Soviet authorities
sent a photostat of four pages to the court at Berne. The
title-page carries no date, but the late Boris Nicolaevsky was
convinced, after careful inspection, that this was indeed

[1] A facsimile of the Russian affidavit is in L. Fry, *Waters Flowing
Eastwards*, Paris, 1933, after p. 100; a French translation (with some
errors) in L. Fry, *Le Juif notre maître*, Paris, 1931, pp. 95–6.

Stepanov's hectograph.[1] The hectograph was made from a hand-written Russian document with the title *The Ancient and Modern Protocols of the Meetings of the Elders of Zion*. Unfortunately it can no longer be inspected – two years of assiduous inquiry extracted nothing from the Lenin Library except a statement that no such manuscript can be traced – but the Wiener Library possesses a German translation of the extracts sent to Berne. This shows that the text must have been practically identical with that later edited by Nilus, which directly or indirectly provides the basis for almost all later editions throughout the world.

Among the 'White' Russians there also existed a firm tradition concerning the identity of the lady who brought the handwritten Russian document from Paris and gave it to Sukhotin. She was said to be Yuliana (or, in France, Justine) Glinka.[2] A good deal is known about her too, and again all the evidence fits. Yuliana Dmitrievna Glinka (1844–1918) was the daughter of a Russian diplomat who ended his career as ambassador in Lisbon. She herself became a lady-in-waiting to the Empress Maria Alexandrovna and lived much of her life in great style in St Petersburg, associating with the spiritualists around Mme Blavatsky[3] and indeed squandering her fortune in supporting them. But there was also another and more sinister side to her life. In Paris in 1881–2 she tried her hand at the game which Rachkovsky was to play so brilliantly shortly afterwards – watching and denouncing the Russian terrorists in exile. General Orzheyevsky, who was a prominent figure in the secret police and ended as Assistant Minister for Internal Affairs, had befriended her ever since her childhood; and she sent her secret reports to him. But she was not really gifted for the work, feuded constantly with the Russian ambassador and ended by being unmasked in the left-wing newspaper *Le Radical*.

Glinka continued to spend a good deal of her time in Paris until, on a visit to St Petersburg somewhere around 1895, she

[1] Private communication to the author.
[2] Cf. L. Fry, *Waters Flowing Eastwards*, pp. 87–9.
[3] Yelena Petrovna Blavatsky (1831–91), Russian theosophist and spiritualistic medium. At one time she herself tried – in vain – to find employment in the Russian secret service.

found that she had lost the imperial favour. The Tsar had been deeply offended by a series of books which her great friend Juliette Adam had published in Paris and which contained all kinds of rumours and revelations about the Russian court. Rightly or wrongly he suspected Glinka of complicity and exiled her to her estate in the government of Orel, which bordered on the government of Tula. The natural protector for Glinka in her distress would have been the Marshal of Nobility for the district – and that was Alexey Sukhotin, the same person from whom Stepanov claimed to have received the *Protocols*.[1]

Glinka was exiled only temporarily and in later years she was once more comfortably established in St Petersburg. To judge by an article which the right-wing St Petersburg newspaper *Novoe Vremya* printed in its issue of 7 April 1902, she may have developed a proprietory attitude to the *Protocols*. The well-known journalist M. Menshikov reported how a lady of fashion had invited him to her house to see a document of vast importance. Seated in an elegant apartment (in Paris Glinka had been noted for her fine picture-collection) and speaking perfect French, the lady informed him that she was in direct contact with the world beyond the grave and proceeded to induct him into the mysteries of theosophy (Glinka was a disciple of Mme Blavatsky). Finally she initiated him into the mysteries of the *Protocols*. Of recent years, she explained, the original French manuscript had been kept at Nice, which had long been the secret capital of the Jews; but they had been stolen by a French journalist, who had passed them on to her. In great haste she had translated extracts from French into Russian. Menshikov took one glance at the

---

[1] There exists in the Freyenwald Collection at the Wiener Library a copy of a statement, dated 13 December 1936, by a female cousin of Alexey Sukhotin. It says that about 1895, when visiting her cousin on his estate, she saw the manuscript of the *Protocols* being copied out by Sukhotin's sister and by another young lady, who is named and who in 1936 was living in Paris. This statement would have little value by itself, but has some as corroboratory evidence. It could even be that they were retranslating the Russian text into French; for the text which du Chayla claims to have seen in Nilus's possession, written in bad French by various hands, was certainly not the original French version; there is no evidence that *that* ever left France.

Protocols and immediately recognized them as a forgery of a
very familiar type. And he adds that there were other copies
in St Petersburg, one of them in the possession of a journalist –
one guesses, Krushevan, since his *Znamya* published the
Protocols the following year.

There are, then, reasonable grounds for thinking that
Yuliana Glinka and Filip Stepanov really were involved in
the first publication of the *Protocols*. As for the date, internal
evidence suggests that in saying he received the *Protocols* in
1895 and published them in 1897 Stepanov was erring no more
than is to be expected after thirty years. There is for instance
the remark, at the end of 'protocol' 16, that as part of the plan
to stupefy the Gentiles one of the Elders' agents, Bourgeois, is
advocating a programme of teaching by object lessons. The
reference is to Léon Bourgeois, a highly suspect figure in the
eyes of the French right wing since, as Prime Minister in 1895–
6, he had included nine Freemasons in his cabinet. From 1890
to 1896 he frequently spoke in favour of a system of teaching
by object lessons, and in 1897 these speeches were published
in a book, *L'éducation de la démocratie française*; in 1898, as
Minister of Education, he issued decrees on the subject. A
similar reference which points in the same direction is the
passage in 'protocol' 10 where the Elders recommend the
election of presidents with some 'Panama' in their past. This
refers almost certainly to Emile Loubet, who was Prime
Minister of France when the Panama scandal reached its
climax in 1892. Though certainly not involved in the scandal
itself, Loubet showed no eagerness to institute inquiries against
those who were; and this made him a suspect figure. In 1895
Loubet was elected President of the Senate, which made him a
candidate for the presidency of the Republic, and in 1899 he
was elected President of the Republic. The passage in the
Protocols could have been inspired by either event.

As for the Paris underground, the *Métro*, plans for it were
announced in 1894, but it was only in 1897 that the municipal
council granted the concession, and it was in 1900 that the
first line was opened. In view of the threat in the *Protocols*
to blow up capital cities from the underground railways, it is
worth noting that in 1897 Drumont's *Libre Parole* was lament-
ing the number of Jewish shareholders in the *Métro*. Again, it

was in 1896 that the Russian Minister of Finance Sergey Witte
first proposed the introduction of the gold-standard in Russia,
in place of the gold-and-silver standard then in force; and in
1897 it was in fact introduced. This too figures in the *Protocols*
– in 'protocol' 19 there is the observation that the gold standard has ruined every state that has adopted it. But, above
all, there is the title of the forgery itself. One would normally
expect the mysterious rulers to be called Elders of Jewry or
Elders of Israel. There must be some reason why they bear the
absurd name of Elders of Zion, and there is in fact a very
plausible one. As we have seen, the first Zionist congress at
Basel was interpreted by antisemites as a giant stride towards
Jewish world-domination. Countless editions of the *Protocols*
have connected that document with the congress; and it does
seem likely that this event inspired if not the forgery itself,
then at least its title. The year of the congress was 1897.

All in all it is practically certain that the *Protocols* were
fabricated some time between 1894 and 1899 and highly probable that it was in 1897 or 1898. The country was undoubtedly France, as is shown by the many references to French
affairs. One may assume that the place was Paris and one may
even be rather more precise: one of the copies of Joly's book in
the Bibliothèque Nationale bears markings which correspond
strikingly with the borrowings in the *Protocols*. So the job was
done in the midst of the Dreyfus affair – somewhere between
the arrest of Alfred Dreyfus in 1894 and his pardon in 1899,
and probably at the very height of the great debate which so
bitterly divided France. And nevertheless the forgery is clearly
the work of a Russian and oriented towards the Russian right
wing. Can one, then, be certain that it was done at the behest
of the head of Okhrana in Paris, the sinister Rachkovsky?

As we have seen, there are very substantial grounds for this
view – and nevertheless the question is less simple than it
seems. Rachkovsky's political master and patron was Sergey
Witte, the all-powerful Minister of Finance, and Witte's
enemies were also Rachkovsky's enemies. And there is no
doubt that Witte's enemies had a hand in the *Protocols*.
When Witte took office in 1892 he took up the task begun by
Peter the Great and largely neglected by later rulers: the
transformation of backward Russia into a country as modern

as the countries of western Europe. During the following decade the production of coal and of iron and steel was more than doubled; the construction of railways, which at that time was the surest index of industrial development, proceeded at a rate attained in only one other country, the United States. But this rapid economic development brought grave disadvantages to those classes whose wealth was bound up with the traditional, agricultural order; and in these circles Witte was detested. Moreover in 1898 there came a serious slump which brought heavy losses even to those who had benefited most from the economic expansion. Witte was under heavy pressure to resort to inflation, even if this meant abandoning the newly adopted gold-standard. He resisted, and his unpopularity became still more widespread.

The *Protocols* have all the appearance of a weapon for use in the campaign against Witte. In the *Protocols* it is argued that slumps are used by the Elders as a means of getting control over all money and of fomenting unrest in the proletariat; and as we have seen, it is also argued that the gold-standard ruins the countries that adopt it. Moreover, if one compares the *Dialogue aux Enfers* with the *Protocols* one finds that the only economic and financial reflections which have been preserved from Joly's book are those which applied to developments in Russia under Witte. The intention seems obvious enough: it is to present Witte as a tool in the hands of the Elders of Zion.

The *Protocols* are not the only piece of propaganda directed simultaneously against the Jews and against Witte. There is an even more bizarre document called *Tayna Yevreystva* (*The Secret of Jewry*),[1] which carries a date – February 1895 – and which looks like a first, ham-handed attempt at the *Protocols*. *Tayna Yevreystva* came to light when, on instructions from the Minister of the Interior, Stolypin, in the first year of this century, the police archives were combed for evidence as to the origin of the *Protocols*. It is a ridiculous essay about an imaginary secret religion which, after being held by the Essenes in the time of Jesus, is now supposed to be cherished by the unknown rulers of Jewry. But it is at one with the *Protocols* in warning us that the secret Jewish government is

[1] Text in Yu. Delevsky, *Protokoly Sionskikh Mudretsov*, Berlin, 1923, pp. 138–58. Cf. J. Gwyer, *Portraits of Mean Men*, London, 1938.

now striving to turn Russia from an agrarian, semi-feudal
country into a modern state with a capitalistic economy and
a liberal middle class. 'Already in the West the latest economic
factor, capitalism, served Freemasonry as a weapon, which
had now been skilfully appropriated by the Jews. Naturally it
was decided to employ the same weapon in Russia, where the
autocracy rests entirely on the support of the landed aristocracy, whereas the child of capitalism, the bourgeoisie, is
benevolently disposed towards revolutionary liberalism.'[1]
And like the *Protocols*, *Tayna Yevreystva* contains an attack on
Witte's innovation, the gold-standard.

According to one 'White' Russian tradition, this extraordinary production was sent by Yuliana Glinka to her friend
General Orzheyevsky, who passed it to the commander of the
Imperial Guard, General Cherevin, who was supposed to pass
it on to the Tsar but failed to do so. And there is little doubt
that the *Protocols* too were intended to be read by the Tsar,
and for a quite specific reason. Compared with his formidable
father Alexander III, Nicholas II was a mild and kindly man
who in the first years of his reign had been reluctant to persecute anyone – even the Jews – and who moreover had shown
a certain willingness to let Russia be modernized, perhaps even
slightly liberalized. The ultra-reactionaries were much concerned to cure the Tsar of these disconcerting traits, and the
way they set about it was to persuade him that the Jews
formed a deadly conspiracy intent on undermining the foundations of Russian society and Orthodox Christianity; and
that the Jews' chosen instrument was the great modernizer,
Witte.

Who, in the end, forged the *Protocols*? Boris Nicolaevsky
and Henri Rollin have argued that much of the *Protocols*
could have come from the eminent physiologist and political
journalist known as Ilya Tsion in Russia and Elie de Cyon in
France.[2] De Cyon certainly was a fanatical opponent of Witte,
and many passages in his political writings do resemble those
parts of the *Protocols* which are directed against Witte's
policies. He even composed one of his attacks on Witte by the

[1] Delevsky, op. cit., p. 155.
[2] Nicolaevsky in a private communication to the author, Henri Rollin
in *L'Apocalypse de notre temps*.

very same method employed in the *Protocols*, i.e. by taking an old French satire on a long-dead statesman and simply changing the names. Also, he was a Russian expatriate who lived in Paris and belonged to the circle around Juliette Adam – who in turn was a close friend of Yuliana Glinka. But there is an important qualification to be made: if de Cyon really is the forger, what he forged cannot have been the *Protocols* as we know them today.

It is inconceivable that a person of such seriousness and intellectual calibre as de Cyon should have sunk to writing a crude antisemitic fabrication. Moreover he was himself of Jewish origin, and though converted to Christianity he never turned against the Jews. In his book *La Russie contemporaine* (1892) he shows a lively sympathy with the persecuted Russian Jews, demands equal opportunities for them, bitterly attacks antisemitic propagandists and instigators of pogroms. If de Cyon did indeed have a hand in the concoction we know as the *Protocols*, then somebody must have appropriated his work and transformed it, replacing the Russian Minister of Finance by the Elders of Zion.

And so we come back to Rachkovsky. For in 1897 Rachkovsky and his men, on instructions from Witte, burgled de Cyon's villa at Territet, Switzerland, and removed quantities of papers. They were looking for writings directed against Witte, and it may well be that they found an adaptation of Joly's book. It remains rather puzzling that Witte's devoted servant Rachkovsky should have propagated a document which, even when transformed, is still largely directed against his master's policies. Perhaps his intention was that the book should be generally ascribed to de Cyon? Such a manoeuvre would serve two purposes: antisemites would be able to claim that the Jewish world-conspiracy had been unmasked by someone who was himself of Jewish birth; and de Cyon would be cruelly mortified and at the same time quite unable to defend himself. And when one recalls that in Russia de Cyon was called Tsion – the same word as Zion – the title of the *Protocols* takes on an added meaning as a malicious private joke. All this would be very much in Rachkovsky's style.

All in all, the most likely hypothesis is that Joly's satire on Napoleon III was transformed by de Cyon into a satire on

Witte which was then transformed under Rachkovsky's guidance into the *Protocols of the Elders of Zion*. But some mystery remains and it is unlikely ever to be cleared up now. The Okhrana archives at the Hoover Institution, Stanford University, reveal nothing; and Rachkovsky's private archives in Paris (now lost) also revealed nothing when Boris Nicolaevsky inspected them in the 1930s. De Cyon's papers, which were kept by his widow in Paris until the Second World War, have disappeared. There is also the riddle of *Tayna Yevreystva*, which can hardly be attributed either to de Cyon or to Rachkovsky. And there one must leave the matter – to be pursued perhaps some day by a specialist in the 1890s with time and energy to spare.

As for the early editors of the *Protocols*, comparison with the fragments of the hectograph in the Wiener Library show Nilus's version to be the nearest to the original, even though it was not the first to be published. Sergey Nilus is in fact the key figure in the launching of the forgery. How it came into his hands remains, like so much else, uncertain. He himself said, in the preface to the 1917 edition of his book, that Sukhotin gave him a copy in 1901; while a letter from Filip Stepanov's son, now in the Freyenwald Collection in the Wiener Library, says that this was a mistake for Stepanov. In any case it is true that in 1901 Nilus was living fairly near to the estates of Sukhotin, Stepanov, and Glinka. But as we have seen, there is also good reason for thinking that Rachkovsky had some contact either with Nilus or with Nilus's copy of the *Protocols*.

Again and again, in trying to unravel the early history of the *Protocols*, one comes up against ambiguities, uncertainties, riddles. There is no need to take them very seriously. It was necessary to glance at the strange vanished world in which, a mere seventy years ago, the *Protocols* were born – the world of counter-revolutionary agents and pseudo-mystics that flourished on the decay of the Tsar's empire.

But what is really important about the *Protocols* is the great influence which – incredibly yet incontestably – they have exercised on twentieth-century history.

CHAPTER V

The *Protocols* in Russia

1

WHATEVER the origin of the *Protocols*, they were adopted and preserved and in the end launched on the world by *pogromshchiki*, professional instigators of pogroms. For the hundreds of local massacres of Jews which occurred in Russia between 1881 and 1920 were by no means spontaneous outbreaks of popular fury – they demanded long-term planning, careful organization, above all intensive agitation. Sometimes this work was carried out by the police, but sometimes private individuals – above all, unscrupulous journalists – took a hand. These were the people who made the *Protocols* their own.

The first person to publish the *Protocols*, Pavolachi Krushevan, was a typical *pogromshchik*. Just four months before he printed the *Protocols* in his St Petersburg newspaper *Znamya*, his other newspaper *Bessarabets* succeeded in provoking a pogrom in his native province of Bessarabia – in fact in the provincial capital, Kishinev, where it was published. How this was achieved was established by Irish and American travellers who visited the town just after the massacre.[1] They found a fertile and prosperous country where traditionally relations between the mass of the population and the large Jewish minority had been very good – so good in fact that in 1881–3, when the whole of south Russia was swept with pogroms, the Bessarabian peasants refused to take part: 'If the Tsar wills that the Jews be slain,' they said, 'he has his army. But we

[1] See I. Singer, *Russia at the Bar of the American People: A Memorial of Kishinev*, New York and London, 1904, and the report of the celebrated Irish nationalist Michael Davitt, who visited Kishinev just after the massacre: *Within the Pale: The true story of antisemitic persecutions in Russia*, London, 1903.

will not strike the Jews.' The situation changed only in 1898, when Krushevan launched his local newspaper and began to publish fanatical attacks on the Jews. A group of journalists, civil servants, and other professional men was formed and, guided by Krushevan from St Petersburg, deliberately began to prepare the way for massacre. In 1902, at Easter – always the favourite time for pogroms – Krushevan announced that a Christian youth, found dead in a well, was the victim of a Jewish ritual murder. That time he was unsuccessful, as the real murderer was quickly identified; but the following year the murder of a boy at Dubossary enabled him to renew the charge, this time with success. He also put it about that an imperial ukase had been issued permitting Christians 'to execute bloody justice on the Jews during the three days of Easter'.

But this was not all. In preparing for the massacre Krushevan's men also made use of the more modern fantasy of the Jewish world-conspiracy. They distributed copies of *The Rabbi's Speech*, and they also elaborated on it. The delusions they fostered emerge clearly from the utterances of Krushevan's leading representative in Kishinev, an agitator called Pronin. At the farcical trial which was held – largely under pressure from abroad – some months after the massacre, this man stated in evidence that a meeting of Jews from all countries had taken place in the Kishinev synagogue just before Easter. The meeting decided to organize a revolt against the Government; whereupon the Jews attacked the Christian population, which merely defended itself. Pronin also published in *Znamya* an article in which he praised the rioters as true patriots who were concerned only to defend the Tsar and Holy Russia against a fearsome international conspiracy. All this when at Kishinev no single Christian had been injured but forty-five Jews had been killed and hundreds injured – almost all of them artisans, miserably poor and completely helpless – and some 10,000 reduced to destitution. Such was the milieu in which the *Protocols* began their public career.

Meanwhile the struggle to modernize and liberalize the Russian political régime was reaching a new intensity. Particularly in 1904–5, against the background of the disastrous war with Japan, there was overwhelming pressure for fundamental reforms, and notably for the establishment of a national representative assembly, freedom of speech, and guarantees of individual liberty. A nation-wide general strike in September 1905 forced the Government to yield, and in October the Tsar reluctantly issued a manifesto promising a constitution based on the principles of modern liberalism. But these developments did not, needless to say, go unopposed. The Tsar himself was surrounded by reactionary influences – notably his mother, some of the grand-dukes, the Procurator of the Holy Synod Pobedonostsev, the Governor-General of St Petersburg Trepov, not to mention the organization known as the Union of the Russian People, or more popularly as the Black Hundreds.[1]

One of the freedoms granted by the Tsar's October manifesto was the freedom of association – and none were quicker to avail themselves of it than the extreme right-wing. On 4 November 1905 the Union of the Russian People was founded in St Petersburg by a doctor, A. Dubrovin, and a politician, V. M. Purishkevich, who was the driving force behind the organization. Like those other members of the Black Hundreds, Krushevan and Butmi, Purishkevich came from Bessarabia – in fact he had graduated at Kishinev – and his political aim was precisely the same as theirs: to fight the liberalization of Russia by presenting it as a Jewish plot, and to get Jews massacred to show how real the plot was. Proclamations began to appear in towns and villages, of which the following is a fair sample:

The efforts to replace the autocracy of the divinely appointed Tsar by a constitution and a parliament are inspired by those bloodsuckers, the Jews, the Armenians and the Poles. Beware of the Jews! All the evil, all the misfortune of our country comes from the Jews. Down with the traitors, down with the constitution![2]

[1] On the Union of the Russian People see W. Laqueur. *Russia and Germany*, notably pp. 79–86. Strictly speaking the Black Hundreds were armed bands recruited for purposes of terror by the Union of the Russian People and similar political organizations; they consisted largely of small shop-keepers, vagabonds and professional criminals. But in popular speech the members of these political organizations themselves were often referred to as 'Black Hundredists'.

[2] Quoted in B. Segel, *Die Protokolle der Weisen von Zion*, Berlin, 1924, p. 214.

And when the national assembly – the Duma of the Empire
– came into being, the propaganda of the Black Hundreds
concentrated on discrediting it as an instrument in the hands
of the Jews. The elections to the first Duma in 1906 and to the
second and third Dumas in 1907 were accompanied by a spate
of pamphlets stating that most of the candidates were Jews,
that the liberal parties were financed by the Jews, that the
Jews were enslaving Russia through the Duma. Among the
electioneering pamphlets published by the Black Hundreds
Butmi's version of the *Protocols*, *The Enemies of the Human
Race* – four editions in 1906–7 – finds its rightful place.[1]

Even in the lamentable context of Russian political life,
the Black Hundreds were widely regarded as being beyond the
pale. Witte for one had no doubts:

This party is patriotic to the depths of its soul . . . but its
patriotism is primitive, it is based not on reason and generosity but
on passion. Most of its leaders are political upstarts, people with
unclean ways of thinking and feeling; they have not a single viable
political idea and concentrate all their efforts on unleashing the
lowest possible impulses in the benighted, savage masses. Sheltered
by the wings of the two-headed eagle this party can instigate the
most frightful pogroms and convulsions, but it is incapable of anything positive. It embodies a wild, nihilistic patriotism which
thrives on lies, slander and deceit, it is a party of wild and cowardly
despair but has no room for courageous, far-sighted, creative
thinking. The bulk of the membership comes from the wild,
ignorant masses, its leaders are political villains, it has secret
sympathizers in court circles and amongst nobles with all kinds of
titles – people who seek their salvation in lawlessness and have as
their slogan: 'Not we for the people, but the people for the good of
our stomachs'. . . . And the Tsar dreams of restoring greatness to
Russia with the help of this party. Poor Tsar . . .[2]

These people were in fact true precursors of the Nazis.
Words such as 'proto-Fascist' have been so monstrously
misused that one hesitates to use them at all – yet there is no
denying that the Black Hundreds mark an important stage in

[1] An account of these Black Hundred publications is given in the
article on Antisemitism in the *Yevreyskaya Entsiklopediya*, Vol. II, pp.
746–52.

[2] Translated from the German version of Witte's memoirs: *Erin-
nerungen*, Berlin, 1923, pp. 144 seq.

the transition from reactionary politics as they were understood in the nineteenth century to the right-wing totalitarianism of the Nazis. In their allegiance to throne and altar they
belonged to the past – but as political adventurers dedicated to
sabotaging, by means of antisemitic agitation and terrorism,
the development of liberal democracy, and as romantic reactionaries who could also talk the language of radical demagogy,
they certainly did look forward to Hitler and his associates.
Like the Nazis, they pretended that Jews formed a capitalist-
revolutionary conspiracy, and that in order to prevent this
conspiratorial body from establishing a monstrous tyranny
the workers and peasants must stand firmly by the 'native'
ruling class. And they forestalled the Nazis, too, in their ideas
as to what should be done to the Jews. If some wanted to deport them to the Kolyma region in the Arctic or beyond the
Altai mountains in southern Siberia, others looked forward to
their physical annihilation. One leading member, 'Markov II',
who in the 1930s was to be employed by the Nazis as an expert
on the *Protocols* and the Judeo-Masonic conspiracy, was already prophesying in 1911, in a speech in the Duma, that 'all
the Yids, down to very last, will be killed'.[1]

It was well known that the Black Hundreds employed
criminals to carry out assassinations and to lead pogroms, and
Black Hundred politicians were not received in decent society
– but that did not prevent the organization from receiving
abundant support from church and state. A bishop was among
its leaders, monasteries published leaflets in support of it, its
emblems and banners were displayed in churches, priests
urged their congregations to pray for its success and to parti-
cipate in its activities. The Government for its part gave
every kind of assistance. It is estimated that in the single year
the Union of the Russian People received 2,500,000 roubles[2]
in government subsidies. It was granted the right to apply for
a free pardon for any member arrested for participating in
pogroms. Above all, it enjoyed the full approval of the Tsar,
who praised it as a shining example of justice and order and
was pleased to wear its badge on his uniform. During the

---

[1] Quoted in A. B. Tager, *The Decay of Czarism: the Beiliss trial*,
Philadelphia, 1935, p. 44.
[2] At that time the rouble was worth about two shillings.

Beiliss ritual murder trial he even sent a telegram thanking the leaders for their attempt to obtain a conviction.

Then there is the story of the Lamsdorf Memorandum to show how even foreign policy could be affected by the outlook of the Black Hundreds. Faced with the advance of liberalism in Russia the Minister for Foreign Affairs, Count Lamsdorf, prepared in 1906 a secret memorandum in which he recommended that Russia, Germany, and the Vatican should take common action against the Alliance Israélite Universelle and its supposed instrument, France. The campaign to extend the franchise and liberalize the régime, he explained, was simply a trick to modernize Russia which, as 'a state of peasants, Orthodox and monarchist', still stood in the way of world-domination by the Judeo-Masons controlled from Paris. It is true that the Lamsdorf Memorandum was quickly buried by Lamsdorf's successor, Isvolsky (it was published only in 1918, by the Bolsheviks), but it is worth noting what the Tsar wrote in the margin: 'Negotiations must be started *at once*. I entirely share the opinions expressed here'.[1]

In this atmosphere the *Protocols* enjoyed their first vogue. How seriously they were taken in some quarters, and how blindly they were believed, is shown by an unpublished letter which a former conservative Russian journalist, I. Kolyshko, otherwise known as 'Bayan', wrote to Burtsev at the time of the Berne trial, when both of them were refugees in France:

7 September 1934

Much esteemed Vladimir Lvovich,

You ask whether, as a former journalist . . ., I know anything about the so-called *Protocols of the Elders of Zion*. . . .

To help you evaluate my recollections, I think it necessary to tell you that at that time my sympathies drew me to right-wing circles in Russia . . . to people who tended to be antisemitic . . . as a result I paid most attention to what came to me from the anti-semitic camp. I cannot deny that when they first appeared these *Protocols* made a really overwhelming impression in these circles,

---

[1] The Lamsdorf Memorandum was published by the Soviet Commissariat of Foreign Affairs in 1918. A French translation appeared in the *Mercure de France*, issue of 1 October 1918, pp. 547–51, and an English translation in L. Wolf, *Diplomatic History of the Jewish Question*, London, 1919, pp. 54–62.

and on me personally. As you know, one believes what one wants to believe. The people amongst whom I moved began by believing *absolutely* in the authenticity of this document. Then gradually the efforts of the Left began to undermine this belief, we began to have doubts and the construction . . . began to crumble, under the corroding effect of criticism (and of the facts); slowly at first, then more and more quickly. So far as I can recall . . . it finally collapsed at the beginning of the war. During the Great War I heard no mention of the *Protocols* in Russia, until after 1917. . . .

Inside Russia the controversy came to an end. I was not interested in how or when it spilled over into the west – into France, England and Germany. Because I regarded this matter as settled *once and for all*. . . . There seemed no possibility that the *Protocols* would ever again revive and upset mankind. . . .

> With the greatest esteem and devotion,
> I. Kolyshko (Bayan)[1]

The success of the *Protocols* before the war was in fact limited. Zhevakhov tells how in 1913 Nilus complained to him: 'I cannot get the public to treat the *Protocols* seriously, with the attention they deserve. They are read, criticized, often ridiculed, but there are very few who attach importance to them and see in them a real threat to Christianity, a pro- gramme for the destruction of the Christian order and for the conquest of the whole world by the Jews. That nobody be- lieves . . .'[2] Years later 'Markov II', in a letter preserved in the Wiener Library, lamented that the Union of the Russian People, by its half-hearted use of the *Protocols*, had failed to avert the Russian Revolution.

One has to bear in mind that in these matters everything depended on the attitude of the Tsar himself – and in the end the Tsar, however besotted by the Judeo-Masonic conspiracy, had to recognize the *Protocols* as spurious. How this came about is described in a statement from General K. I. Globa- chev, one-time commandant of the St Petersburg division of the Okhrana, which Burtsev produced at the Berne trial. Globachev describes how, after many unsuccessful attempts, the *Protocols* were at last brought to the Tsar's notice in the revolutionary year 1905. 'Reading the *Protocols*,' he continues,

---

[1] A copy of Kolyshko's letter is in the B. I. Nicolaevsky Collection at the Hoover Institution, Stanford University, California.

[2] N. D. Zhevakhov, *Sergey Alexandrovich Nilus*, Novi Sad, 1936, p. 35.

'made a very deep impression on Nicholas II, who made them his handbook for politics.' Typical in this respect are the marginal annotations which Nicholas II made on the copy of the *Protocols* which had been submitted to him: 'What depth of thought!' – 'What foresight!' – 'What precision in the realization of the programme!' – 'Our year 1905 has gone as though managed by the Elders.' – 'There can be no doubt as to their authenticity.' – 'Everywhere one sees the directing and destroying hand of Judaism.' And so on. Keenly interested in the 'discovery' of the *Protocols*, Nicholas II gave his attention to the foreign branch of the Russian secret police and handed out a great number of rewards, decorations, and gratuities. . . . The leaders of the Union of the Russian People, like Shmakov, Markov II, etc., addressed a request to the Ministry of the Interior, asking for authorization to use the *Protocols* on a large scale in the struggle against militant Judaism, and for subsidies for the purpose. But the Minister of the Interior, Stolypin . . . entrusted two officers of the corps of gendarmes,[1] Martynov and Vassilyev, with a secret inquiry into the origin of the *Protocols*. This inquiry revealed clearly the spuriousness of the *Protocols*. The results of the inquiry were presented by Stolypin to Nicholas II, who was completely bowled over. And this is the resolution of Nicholas II on the report concerning the employment of the *Protocols* for anti-semitic propaganda: 'Drop the *Protocols*. One cannot defend a pure cause by dirty methods'[2].

This situation changed in 1917–18, when first the Tsar and then the Provisional Government were overthrown, the Bolsheviks seized power and the civil war began. Indeed, what launched the *Protocols* on their career across the world was above all the murder of the imperial family at Yekaterinburg (now Sverdlovsk) on 17 July 1918. Here chance played an extraordinary part. Some months before her murder at Yekaterinburg the deposed Empress had received from a friend, Zinaïda Sergeyevna Tolstaya, a copy of Nilus's book containing the *Protocols*. It seems to have meant little to her, to judge

---

[1] The corps of gendarmes was a semi-military police force which, while concerned with political matters, was independent of the Okhrana.

[2] Burtsev later published this document in his book *Protokoly Sionskikh Mudretsov*, Paris, 1938, pp. 105–6.

by a letter which she sent to her great friend Anna Vyrubova
on 20 March 1918: 'Zina has sent me a book: *The Great in the
Small,* by Nilus, I am reading it with interest.'[1] This terse
comment hardly suggests enthusiasm; and the Tsaritsa, though
a stupid, superstitious, and hysterical woman, was in fact far
less of an antisemite than her husband. In her correspondence
one even finds her remonstrating with the Tsar over his antisemitic policy. There is therefore much irony in the fact that
the Tsaritsa's death should, more than any other event, have
brought world fame to an old and half-forgotten antisemitic
forgery.

As luck would have it, the Empress took Nilus's book with
her to her last home, the house of Ipatyev at Yekaterinburg.
A week after the murder of the imperial family Yekaterinburg
was evacuated by the Bolsheviks and occupied by the 'Whites';
on 28 July the remains of the Tsar, the Tsaritsa, and their
children, dismembered and incinerated, were discovered at the
bottom of a disused mine-shaft in a nearby forest. Meanwhile
the examining magistrate Nametkin was engaged in drawing
up an inventory of the belongings found at Ipatyev's house.
He found three books belonging to the Empress: the first
volume of *War and Peace,* the Bible in Russian, and *The Great
in the Small* by Nilus.

Another curious circumstance came to light: the Tsaritsa
had drawn a swastika in the embrasure of a window in the
room occupied by her and her husband. It is known that she
had long had a special partiality for this ancient symbol[2] – she
wore a jewelled swastika and had swastikas engraved on the
gifts which she sent to her friends. It is also known that for
this profoundly superstitious woman the swastika was a
talisman intended to bring good luck. But already then there
were people for whom it meant something quite different.
Well before the war the Austrian writer Guido von List had
taught, in a whole series of popular books on 'the Germano-

[1] Anna Vyrubova, *Souvenirs de ma vie,* Paris, 1927, p. 269.
[2] The swastika is found in remains from the bronze age in various
parts of Europe, and was also known in ancient Persia, India, China,
Japan, and among the Indian tribes of north, central, and south
America. Its commonest significance is as a symbol of good luck or
benediction.

Aryans', that the swastika symbolized the purity of Germanic
blood and the struggle of the 'Aryans' against the Jews. These
ideas had penetrated to Russia; and to Russians who were
familiar with them the discovery of the Empress's swastika
together with the copy of Nilus came as a revelation from on
high. This, they believed, was a testament from their dead
Empress; and what it said was that the reign of Antichrist was
beginning, that the Bolshevik revolution was the supreme
assault of the Satanic powers, that the imperial family had
been destroyed because they represented the divine will on
earth – and that the forces of darkness were incarnated in the
Jews.

It was all the easier to arrive at such a conclusion because
some Jews really were playing a conspicuous part in the revolution. Among the officers in the 'White' armies, some failed to
reflect that this might be connected with the oppression to
which Jews had been subjected under the tsarist régime; or
that earlier tsars had been assassinated also, and by pure-
blooded Russians. This is not surprising, for these men
had grown up in a society where 'the Jew' had been regarded as the source of all evil. They had been taught that
the whole Russian people loved the Tsar and his autocracy, and
they had every reason for concealing from themselves that this
had long ceased to be true. They needed a simple explanation
for the catastrophe which was overwhelming them and their
world. They found it in the union of the swastika and the
Protocols in Ipatyev's house. And soon the *pogromshchiki* were
at hand to exploit the great discovery.

2

When the Tsar and his family were murdered the civil war was
still in its early stages. It continued for another two years,
during which the Soviet Government was repeatedly on the
brink of defeat, before the 'White' armies were finally routed in
1920. It was during those two years that the *Protocols* first
showed their power to incite men to murder.

The people behind the *Protocols* were still the same. As a
unified organization the Union of the Russian People had

hardly existed since about 1910, but now the former leaders attached themselves to the various 'White' armies, founded new political groups with names like the Union of the Russian National Communities or the Russian Assembly, and above all carried on a vigorous agitation in favour of pogroms. The Frenchman du Chayla, who was with the 'White' armies at that time, has described the zeal of these men in disseminating the *Protocols*. A Moscow lawyer, Ismailov, and a lieutenant-colonel, Rodionov, combined forces to produce a new, cheap edition for the armies in the Don region; and this was distributed to the troops by Purishkevich, a founder of the Black Hundreds, who had got himself a job in General Denikin's propaganda department at Rostov. In the Crimea too, under the régime of General Wrangel, professors and journalists 'shouted at every street-corner about the menace of the *Protocols* and the Judeo-Masonic world-conspiracy'.[1]

To this one may add that further editions of the *Protocols* were published in Siberia. One was printed at Omsk, for the army of Admiral Kolchak. The Admiral himself was obsessed by the *Protocols*; G. K. Gins, who saw much of him at that time, has recorded that he 'literally devoured the *Protocols*. His head was crammed with anti-Masonic ideas. He was ready to see Freemasons everywhere, even in his own entourage . . . and amongst the members of the military missions of the Allies'.[2] Other editions of the *Protocols* appeared in the easternmost parts of Siberia, such as Vladivostok and Khabarovsk. An edition was even published by 'White' Russians in Japan.

The interpretation that was now put upon the *Protocols* emerges clearly from the preface which was attached to the first of the new editions, that produced by the Moscow lawyer Ismailov and the Cossack officer Rodionov at Novocherkask under the title *Zionist Protocols, Plan for World Conquest by the Judeo-Masons*:

> The *Protocols* are a programme, carefully worked out in every detail, for the conquest of the world by the Jews. The greater part of this programme has already been realized, and if we do not take thought, we are irretrievably doomed to destruction. . . . These *Protocols* are in fact not only the key to our first, unsuccessful

---

[1] A. du Chayla, in *La Tribune Juive*, Paris, 14 May 1921, pp. 6–7.
[2] G. K. Gins, *Sibir, Soyuzniki i Kolchak*, Peking, 1921, Vol. II, p. 39.

revolution (1905), but also to our second revolution (1917), in which the Jews have played such a disastrous role for Russia. . . . For us who are witnesses of this self-laceration, for us who hope to see Russia's rebirth, this document is all the more significant because it reveals the means employed by the enemies of Christianity to subjugate us. Only if we reach an understanding of these means, shall we be able to fight successfully the enemies of Christ and of Christian civilisation.[1]

The *Protocols* were of course far too complicated and sophisticated to be understood by the common soldiers – most of whom were in any case illiterate. At the Berne trial of 1934 Chaim Weizmann recalled the first time he saw the *Protocols*. British officers attached to the 'White' armies brought to Palestine a document of four or five typewritten pages, and explained that just such a document was to be found in the possession of every 'White' officer and N.C.O. On inspection it turned out to consist of extracts from the *Protocols*. From other sources it appears that material of this kind was distributed on a vast scale to literate members of the various 'White' and Ukrainian armies, who used to read and explain it to the illiterate.

New forgeries were also produced to supplement the *Protocols* and bring them up to date. The most celebrated of these was a document said to have been found on a Jewish Bolshevik commander in the Red Army, of the name of Zunder. Copies of this document seem to have been circulated as early as May 1918; and in the winter of 1919–20, when the tide of battle was turning and the 'White' armies, hitherto victorious, were losing battle after battle, it began to figure in newspapers run by the 'White' armies – sometimes in new and considerably expanded versions. It reads as follows:

Secret. To the representatives of all the branches of the Israelite International League.

Sons of Israel! The hour of our ultimate victory is near! We stand on the threshold to the command of the world. That which we could only dream of before is about to be realized. Only quite recently feeble and powerless, we can now, thanks to the world's catastrophe, raise our heads with pride.

We must, however, be careful! It can surely be prophesied that,

[1] *Sionskiye Protokoly* (ed. A. Rodionov), Novocherkask, 1918.

after we have marched over ruined and broken altars and thrones, we shall advance further on the same indicated path.

The authority of the to us alien religions and doctrines of faith we have, through very successful propaganda, subjected to a merciless criticism and mockery. We have brought the culture, civilization, traditions and thrones of the Christian nations to stagger, wherein, among these nations, we found more men than was necessary for our work. We have done everything to bring the Russian people under the yoke of the Jewish power, and ultimately compelled them to fall on their knees before us.

We have nearly completed all this, but we must all the same be very cautious, because the oppressed Russia is our arch-enemy. The victory over Russia, gained through our intellectual superiority, may in future, in a new generation, turn against us.

Russia is conquered and brought to the ground. Russia is in the agony of death under our heel, but do not forget – not even for a moment – that we must be careful. The holy care for our safety does not allow us to show either pity or mercy. At last we have been allowed to behold the bitter need of the Russian people, and to see it in tears! By taking from them their property, their gold, we have reduced this people to helpless slaves.

Be cautious and silent. We ought to have no mercy for our enemy. We must make an end of the best and leading elements of the Russian people, so that the vanquished Russia may not find any leader! Thereby every possibility will vanish for them to resist our power. We must excite hatred and disputes between workers and peasants. War and class struggle will destroy all treasure and culture created by the Christian people. But be cautious, Sons of Israel! Our victory is near, because our political and economic power and influence upon the masses are in rapid progress. We buy up Government loans and gold and thereby we have controlling power of the world's exchanges. The power is in our hands, but be careful – place no faith in traitorous shady powers.

Bronstein (Trotsky), Apfelbaum (Zinovyev), Rosenfeld (Kamenev), Steinberg – all of them are like unto thousands of other true sons of Israel. Our power in Russia is unlimited. In the towns the commissariats and committees of food, house committees, etc., are dominated by our people. But do not let victory intoxicate you. Be careful, cautious, because no one except yourselves will protect us.

Remember, we cannot rely on the Red Army, which one day may turn its warfare on ourselves.

Sons of Israel! The hour for our long-cherished victory over

Russia is near; close your ranks! Make known our people's national policy! Fight for our eternal ideals! Keep holy the old laws, which history has bequeathed to us! May our intellect, our genius, protect and lead us!

Signed, The Central Committee of the Israelite International League.[1]

For all its absurdity, the Zunder document was a portent; for the idea underlying it – that the Bolshevik revolution was the result of a Jewish plot and fulfilled the age-old strivings of the Jewish people – was to leave its mark on history. Already at that time the idea had become an obsession with many of the 'White' Russians, later it was to become an article of faith with the Nazis, within a generation it was to influence the policy of the German Government at home and abroad. It is worth considering what basis, if any, it had in historical fact.

Until the last few generations, to be a Jew meant one thing only: to be an adherent of the Jewish religion. For Jews in this sense of the word the Bolshevik revolution meant not fulfilment but renewed peril. In the event religious Jews have been at least as much persecuted in the Soviet Union as have religious Christians. At the very time when the Zunder document was circulating in the 'White' armies, the Soviet Government was converting synagogues into workers' clubs, dissolving Jewish religious, cultural, and philanthropic institutions, and banning all Hebrew books, irrespective of their contents. Bolsheviks of Jewish descent felt not the slightest solidarity with religious Jews – on the contrary. When a deputation of Jews called on Trotsky and asked him to do nothing which could provoke the 'White' soldiery to pogroms, he answered: 'Go home to your Jews and tell them I'm not a Jew and don't care about the Jews or what happens to them'.[2] Here is a gulf, and an unbridgeable one, which antisemitic propagandists have done their best to conceal.

There was another reason why the great mass of Russian Jews could not conceivably support the Bolsheviks: they were mostly small shop-keepers and self-employed artisans. As

[1] Reprinted in *Four Protocols of Zion* (*not the Protocols of Nilus*), London, 1921.

[2] H. Valentin, *Antisemitenspiegel*, Vienna, 1937, pp. 179–80.

such, though mostly miserably poor, they were from the
Leninist point of view class-enemies. Although these people
were inevitably opposed to the tsarist régime which persecuted
them, they were anything but Communist. During the short
period when the free expression of political opinion was
possible, they emerged mainly as supporters of the bourgeois
reformist Constitutional Democrats. Under the Soviet régime
they suffered even more than other Russians – in the 1920s
more than a third of the Jewish population was without civil
rights, as compared with 5–6 per cent of the non-Jewish
population.

It remains true that Jews, in the sense of persons of Jewish
descent, provided a disproportionate part of the leadership
(though not of the total membership) of the two Marxist
parties, the Bolsheviks and the Mensheviks. The reason is not
far to seek. These were people who had broken with the traditional Jewish community and abandoned the Jewish religion
but who nevertheless suffered discrimination and persecution
under the tsarist autocracy; and this was sufficient to lead
them towards the parties of the Left. Moreover they were
mostly former university students – and owing to the *numerus
clausus* a Jew had to be of quite outstanding ability to get to a
university at all. Once they had joined a political party such
people were well qualified to rise to positions of leadership.
It is a situation which has been repeated in other countries
where Jewish intellectuals have had to cope with antisemitism
without the support and consolation of religious faith.

Such Jews are usually idealists inspired by a vision of a
society from which all forms of discrimination are banished.
In general they make poor politicians and they tend to be
ousted soon after a successful revolution. In Russia Jews were
in fact far more numerous in the Menshevik than in the
Bolshevik leadership; and these Menshevik leaders were all
exiled or imprisoned or executed by the Bolsheviks. As for
the Jews among the Bolshevik leaders, they too were almost all
shot in the 1930s.

Such are the facts. But fantasy does not wait upon facts,
and the myth of the Judeo-Communist conspiracy was to
prove even more potent than the myth of the Judeo-Masonic
conspiracy. The Russian civil war provided a first indication

of its power. Some of the army commanders, such as General Denikin, might themselves be revolted by the propaganda which was being carried on among their troops, but this made no difference. The Black Hundred organizations had formulated their war aim very clearly, and they effectively imposed it on the troops: 'Kill the Jews, Save Russia.'

The enormous massacres of Jews carried out by the Nazis have overshadowed everything that went before, so that few people now are much aware of the prelude which was acted out in Russia between 1918 and 1920. The number of victims was nevertheless very considerable – over 100,000 killed and an unknown number of wounded and maimed. Many of the accounts given by witnesses of these pogroms are too horrible to bear re-telling. The following extracts from a report by the Russian journalist Ivan Derevensky on the pogrom carried out by a Cossack regiment at Fastov, near Kiev, in September 1919, will suffice to give some idea of what a pogrom was like and how it was set in motion. This is what happened after an unsuccessful attempt by the Bolsheviks to capture the town:

In the first three days robbery and murder were perpetrated mainly at night. During the nights the whole population could hear shooting and desperate cries now from one direction, now from another. At first murders were not so frequent, but they became more and more so. By about the third day Cossacks were already walking about the town, quite openly looking for Jewish houses and when they found one, doing whatever they liked. They were also stopping Jews in the streets. Sometimes they would simply ask, 'A Yid?' and put a bullet through his skull. More often they would search the man, strip him naked, and then shoot him. Many of the killers were drunk. . . .

About the second or third day they began to set fire to Jewish homes. The reason for this was that the *pogromshchiki* wanted to destroy the traces of their worst crimes. In one house on the corner of the Torgovy Square, for instance, were fifteen corpses, including many young girls who had been killed after being raped. They set that house alight to cover up those crimes. . . .

I shall describe the excesses committed, dividing them into their different kinds.

Murders. When I was in Fastov it was not yet possible to establish the number of victims with any certainty. According to the Red Cross, 550 bodies had been buried in the Jewish cemetery.

But the total number of dead was thought to be much higher. The general view amongst both Christians and Jews was that between 1,500 and 2,000 Jews had been killed in Fastov. . . . By the time I arrived all bodies had been removed from the streets and buried, but they were still finding bodies in woods and ditches and in some of the houses. Apart from that it is agreed that many bodies were burnt when the houses were set on fire. People are still searching for the remains. Near some of the burnt-out houses there is a strong smell of dead bodies. Unidentifiable bones are often found in the ashes. Many of the victims cannot be traced by their relatives at all and are presumed dead. Behind the house of prayer many corpses were eaten by pigs and dogs. . . .

Woundings. The number of wounded is put at 300–400. Some of these wounded die every day. Owing to shortage of personnel medical aid is very inadequate. The wounded are in the class-rooms of the local school. They lie there without bandages, and in such a state of overcrowding that one can hardly walk between them.

Atrocities. I was told of one case of a man being thrown into the fire alive. A man called Kiksman had his tongue cut out and died after being shot with a dumdum bullet. Everyone talks of how dumdum bullets were used, including the medical personnel from the hospital. A man called Markman had both ears cut off, another member of the same family got twelve slashes with a sabre, another got eight. The corpse of a small girl, M. Polskaya, showed that she had suffered burning while alive. One of the lists of the buried (available from the police clerk) contains the names of two six-month-old babies, Avrum Slobodsky and Ruvin Konik. A man was killed by being cut in two. In front of the synagogue about twenty Jews were stripped naked and then shot. The same happened to four Jews in Voksal Street. . . .

Very often people were got ready for hanging, in order to make them give up their money. . . . But many were hanged until they were dead – for instance Moshko Remenik (on a tree in his garden) and a father and his school-boy son, Meyer and Boris Zabarsky. These two were experimentally half-hanged first, and the boy was forced to tighten the noose around his father's neck. . . .

Rape. Understandably, the names of victims of rape who survived are not available. There were very few of these – I heard only of two young girls, who were in some hospital. But according to witnesses rapes were very numerous; the victims were usually killed afterwards. I was told of rapes committed on very young girls. . . .

Arson. Altogether about 200 buildings were burnt down, half of them dwellings. . . . About a thousand families have been rendered homeless and are sheltering in the synagogue, the school or simply on the street.

To the question, 'Who perpetrated this pogrom?' it is possible to give a quite definite answer: the Cossacks of the 2nd Brigade from Tersk. It is commanded by Colonel Belogortsev. . . .

I must point out that the victims of the pogrom are convinced that the pogrom was 'permitted' by brigade headquarters. They drew this conclusion from the fact that the officers were at best indifferent and often came out in support of the pogrom, and that individual Cossacks said such things as 'We were ordered to beat the Yids,' and 'We had leave to *have a party* for three days,' and 'Nobody is going to punish us for this,' and so on. But I must add that some officers of that same brigade tried to stop the pogrom, to defend certain houses and in general to help the Jews in their plight. Lieutenant Ilyushkin, who was in command of the artillery, persuaded his Cossacks to defend a whole block of buildings. . . .

Now as for the causes of the pogrom: although this was just what interested me most, I could find no real reason for the pogrom at all. One thing only is certain – that there was amongst the Cossacks a general belief – though an entirely vague and baseless one – that Jews sympathized with Bolshevism. Lieutenant Ilyushkin told me that, 'obviously for purposes of provocation', somebody spread a rumour amongst the Cossacks to the effect that Jews welcomed the Bolsheviks with joy when for a short time they occupied Fastov . . . and that they fired at the Volunteer forces[1] as these withdrew from Fastov. This rumour was not confirmed by any of my many informants. On the contrary, everybody – including people who were very hostile to the Jews – denied absolutely that such things could possibly have happened. At the time when the Bolsheviks penetrated into Fastov the Jews – like the rest of the inhabitants – hid in the cellars. . . . [2]

While these things were happening in Russia the *Protocols* and the myth of the Judeo-Bolshevik conspiracy were penetrating westwards and establishing themselves above all in Germany.

---

[1] i.e. 'White' forces.

[2] Derevensky was sent to Fastov by an organization founded in Kiev in 1919 for collecting data about the pogroms in the Ukraine, later called the Central Archives of Pogrom-materials and located in Berlin. Derevensky arrived in Fastov on 17 September 1919; the pogrom had taken place on 10–13 September. His report is printed in I. B. Shekhtman, *Pogromy dobrovolcheskoy armii na Ukraine*, Berlin, 1932.

CHAPTER VI

The *Protocols* reach Germany

1

IN the course of the Russian civil war the *pogromshchiki* and the 'White' officers whom they influenced built up a whole corpus of antisemitic legends and forgeries. For instance, in September 1919 a monarchist journal at Rostov on the Don printed a forged document which it falsely attributed to the American secret service.[1] The purport of the document was that the Bolsheviks had received a subsidy of many millions of dollars from the American Jewish banker Jacob Schiff on behalf of the New York banking house of Kuhn, Loeb and Co., and that this had enabled them to carry out their revolution. It is easy to see why Schiff was singled out in this way. During the pogroms of 1905 he really had tried to persuade the United States Government to exert itself on behalf of the Russian Jews – and that was something no *pogromshchik* could forgive. But some of the foreign correspondents and members of the military missions with the 'White' armies took this kind of stuff seriously and helped to channel it to western Europe. Before long Mgr Jouin in Paris was blithely reprinting the forgery about Schiff in his edition of the *Protocols*; while for the Nazis the story was to provide an inexhaustible theme for propaganda.

Meanwhile the *Protocols* themselves travelled west. Some twenty years after the original French manuscript of the forgery had gone from Paris to Russia, printed copies of the Russian translation came out of Russia in the baggage of 'White' Russian officers. In 1919 typewritten copies in various languages began to circulate among the delegates to the Peace

---

[1] *V Moskvu*, issue No. 1, 23 September 1919.

Conference; they also began to appear on the desks of cabinet ministers and civil servants in London, Paris, Rome, and Washington. The aim of this manoeuvre was to persuade the governments of the various powers to continue and intensify their intervention in Russia. All kinds of objections could be raised against intervening in a genuine civil war – but what if the conflict in Russia were no civil war but simply the unfolding of an international Jewish plot to subjugate the Russian people? Crazy as the argument may seem now, it appears to have had some effect on governmental policies.

Not that all dealers in the *Protocols* thought in terms of high policy. In the summer and autumn of 1919 a mysterious Lithuanian, a former employee of the Okhrana, called on a Jewish delegation to the Peace Conference and offered to hand over, for £10,000, a book which could be exceedingly dangerous to the Jews. Needless to say no business was done; but the delegation saw the book, and it was a copy of the *Protocols*. And this was no isolated incident: the American Jewish Committee had occasion to report, in its yearbook for 1920, how it had been approached by certain Russians with an offer to destroy, for a handsome consideration, the original manuscript of the *Protocols*. But the time for such private intrigues was drawing to a close. By the end of 1919 the *Protocols* had begun their rise to world fame, thanks to the efforts of a pair of Russian fanatics settled in Berlin, Pyotr Nikolaevich Shabelsky-Bork and Fyodor Viktorovich Vinberg.[1]

Shabelsky-Bork was born in the Caucasus in 1893. His father was a rich landowner; his mother was a leading member of the Union of the Russian People, the editor of a Black Hundred periodical in St Petersburg and the author of an antisemitic and anti-Masonic book called *The Satanists of the Twentieth Century*. Shabelsky-Bork himself belonged from an early age to the Union of the Russian People and to another similar organization, the Confraternity of St Michael the Archangel. He served as an officer in the World War and, briefly, in the civil war. In September 1918 he was at Yeka-

[1] On the part played by Vinberg and Shabelsky-Bork see H. Rollin, *L'Apocalypse de notre temps*, Paris, 1939, notably pp. 153 seq., and W. Laqueur, *Russia and Germany*, London, 1965, pp. 109 seq.

terinburg, claiming that he had been commissioned by certain
highly placed persons to inquire into the circumstances attending the murder of the imperial family. He interrogated a
number of people there and must certainly have heard about
the Tsaritsa's swastika and her copy of Nilus.

Vinberg was a much older man, having been born in 1871 at
Kiev, as the son of a general commanding a cavalry division.
He himself became an officer, and eventually a colonel, in the
Imperial Guard. He was a member of the Confraternity of St
Michael the Archangel and wrote for Black Hundred periodicals. In 1918 he was arrested for counter-revolutionary activities and imprisoned in the fortress of St Peter and St Paul in
Petrograd;[1] but soon he escaped or was released. He made his
way to the Ukraine, where he joined the 'White' propagandists
and *pogromshchiki* at Kiev. The murder of the Tsaritsa and the
discoveries made in her room at Yekaterinburg had a very
special significance for him. When he died in France in 1927
the obituary in the *Revue Internationale des Sociétés secrètes*
noted that the Tsaritsa had been honorary colonel of Vinberg's
regiment: 'He really worshipped her, and all his writings
against the Jews and Freemasons are permeated by this cult.'[2]

Shabelsky-Bork and Vinberg both left Russia at a fairly
early stage in the civil war. When the German troops evacuated
the Ukraine after the armistice of November 1918 the German
authorities provided a train for any Russian officers wishing
to accompany them. Shabelsky-Bork and Vinberg took the
opportunity and moved to Germany. It seems that immediately on arrival, in a Germany still in the first throes of defeat and
revolution, Vinberg established contact with the man who
was to produce the first German translation of the *Protocols*,
Ludwig Müller. Müller, who liked to call himself Müller von
Hausen and also used the pen-name Gottfried zur Beek, was a
retired army captain and the editor of a conservative and antisemitic monthly, *Auf Vorposten* (*On Outpost Duty*). Before
November was out, this man possessed a copy of the 1911
edition of Nilus's book, *The Great in the Small*, with the *Protocols*
– and he had it either from Vinberg or from some associate of

---

[1] St Petersburg, now Leningrad, was called Petrograd from 1914 to
1920.
[2] On the *Revue Internationale des Sociétés secrètes* see below, pp. 164–5.

Vinberg's. The contacts between these obscure, half-crazy, half-criminal characters were to have important consequences. Mgr Jouin, who did so much to disseminate the *Protocols* in France, considered that Vinberg's activity in Germany was 'the starting-point for the crusade against the Judeo-Masonic peril'; and if this was an exaggeration it had some truth in it. Certainly from that moment antisemitic agitation took on a murderous intensity which was new in western Europe.

In Berlin Vinberg and Shabelsky-Bork collaborated in producing a yearbook, *Luch Sveta* (*A Ray of Light*), the third issue of which (May 1920) contains the complete text of the 1911 edition of Nilus. The other issues are also obsessively concerned with the imaginary Judeo-Masonic-Bolshevik conspiracy; and so is Vinberg's book *Krestny Put* (i.e. *Via dolorosa*) which was translated into German. In all these writings Vinberg insists that in one way or another the Jews must be got rid of. Of course he realizes that this cannot be done in a democracy, but this worries him not at all, for in his view democracy is in any case a monstrous aberration – in fact it is a devilish device invented by the Jews as a means of securing their domination. Vinberg accordingly demands that the natural leaders of the nations shall once and for all recognize the political incompetence of the masses, turn their backs on democratic politics, seize power and impose their dictatorship on these 'anthropoid herds'. Then the time will be ripe to unite the nations in a common front against the world-conspiracy of the Jews.

Meanwhile Vinberg sees one great consolation: Germany is relatively free from the democratic malady. 'In Germany the *Protocols of the Elders of Zion* circulate freely, and the workers are revising their socialist programmes at extra meetings. . . . Lectures on Jewish domination are being given every-where. . . .'[1] And it is Germany's enemies, England and France, that constitute the stronghold of the Elders. Already in the eighteenth century England, at the behest of the Elders, paid such men as Rousseau, Voltaire, and the Encyclopedists to undermine France; more recently she paid Tolstoy and Gorky to undermine Russia. The French Revolution was planned by the Elders and so were the Russian and German

[1] F. V. Vinberg, *Krestny Put*, Munich, 1922 edition, p. 246.

revolutions of 1917–18. 'The link connecting the German and Russian revolutions consists in the fact that the two *coups d'état* were artificially provoked by means of the world-wide ... network of Judeo-Masonic organizations. In these organizations, low-grade Freemasonry plays the part of a blind weapon of the notorious ... Alliance Israélite Universelle, that secret council of the Elders of the People of Israel. ...'[1] Moreover not only the revolutions but the World War itself was the work of the Elders, operating through British and French foreign policy. The Kaiser and the Tsar did their best to avoid war but they were no match for the Elders. The only remedy now lies in an alliance of the true Germany and the true Russia – meaning a Germany and a Russia under dictatorships of the Right. Such an alliance may yet challenge and overthrow the Judeo-Masonic conspiracy and its French and British puppets. There must be a new slogan: 'Germany and Russia above everything! above everything in the world!' 'In this way,' comments Vinberg, 'the two peoples will realize their dream, magnanimous and beneficent but hitherto unrealizable, of peace in the world. ...'[2]

As a political programme Vinberg's utterances cannot be taken seriously. Among the Russian émigrés only a minority even of the right-wing extremists was willing to call on German help to restore the tsarist régime, while among German right-wingers only a few – such as Ludendorff – were so unrealistic as to contemplate such a restoration. On the other hand Vinberg was absolutely right in thinking that the *Protocols* would have a greater appeal in Germany than in any other country. He knew, of course, that ever since the emergence of antisemitism as a political force, around 1870, it had been far stronger and more widespread in Germany than in England or France. But this was not all: as soon as it became apparent that Germany was going to lose the war, those who had led the country to disaster hastened to throw the blame upon the Jews, who were held responsible both for the war itself and for Germany's failure to win it.

Already in January 1918 the right-wing monthly *Deutschlands Erneuerung* (*Germany's Renewal*) produced a variation

---

[1] *Luch Sveta*, Berlin, Vol. I (1919), p. 50.
[2] F. V. Vinberg, *Krestny Put*, p. 49.

on *The Rabbi's Speech*, adapted to the needs of the moment. In 1913, it declared, an international group of Jewish bankers met in Paris and decided that the time had come for high finance to oust kings and emperors and openly impose its authority upon the whole world; what had hitherto been secret control must now become avowed dictatorship. These were the men who had plunged the world into war. They had also seen to it that 'all-Jewish agitators' should undermine Germany to such an extent that foreign powers felt free to attack her, in the certain knowledge that war would plunge her into revolution. This idea quickly caught on in right-wing circles. As, during the last desperate months of the war, strikes spread in Germany and Austria, leaflets were distributed stating that 'American, English and Russian Jews have raised 1,500,000,000 marks . . . to incite Germans against Germans, brothers against brothers'. In August 1918, when the German Army was in full retreat on the western front, Prince Dr Otto zu Salm-Horstmar – who in due course was to become a very active sponsor of the *Protocols* – explained that Germany was losing the war because the democratic philosophy was undermining the aristocratic philosophy which was natural to Germans; and this democratic philosophy found its strongest support in the international Jewish race, operating through the Masonic lodges. For good measure he added that Lenin was a Jew and belonged to a Masonic lodge in Paris, to which Trotsky also belonged. All this the prince said in a formal speech in the upper house of the Prussian Diet.

In the very moment of Germany's final defeat the periodical *Auf Vorposten* was ready with its explanation: 'The blue and white flag of the Jewish people and the blood-red banner of the Scottish high-grade[1] have won for the present! The thrones of the Romanovs, the Habsburgs and Hohenzollerns . . . are deserted, and Germany groans under the tyranny of the workers' and soldiers' councils.'[2] And early in 1919, as the German population tasted the full bitterness of defeat, whole books began to appear in which the war and its outcome were explained in this way. Two particularly influential works were *Judas Schuldbuch, eine deutsche Abrechnung (Accounts to be*

---

[1] I.e. 'the old and accepted Scottish rite', see above, p. 49.
[2] *Auf Vorposten* for 1918, Heft 4–6, p. 82.

settled by Germany with the Jews), which appeared over the pseudonym 'Wilhelm Meister',[1] and *Weltfreimaurerei, Weltrevolution, Weltrepublik, eine Untersuchung über Ursprung und Endziele des Weltkrieges* (*World Freemasonry, World Revolution, World Republic, an investigation into the origin and final aims of the World War*), by Dr F. Wichtl – both of them published in Munich, where Adolf Hitler was just beginning his political career. Their object is stated with remarkable naïveté by Wichtl himself: 'to convince the reader that it is not we Germans who are to blame for all the horrible bloodshed' but the Judeo-Masonic world-conspiracy, 'the invisible master of all peoples and states'.[2] It is of course taken for granted that Russia is firmly in the hands of that power – but the British Empire is no less so. Englishmen and Jews together plotted the war as a means to world-domination; the Entente was organized by Jews from their stronghold in the City of London, and so of course was the pacifist propaganda that undermined Germany. And if Trotsky is the agent both of Jewish high finance and of the rabbinate, the Jewish monarch who was about to be established as world-ruler is none other than King George V. A country where such stuff could enjoy big sales (between them these two books sold some 50,000 copies within a year) was indeed ready for the *Protocols*.

But the *Protocols* hung fire. It had been intended to publish them simultaneously in Germany and in Britain, with appropriately varied commentaries – only it proved no easy matter to find them a British publisher. Publication in Germany was accordingly delayed until the beginning of 1920; but meanwhile there were many hints of joys to come. In April 1919 old Theodor Fritsch, 'the Nestor of German antisemitism', printed in his *Hammer* a prophecy which a Jewish revolutionary was supposed to have made in Paris in 1895, i.e. about the time of origin of the *Protocols*: 'In about thirty years Germany will be involved in a great war, which it will be bound to lose. Then on the ruins of the German Empire we shall build our empire,

---

[1] 'Wilhelm Meister' was really Paul Bang, the economic expert of the Deutschnationale Volkspartei, the successor to the pre-1918 Conservative party of Prussia.

[2] F. Wichtl, *Weltfreimaurerei, Weltrevolution, Weltrepublik*, ninth edition, Munich, 1922, p. 268.

as Jehovah promised us, with a second Solomon as king.'
Fritsch, one feels, must have been reading a copy of the
Protocols (soon he was to produce an edition of them, at great
profit to himself). Also in April 1919 Vinberg in *Luch Sveta*
talked of a German edition as being imminent; and in the
same month *Auf Vorposten* carried an advertisement which
remains a most significant document:

In Germany the reports of the Elders of Zion were known before
the war only in Jewish and Masonic circles. World history would
certainly have followed another course if the princes of Europe had
known the *Secrets of the Elders of Zion* early enough and had drawn
the right conclusions from them. . . .
In view of the softness shown by the peoples of central Europe,
and particularly by the Germans, in their handling of the Jewish
question, any revelation of Jewish aims would probably have been
rejected before the war with an incredulous smile. Even during the
world war only a few realized that there must exist some great
plan for the destruction of Germany; those who were initiated
knew that the Freemasons and Jews had prepared this plan
decades in advance, for the purpose of overthrowing the princely
houses of Europe and then launching a struggle against the
Church. . . . Let an impartial tribunal examine who is to blame for
the war! We summon the leaders of international Freemasonry,
the Jewish world-alliances and all the chief rabbis to appear
before it.[1]

This much at least was true: people who before the war
would have laughed the *Protocols* to scorn were ready to take
them seriously now. The development which had taken place
in Russia after the October revolution was about to be repeated, on an infinitely vaster scale, in Germany. Once more
defeated and ruined men were to invoke this ridiculous fake
to explain their misfortunes and excuse their failures. Above
all a handful of political adventurers were to use it as a device
for capturing influence, privilege, and power – and in this
some of them were to succeed far beyond the dreams of any
Black Hundred *pogromschchik*.
A good deal is known about the promotion of the first
German edition of the *Protocols*. The book was published in
mid-January, 1920, under the title *Die Geheimnisse der Weisen*

[1] *Auf Vorposten* for 1919, Heft 4–6, pp. 78–80.

von Zion (The Secrets of the Elders of Zion). The publisher was
the same organization as published *Auf Vorposten* – the
Verband gegen Ueberhebung des Judentums (Association
against the Presumption of the Jews), which had been founded
in 1912 or 1913 for the purpose of 'enlightening the spiritual,
social and economic élite of the people'. The editor was the
founder of that organization – the same Ludwig Müller, *alias*
Müller von Hausen, *alias* Gottfried zur Beek, to whom the
copy of Nilus had been passed in November 1918. Though the
book quickly became a best-seller it started by being heavily
subsidized – and we know from what quarters. The upper
house of the Prussian Diet might have been abolished under
the new constitution but its conservative wing still functioned
as an entity, notably by subscribing funds to various organizations which aimed at discrediting the republic and restoring
the monarchy. Prince Dr Otto zu Salm-Horstmar raised
money for the *Protocols* from this source. It seems certain
moreover that members of the deposed Hohenzollern family
also contributed; at any rate, when this charge was brought
the usually vociferous *Auf Vorposten* remained prudently
silent.

The Hohenzollerns certainly had cause to be pleased with
the book: it carried a dedication 'To the Princes of Europe'
and a portrait of their illustrious ancestor, the 'Great Elector',
with the motto: 'May an avenger arise some day from our
bones.' No wonder Prince Joachim Albrecht of Prussia made
a practice of handing out copies of the book to the staff of the
hotels and restaurants he frequented. As for the exiled Kaiser,
when Lady Norah Bentinck visited him in the summer of 1921
she found him utterly convinced that his fall was due to the
Elders.[1] To Germany's great war-hero, General Ludendorff,
the *Protocols* also came as a revelation – and one which he
refused to reject even after *The Times* had proved its spuriousness. 'The supreme government of the Jewish people,' he
wrote in 1922, 'was working hand in hand with France and
England. Perhaps it was leading them both.'[2] And he reflect-

[1] Lady Norah Bentinck, *The Ex-Kaiser in Exile*, London, 1921, pp.
99–108.
[2] E. Ludendorff, *Kriegsführung und Politik*, second edition, Berlin,
1922, p. 51.

ed: 'Several publications have recently appeared which throw more light on the position of the Jewish people. The German people, but also the other peoples of the earth, have every reason to make a thorough study of the historical development of the Jewish people, its organizations, its methods of fighting and its plans. One suspects that in many instances we shall arrive at another version of world history.'[1] Ludendorff's need for a scapegoat was of course great, for by recommending the most ruthless submarine warfare he had done as much as anyone to bring the United States into the war against Germany.

If Ludendorff and the Kaiser were perhaps genuinely deceived, the professional politician Count Ernst zu Reventlow knew perfectly well what he was doing. This Prussian aristocrat, who was a leading member of the *völkisch*[2] bloc in the Reichstag and was in due course to become a Nazi, was wholly committed to propagating the *Protocols*. He did so in *Auf Vorposten*, in his own newspaper *Der Reichswart* (*The Guardian of the Reich*) and also in newspapers with mass circulations, such as the *Deutsches Tageblatt*; and when *The Times* produced its revelation he defended the authenticity of the *Protocols* more vigorously than ever. 'The revelations of *The Times*,' he wrote, 'cannot touch, let alone destroy, the genuineness of the *Protocols*. On the contrary, these revelations throw a most interesting and valuable light on Jewish manoeuvres. . . . Let people in Germany draw the practical conclusion and see to it that the book, which is already widely distributed, is distributed as widely as ever possible!'[3] Thus Count Reventlow – who, as we shall see, believed not a word of it.[4]

Amid the chorus of praise the voice of the Association against the Presumption of the Jews sounded loud and clear. These enterprising publishers did not talk merely of politics, of such things as wars and revolutions – in their publicity, as later in Nazi propaganda, the unmasking of the Judeo-Masonic conspiracy is presented as a turning-point in the

---

[1] Ibid., p. 322, footnote.
[2] Extreme nationalists who were more radical and 'popular' than the German National People's party, and frankly racist and antisemitic in outlook. [3] In *Deutsches Tageblatt*, issue for 23 August 1921.
[4] See below, p. 140.

spiritual history of mankind. According to *Auf Vorposten* the
new book revealed a plot

'to destroy Christianity and other forms of belief in God and to
establish the Mosaic–Talmudic faith as the religion for the world.
The great struggle, which far-sighted men foretold decades ago, has
now begun. If the civilized peoples of Europe do not now rouse
themselves for the struggle against the common enemy, our
civilization will be destroyed by the same disruptive fungus as was
the civilization of antiquity two thousand years ago. . . . A few
days ago a Berlin professor told us that this book will surely bring
salvation to our people, and a south German scholar wrote to say
that no book has ever provoked such a revolution in people's
world-view as does the work of Gottfried zur Beek – not since the
invention of printing, nay, since the discovery of the alphabet.
From all levels of the German population, from the courts of princes
to the workers' cottages, there come to us messages of rejoicing
and approval that at last a brave man has solved the question on
which the destiny of the German people depends.'[1]

Publishers' blurbs admittedly tend to exaggerate – but the
popular reception accorded to the Müller von Hausen (or
Gottfried zur Beek) edition of the *Protocols* really was extraordinary. It was reprinted twice within a month of publication
and another three times before the end of 1920; sales quickly
reached 120,000 copies. And the book certainly did much to
foster the Nazi madness already under the democratic and
liberal régime of the Weimar Republic. This, for instance, is
what a Jewish observer found in the early 1920s:

In Berlin I attended several meetings which were entirely devoted to the *Protocols*. The speaker was usually a professor, a
teacher, an editor, a lawyer or someone of that kind. The audience
consisted of members of the educated class, civil servants, trades-
men, former officers, ladies, above all students, students of all
faculties and years of seniority. . . . Passions were whipped up to
boiling-point. There, in front of one, in the flesh, was the cause of
all ills – those who had made the war and brought about the defeat
and engineered the revolution, those who had conjured up all our
suffering. This enemy was quite close by, he could be caught by our
hands, and yet he was the enemy who slunk about in the darkness,
one shuddered to think what secret designs he was harbouring.

<hr>

[1] *Auf Vorposten*, for 1920, Heft 1–2, pp. 35–7.

I observed the students. A few hours earlier they had perhaps been exerting all their mental energy in a seminar under the guidance of a world-famous scholar, in an effort to solve some legal or philosophical or mathematical problem. Now young blood was boiling, eyes flashed, fists clenched, hoarse voices roared applause or vengeance. Sometimes a speech from the floor was permitted; whoever dared to express a slight doubt was shouted down, often insulted and threatened. If I had been recognized as a Jew, I doubt whether I would have got away without physical injury. But German scholarship allowed belief in the genuineness of the *Protocols* and in the existence of a Jewish world-conspiracy to penetrate ever more deeply into all the educated sections of the German population, so that now[1] it is simply ineradicable. Here and there a serious Christian newspaper expressed slight doubts, raised mild and timid objections, but that was all. None of the great German scholars (save for the late lamented Strack) rose to unmask the forgery. . . .[2]

This account is confirmed by others from the same period – and all agree that the *Protocols* were predominantly a middle-class preoccupation. The Social-Democratic newspapers were staunch in denouncing them, whereas the bulk of the 'bourgeois' press remained at best non-committal. And the most zealous students of the *Protocols* were to be found not among the industrial workers, whether skilled or unskilled, but in the professional classes. Former officers were particularly addicted to them – but they also circulated in institutes of technology, often with the approval of the staff, and helped to form the outlook of students who later occupied positions at all levels of industry, including the highest. (Incidentally Techow, the murderer of Rathenau, had been through an institute of technology.)[3] No doubt the most enthusiastic believers were those who subscribed to the racialist and *völkisch* outlook – at which we shall be glancing later – but on the other hand even the most orthodox Protestantism was no sure protection. Antisemitic propagandists began to put it about that the authenticity of the *Protocols* was guaranteed by the British Museum, on the grounds that a copy of Nilus's book is to be found in the great library; and that was enough to convince

[1] i.e. in 1924.

[2] B. Segel, *Die Protokolle der Weisen von Zion*, pp. 37–8.

[3] See below, pp. 145–6.

even the most staid and respectable journals of the Lutheran Church.

The appetite of this wide, mainly middle-class public might fluctuate, but it never died away. By the time Hitler came to power in 1933, thirty-three editions of zur Beek's translation had been published. Meanwhile a popular edition had been issued by the publishing house Der Hammer at Leipzig, over the name of Theodor Fritsch; and by 1933 this had sold nearly 100,000 copies. Moreover these editions were accompanied by a stream of works elaborating and justifying the *Protocols*. The German translation of the book on the subject sponsored by Henry Ford, *The International Jew*, ran through six editions between 1920 and 1922. By 1923 the official 'philosopher' of the Nazi Party, Alfred Rosenberg, produced a volume entitled *Die Protokolle der Weisen von Zion und die jüdische Weltpolitik* (*The Protocols of the Elders of Zion and Jewish World Policy*), and this too ran through three editions within a year. Already in the 1920s, then, Germany must have contained hundreds of thousands of copies of the *Protocols* and of commentaries on them.

All this was part of an antisemitic propaganda drive which was far more intensive than anything known before the war. Within a year of the armistice there existed six organizations dedicated to disseminating such propaganda – two in Berlin, three in Hamburg, one in Leipzig – and at least a dozen newspapers and periodicals;[1] this at a time when Hitler and his future party had not even begun to emerge from obscurity. Thanks to these organizations and journals, the *Protocols* did not stand alone but were constantly reinforced by other forgeries and fables concerning the Judeo-Masonic-Communist world-conspiracy. Already in 1919 there appeared two editions of *The Rabbi's Speech*, apart from the variants on it

---

[1] Antisemitic organizations active at the beginning of 1920: Verband gegen die Ueberhebung des Judentums (Berlin), Ausschuss für Volksaufklärung (Berlin), Deutsch-völkischer Bund (Hamburg), Deutsche Erneuerungsgemeinde (Leipzig), Deutsch-völkischer Schutz- und Trutzbund (Hamburg), Reichshammerbund (Hamburg). Antisemitic newspapers and periodicals: *Deutsche Zeitung, Deutsche Tageszeitung, Tägliche Rundschau, Deutsches Wochenblatt, Münchener Beobachter, Deutscher Volksrat, Der Aufrechte, Der deutsche Landtag, Die Tradition, Auf Vorposten, Die deutsche Erneuerung.*

contained in the book of 'Wilhelm Meister'. The Zunder document, after playing its part in provoking pogroms in Russia, penetrated into Germany; it appeared in the newspaper of the Russian right-wingers, *Prizyv (The Call)*, in February 1920 and was at once translated and republished by *Auf Vorposten* and similar journals. In the same month that ancient work, Osman-Bey's *World Conquest by the Jews*, was reprinted. And another rich mine was provided by the long introduction and postscript with which Müller von Hausen ornamented his edition of the *Protocols*.

Even to one hardened by much wandering in these territories it comes as something of a shock to realize just what is contained in this book which was taken seriously by innumerable professors and schoolmasters, business-men and industrialists, army officers and civil servants. For even the *Protocols* are less bizarre than the editorial appendages. These include, for instance, the cartoon 'The Kaiser's Dream', first published in the English weekly *Truth* in 1890.[1] This satirical comment on the Kaiser's ambitions and their probable consequences is interpreted as a Judeo-Masonic production revealing the secret (!) plan to overthrow the European monarchies; after all, was not the editor of *Truth*, Henry Labouchere, a Freemason and what is more a member of the Reform Club? Equally remarkable is a fantasy which Müller von Hausen lifted from *Prizyv*: a black mass had just been celebrated in the Kremlin, where Trotsky and his associates prayed to Satan for help in defeating their enemies; this sacrilegious affair was revealed by a guard, who was thereupon murdered on Trotsky's orders. This stuff, and much more of the same quality, became the stock-in-trade of antisemitic propagandists.

The apex of absurdity was reached in a fabrication called *Die siegreiche Weltanschauung (Neo-Machiavellismus) und wir Juden (The victorious world-view (Neo-Machiavellianism) and we Jews*, which was published within a few weeks of the *Protocols* over the unbelievable name of Dr Siegfried Pentha-Tull. In this pamphlet the author, who is supposed to be a Jew, publicly rejoices over the success of the plan outlined in the *Protocols* – presumably forgetting that the plan itself was

[1] See Plate 4.

supposed to be secret. It did not take long to trace the careless Pentha-Tull. Just at that time the newspaper *Deutsche Zeitung*, which was the organ of the German National People's party (formerly the Conservatives), was publishing a serial novelette with a Jewish villain called Pentha-Tull; and novelette and forgery were in fact by the same person, a well-known antisemite called Hans Schliepmann. But this did not prevent the same newspaper from expressing its horror at the revelations of the imaginary Pentha-Tull. His book, it exclaimed, 'makes one's blood freeze in one's veins'. And it formulated an urgent demand: 'A united Christian phalanx must be formed against the fearful dangers which threaten not only the churches but the whole German people from the direction of the Jews. It is necessary to speak frankly, if we are not to perish miserably. The people can be pulled from the morass . . . only by an energetic struggle against the poisoners of the people; only so can we extricate ourselves from their deadly clutch.'[1]

Nobody was more vocal on the subject of Pentha-Tull than that indefatigable propagator of the *Protocols*, Count Ernst zu Reventlow. In May 1920 he devoted whole articles in the *Deutsche Zeitung* to arguing that the authenticity of the *Protocols* was proved beyond all doubt by Pentha-Tull and the Zunder document; and he did this without himself believing it for a moment. Although one knows that a great deal of antisemitic propaganda consists of deliberate lying, it is rare to find one of the liars admitting as much in writing. Reventlow provides one of the exceptions. In 1940 one of the propaganda offices of the Third Reich thought of resuscitating Pentha-Tull and addressed an inquiry to Reventlow, who was still a member of the Reichstag. The Freyenwald Collection at the Wiener Library contains his reply: 'When I read the pamphlet by "Pentha-Tull" I was clear that it was a pretty clumsy hoax. Nevertheless in public I called it genuine, because this seemed to me to answer the purpose best at that time . . . Heil Hitler!'[2] And we know the purpose for which

---

[1] *Deutsche Zeitung*, issue for 31 August 1920.
[2] A copy of Reventlow's letter, which was dated 5 March 1940 and was addressed to the *Weltdienst*, is in the Freyenwald Collection file 'Pentha-Tull'.

Reventlow did this particular piece of lying. The elections for the first republican Reichstag were due in June 1920. To present the new Republic as a creation of the Elders of Zion was one way of winning votes for the anti-democratic Right.

2

The *Protocols* did much to provoke two political assassinations which occurred in Berlin in 1922.

On his arrival in Berlin Shabelsky-Bork, the friend and collaborator of Vinberg and a very active propagator of the *Protocols*, founded an organization modelled on the Black Hundreds and trained in terrorism. Its major undertaking was carried out on 28 March 1922. A meeting of Russian émigrés was being held in the Berlin Philharmonia, in aid of the victims of famine in the Soviet Union. The chairman of the meeting was Pavel Nikolaevich Milyukov, the eminent historian and the leader of the Constitutional Democrats (Cadets). Milyukov had himself had to flee from Russia to escape being imprisoned or executed by the Bolsheviks; indeed just like Vinberg and Shabelsky-Bork, he had had to attach himself to the German troops withdrawing from the Ukraine. That did not prevent these fanatics from planning his assassination. Shabelsky-Bork and his band suddenly burst into the Philharmonia and opened fire on the platform – missing Milyukov, who threw himself on his face, but killing Vladimir Nabokov, the former ambassador in London of the Provisional Government (and the father, incidentally, of the novelist Vladimir Nabokov). For this murder Shabelsky-Bork was sentenced to fourteen years' hard labour. He was released long before his term was up; and when the Nazis came to power he received a regular pension from Rosenberg's office and, already in 1933, was allowed to collaborate in founding a Russian 'Nazi' movement. It was an appropriate reward, for in trying to kill Milyukov Shabelsky-Bork was acting according to the doctrine of his master Vinberg – who indeed was also implicated in the murder and had to leave Germany as a result. And Vinberg saw in Milyukov the secret, but entirely conscious, agent of the Bolsheviks, who were themselves agents of the Elders of Zion.

This affair was followed within a few months by an assassination, this time by right-wing Germans, which echoed through Europe. In June 1922 a handful of young fanatics murdered Walther Rathenau, the German Minister for Foreign Affairs. And they did so in the conviction not simply that he was acting for the Elders but that he himself was one of the Elders.

Rathenau was a man of extraordinary abilities, who made his mark in the applied sciences, in engineering, in philosophy, in political and economic theory, in addition to being one of Germany's greatest industrialists, an outstanding administrator, a remarkable Foreign Minister. His services to Germany were great. At the very beginning of the war he recognized the mortal threat represented by the British blockade. To counter it he built up, in an amazingly short time, a huge organization for administering raw materials – and which did in fact enable Germany to hold out with raw materials right through the war. After the war he worked tirelessly to overcome Germany's isolation and to secure a lightening of the burden of reparations; at the same time he strove to unite the nations of Europe, still bitterly divided by the experience of the war, in a collective effort at reconstruction. In April 1922, as Foreign Minister, he signed the Rapallo Treaty with the Soviet Union, by which both sides renounced all claims arising from the war.

Rathenau was a fervent patriot, but his patriotism was that of a civilized and liberal European and had nothing to do with chauvinism. Also, he was a Jew. Right-wing fanatics accordingly viewed him with a hatred which became more and more intense as his political status increased. By 1921 the press of the *völkisch* bloc and of the young Nazi party was representing this great idealist as a Satanic being. 'You spread around you hellish justice, hellish practices, hellish morality,' wrote the *Deutsch-völkische Blätter*; while the Nazi *Völkischer Beobachter* complained: 'How long before we have a Walter I of the dynasty of Abraham, Joseph, Rathenau? The day is coming when the wheel of world history will be put into reverse, to roll over many a corpse, of the great financier and his accomplices.'[1] At the same time Theodor Fritsch in the *Hammer* presented Rathenau as the man behind Bolshevism even inside Russia. In 1922 the attacks became more scurrilous still. It was said that in instituting the control of raw materials during the war Rathenau had deliberately organized the starvation of the German people. As for his appointment as Foreign Minister, that had been secured by presenting the Chancellor with an ultimatum threatening to 'sacrifice the German people to Jewish world-power'. And for months before the assassination speeches were being made calling in effect for just such a deed.

In this campaign the *Protocols* were of course invoked constantly, but that was not all – two particular stories were put about which linked Rathenau peculiarly closely with the Elders of Zion. One of these was a weird invention which Müller von Hausen put into his edition of the *Protocols*. Emil Rathenau, the father of the statesman, had once bought and largely reconstructed a house in Berlin; and one of the additions he made was a frieze running round the outside of the building. In reality this frieze consisted of masks with floral decorations, repeated sixty-six times. To the hallucinated gaze of the editor of the *Protocols*, however, it represented sixty-six crowned heads, cut off and resting on sixty-six dishes for receiving sacrificial blood. And who could doubt that in this design the secret of the German and Russian revolutions was symbolically expressed? Had not Emil Rathenau been one of the Kaiser's most trusted counsellors? 'How often,' lamented Müller, 'may our unsuspecting Emperor have crossed the threshold of this house, little suspecting what kindly wishes for the future of the House of Hohenzollern were cherished by the man whom he called his friend?'.[2,3]

---

[1] Both quoted in *C. V. Zeitung* (i.e. the weekly of the Central-Verein deutscher Staatsbürger jüdischen Glaubens), Vol. I, issue for 20 June 1921.

[2] Müller von Hausen seems to have borrowed the idea from a pamphlet called *Versailles Visions*, published in 1919. The author was a dismissed schoolteacher called Leisner, who under the pseudonym of Ellegaard Ellerbek preached a peculiar mixture of occultism, astrology and sun-religion – and who incidentally was taken seriously not only by Alfred Rosenberg but also in certain quite respectable conservative circles.

[3] G. zur Beek, *Die Geheimnisse der Weisen von Zion*, Berlin–Charlottenburg 1919 (really 1920), p. 199.

Like father, like son. Years earlier Walther Rathenau had written a sentence which was to have a long and inglorious history. In the *Neue Freie Presse* for Christmas Day, 1909, there appeared an article by him which was reprinted in his book *Zur Kritik der Zeit* (*A critique of the age*) in 1922. It dealt with economic affairs and contained the following observation: 'Three hundred men, all of whom know one another, guide the economic destinies of the Continent and seek their successors among their followers.' There is no mention whatsoever of Jews; and the context shows what Rathenau intended – which was, to deplore the fact that at that time the leading positions in finance and industry were largely the preserve of a hereditary oligarchy. It seems to have been Ludendorff who first suggested that the 300 men were in fact the secret Jewish government.[1] The suggestion was snatched up by the professional antisemites, and they were quick to draw the obvious conclusion: if Rathenau knew the number of the Elders, that could only mean that he was one of them. Nothing more was required to complete the transformation of the Foreign Minister into a super-criminal. 'The name of the main culprit for the enslavement of our economy is Rathenau,' wrote one right-wing journal. 'Dominion over the productive labour of all the peoples of the earth is passing more and more into the hands of those 300 men who, according to an unnoticed remark of Rathenau's, guide the history of the world, all know one another, and of whom he is one. . . . Many innocent contemporaries still do not recognize the preconcerted operations of these 300 men, who almost without exception belong to the Jewish race. . . .'[2] Alfred Rosenberg, in his pamphlet *Plague in Russia*, stated that Rathenau and his like were 'long since ripe for prison and gallows'. Count zu Reventlow lamented that such a man should still be alive and in excellent health; and his article was reprinted in many newspapers a fortnight before the murder.

Rathenau had frequently been threatened with assassination, but had always refused police protection. He was murdered as he was taking his usual drive from his house to

[1] E. Ludendorff, *Kriegsführung und Politik*, p. 51, footnote.

[2] *Reichsbote*, quoted in *Mitteilungen aus dem Verein zur Abwehr des Antisemitismus*, issue for 12 January 1922, p. 3.

1. MAURICE JOLY (1829-78),
author of the *Dialogue aux
Enfers entre Montesquieu et
Machiavel*

2. PYOTR IVANOVICH RACH-
KOVSKY, head of the foreign
branch of the Okhrana from
1884 to 1902

Within the image, the following handwritten labels appear:

Londres 1648., *Petersbourg 1881.*, *Moscou 1905*, *Paris 1789–1801.*, *Berlin 1871.*, *Kiev.*, *Odessa.*, *Madrid 1552.*, *Rome Sa. Siege.*, *Athènes 429 av. J.C.*, *Constantinople 1910*, *Sion 1920.*

3. 'The Symbolic Snake,' which is supposed to represent the progress of the Jewish plot from the fifth century B.C. onwards. Starting from Palestine the head of the Snake moves through the states of Europe until, with Zionist immigration, it returns to its point of origin. This means that the world is ruled from Palestine, and marks the culmination of the plot. Pictures and descriptions of the Snake have accompanied the *Protocols* throughout their history

4. 'The Kaiser's Dream.' This cartoon was first published in the English weekly *Truth* in 1890 and was intended as a satirical comment on the ambitions of Kaiser Wilhelm II and their possible consequences. It was reprinted in many editions of the *Protocols* as representing the plan of the Elders

5. SERGEY NILUS, whose Russian edition of the *Protocols* in his book *The Great in the Small* formed the basis for most non-Russian editions

6. Antichrist and his emblems, surmounted by the Orthodox cross as talisman against the powers of evil. From the 1911 edition of *The Great in the Small*. The figure labelled 'Antichrist' is really the King in the Tarot pack

„Quand même!"

7. Frontispiece from the year-book *Luch Sveta,* in which the *Protocols* appeared for the first time outside Russia. Here the task of illuminating the dark conspiracy of the Elders is shown as a religious mission

Die Geheimniſſe der Weiſen von Zion

„Alles dieſes wußte ich ſchon vor 11 Jahren; wie ging es aber zu, daß ich es doch nicht glauben wollte?"

Ludwig XVI. bei ſeiner Verhaftung am 22. Juni 1791 in Darennes. Vergl. Joh. Robiſon „Über Geheime Geſellſchaften und deren Gefährlichkeit für Staat und Religion". Deutſche Überſetzung nach der 3. engliſchen Auflage, Königslutter bei B. Culemann 1800, 242. Seite.

Herausgegeben

von

Gottfried zur Beek

3. Auflage

Verlag „Auf Vorpoſten" in Charlottenburg 4
1919

8. Title-page of the first non-Russian version of the *Protocols.* The tusked boar was the emblem of the German anti-semitic society which published this edition

9. From a brochure advertising the *Protocols,* dated 1925. The U. Bodung publishing house belonged to Colonel Fleischhauer of the *Weltdienst*

13. Cover of a popular French edition of the *Protocols,* c. 1934

14. Cover of another popular French edition, c. 1934

Wzór okładki do broszury „W szponach komunizmu".

Po Rosji i Hiszpanji — kolej na Polskę! Trzeba ją skąpać we krwi! Zostawić po niej ruiny i zgliszcza! Żyd już wiedzie kostuchę na żniwo do Polski! Baczmy na ten pochód i czuwajmy, bo gorze nam! Gorze!!!...

Nakł. „Samoobrona Narodu" Poznań   Drukarnia Centralna Poznań

15. Frontispiece to a Polish edition, Poznan, 1937. The caption reads: 'After Russia and Spain—it is Poland's turn! She must have a blood bath! Only ruins and cinders should remain! Already the Jew leads Death to her harvest in Poland! Let us watch this marching column and let us be awake, for woe to us! Woe!!!…'

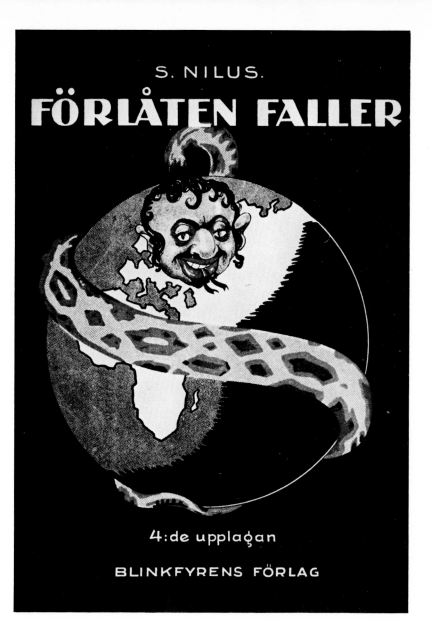

16. Cover of a Swedish edition, Hangö, 1924

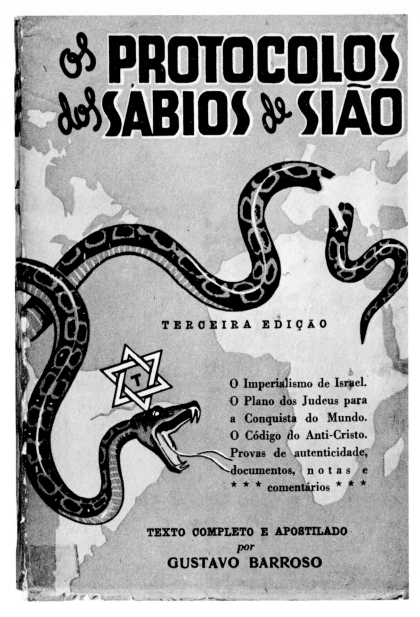

17. Cover of a Brazilian edition, São Paulo, 1937

SABIOS DE SION
PROTOCOLOS

PLAN:
Destruir la Cristiandad
Esclavizar la Humanidad

18. Cover of a very recent Spanish edition, Madrid, 1963. The three heads of the snake represent the Jewish religion, the state of Israel, and Communism

19. A fifteenth-century version of the ritual murder of a Christian boy by Jews. From Schedel's *Liber Cronicarum*

the Foreign Ministry, on the morning of 24 June 1922. The killers were quite young men who belonged to various groups of the extreme Right, such as the Deutsch-völkischer Schutz und Trutzbund (Defensive and Offensive Alliance) and the Ehrhardt Naval Brigade; several of them had taken part in the first attempt by the Right to overthrow the Republic, the Kapp *putsch* of 1920. They were grouped in an organization known as 'Organization Consul' which, like the young Nazi party, was based on Munich. This body was dedicated to terrorism and publicly flaunted its murderous aims. 'Shoot down Walther Rathenau, The God-accursèd Jewish sow,' is a fair sample of the kind of thing it sang about the streets.

The imagination of the assassins was steeped in the *Protocols* and the lore which had gathered around them. The man who planned the murder, Willy Günther, admitted this quite frankly during his preliminary interrogation. The reason why Rathenau had to be killed, he said, was that according to Ludendorff he was the one man in Germany who knew the membership of the secret Jewish government, which had caused the war. The same picture emerged at the trial at Leipzig, in October 1922, of the driver of the car from which Rathenau was shot (of the two who had done the actual killing, one was shot by the police and another shot himself to avoid capture).[1] This is how the accused, Ernst Techow, described the plot as it had been propounded by its originator, the dead Erwin Kern:

Kern said that he proposed to murder Minister Rathenau. And that I must bind myself to help him, whether I wanted to or not. Otherwise he would be prepared to carry the job out alone. And that it was all one to him what the consequences might be. At the same time he gave various reasons which in his opinion were decisive, although that was not my view. He said ... that Rathenau had very close and intimate relations with Bolshevik

[1] The account given by one of the plotters, Ernst von Salomon, in *Die Geächteten*, Berlin 1935, makes no mention of the *Protocols* or the secret Jewish government, and in his famous post-war book *Der Fragebogen · von Ernst von Salomon*, Hamburg 1951, he even denies that Rathenau's Jewishness had anything to do with the murder. But even if some of those involved saw the assassination in other terms, Techow's evidence stands.

Russia, so that he had even married off his sister with the Communist Radek.

To end with, he said that Rathenau had himself confessed, and boasted, that he was one of the three hundred Elders of Zion, whose purpose and aim was to bring the whole world under Jewish influence, as the example of Bolshevist Russia already showed, where at first all factories, etc., were made public property, then at the suggestion and command of the Jew Lenin, Jewish capital was brought in from abroad, to bring the factories into operation again, and so in this way the whole of Russian national property was now in Jewish hands. . . .

The President of the Court: You say that Rathenau had close relations with the Bolshevist Radek, so that he even married his sister off to him.

Techow: That is supposed to be the fact. I don't know.

President: To my knowledge Rathenau has only one sister, who is married to a Dr Andreae in Berlin.

Techow: I don't know.

President: How could this great industrialist come to have such relations with the Russian refugee and Communist Radek? Does it seem likely to you?

Techow: No, it was simply a conjecture, which Kern gave as if it was a fact. So I had to suppose it was right.

President: To continue: Rathenau is supposed to have confessed that he was himself one of the three hundred Elders of Zion. The three hundred Elders of Zion come from a pamphlet. Have you read it?

Techow: Yes.[1]

On the eve of the trial a packet of poisoned chocolates had been sent to one of the accused, Willy Günther, in prison. The public prosecutor, in the statement which he issued, made it clear why: for fear lest 'those who stood behind the murderers of Foreign Minister Rathenau would be betrayed by the evidence which Günther would be giving at the trial'.[2] How far these people can be identified with the leaders of the young Nazi party remains uncertain, but we know what Goebbels wrote to Techow while the latter was serving his sentence of hard labour:

[1] K. Brammer, *Das politische Ergebnis des Rathenau-Prozesses*, Berlin, 1922, p. 26. The book contains a shorthand record of parts of the trial.
[2] Ibid., p. 42.

... the nationalist camp stands by you without any reservations whatsoever. This too shows the difference between true nationalists and 'bourgeois' patriots, who only stand by a man when it is safe to do so and it does not offend against the canons of bourgeois propriety.

And again:

I want to shake your hand – it is an inner need for me – and, as it is not permitted for me to acknowledge your deed, I want to join you and your comrades as a man, as a German, as a young, conscious activist, who believes in Germany's resurrection – in spite of everything![1]

Certainly the assassination of Rathenau as an Elder of Zion foreshadowed the lunatic era when the *Protocols* would be proclaimed as ultimate truth by the government of a great European nation. Certain words spoken by the judge in his summing-up were to take on, retrospectively, a depth of meaning which few would have attributed to them in 1922:

Behind the murderers and their accomplices the chief culprit, irresponsible, fanatical antisemitism, lifts its face, distorted with hatred – antisemitism, which reviles the Jew as such, irrespective of the individual, with all those means of calumny of which that vulgar libel, the *Protocols of the Elders of Zion*, is an example; and in this way sows in confused and immature minds the urge to murder. May the sacrificial death of Rathenau, who well knew to what dangers he was exposing himself when he took up his office; may the insight which this trial has brought concerning the consequences of unscrupulous incitement ... serve to purify the infected air of Germany and to lead Germany, now sinking in mortal sickness in this moral barbarism, towards its cure.[2]

The assassination did indeed act for a time as a salutary shock. A law was introduced for the protection of the Republic, and under its provisions various obscure publicists were prosecuted for continuing to assert that Rathenau had been an Elder of Zion. The Defensive and Offensive Alliance was banned. Ludendorff took fright and in an article in a London newspaper accused the Communists of the murder. Müller von Hausen for his part tried at first to justify the murder by repeating the story of the frieze, but he quickly withdrew it when

[1] E. Techow, *Gemeiner Mörder?!*, Leipzig, 1933, p. 31.
[2] K. Brammer, op. cit., p. 14.

he was sued by Rathenau's mother. And then, from 1924 onwards, the situation in Germany began to change in such a way that even the most fanatical could hardly say just what harm the Elders were doing. A new and more moderate reparations agreement was negotiated, allied troops withdrew from German territory, and in 1926 Germany was received by unanimous vote into the League of Nations. As a result the wave of right-wing extremism ebbed all over Germany. It was a bad time for the *Protocols* – but it was not to last.

CHAPTER VII

The *Protocols* circle the World

1

THE enthusiasm which greeted the *Protocols* in Germany was unique, but that does not mean they were ignored elsewhere. Even in Britain, where antisemitism had never in modern times taken the virulent form familiar on the Continent, and in the United States, where up to that time it had played very little part at all, the forgery attracted serious interest in quarters which might have been expected to know better. Indeed the translations and commentaries which appeared in these two countries in the course of 1920 did a great deal to spread knowledge of the *Protocols* throughout the world – partly of course because they were in English but partly also because of the distinguished names with which they became associated.

In Britain there had been talk of a Jewish world-conspiracy for a couple of years before the *Protocols* appeared. As in Germany, this was conceived as Jewish-Bolshevist affair – but whereas in Germany the Entente was also thought of as allied with the Jews, here the third party to the conspiracy was of course Germany. An early formulation of this odd theory is contained in a book published in 1918, before the end of the war, and entitled *England Under the Heel of the Jew*. Ironically enough, the bulk of this book consists of translated extracts from the German sociologist Werner Sombart – but that does not prevent the original parts from being as anti-German as they are anti-Jewish and anti-Bolshevik. The anonymous author had discovered that the name Ashkenazim, which embraces the great majority of European Jews, is a Hebrew word for Germans – but had overlooked the fact that anything up to six centuries had elapsed since the ancestors of most of these Jews left Germany. The nightmare which this thought inspired seems already to belong to the world of the *Protocols*:

Finance has become international, and international finance is Jewish finance, and Jewish finance is German finance. These two, become one, are penetrating the veins of all the nations of the earth, poisoning their life-blood and sapping the life out of them. . . . When once the Ashkenazi-German alliance was cemented and organized throughout the world, the Kaiser could laugh at his enemies, for he had his allies planted in all their banks, all their brothels, all their businesses, all their Stock Exchanges, all their socialist organizations, all their newspapers, all their council-chambers and war-cabinets, in many of their lawyers' secret closets, and on their judicial benches. When England declared war against him, he was disappointed, but he was not unprepared. . . . He knew he could get a horde of Ashkenazi white slavers with their slaves planted on English soil as Belgian refugees all ready to spread vice and disease among troops and civilians. . . . He had thousands of agents of Rasputinism to carry on his usual work among our rulers and legislators. He knew he could keep in our country tens of thousands of Ashkenazi-Bolsheviks to eat English bread, steal English trade and pollute English life. . . . There is no weapon that the Ashkenazi-Hun finds too low for his handling or too small for his consideration. The same approach – Rasputineries and all – as have proved the downfall of Russia are in intense operation in our islands.

Yet, wily though the Kaiser may be, the author believes him to be less the master of the Jews than their slave, for 'the magic powers of money as wielded by the Lords of Lucre are powers of Black Magic at its blackest'.[1]

This was no voice crying in the wilderness, for soon belief in a German-Jewish-Bolshevik conspiracy became widespread – and by no means only among the semi-literate. Early in 1919 the British ambassador in Copenhagen, Lord Kilmarnock, reported to the Foreign Secretary, Lord Curzon, that the Bolsheviks were said to comprise chiefly Jews and Germans, who, being active and enterprising, were able to tyrannize the dreamy Russians. More remarkable still, the Foreign Office saw fit to publish in an official report the following observations by a naval chaplain recently returned from Russia: '(Bolshevism) originated in German propaganda, and was, and

[1] *England Under the Heel of the Jew*, London, 1918, pp. 60–2.

is being, carried out by international Jews'. Its aims are 'to
buy up all nationalized banks and to open up everywhere
branches of German Government banks . . .' and also 'to
preach the doctrine of the Socialistic form of managing enterprises amongst the working classes, to encourage their efforts
to seize such enterprises and then by means of bankruptcies
to get them into German hands', while at the same time
'spreading amongst the masses such views and teachings as
may at any time be dictated from Berlin'. And of course this
benefits the Jews: 'All business became paralysed, shops were
closed, Jews became possessors of most of the business
houses. . . .'[1]

The press could hardly be expected to be more cautious than
the Foreign Office. By the end of 1919 even the correspondence
columns of *The Times* were opened to a passionate debate as
to whether the horrors through which Russia was passing
could or could not be interpreted as acts of Jewish vengeance.
It was a question on which the newspaper's special correspondent in Russia, Robert Wilton, had no doubts at all. Wilton
was an Englishman who had been brought up in Russia and
who had identified himself completely with the extreme right
wing. In his book *The Last Days of the Romanovs*, published
in 1920, he declared that the Bolsheviks were simply Jewish
agents of the Germans and the revolution nothing but a
Jewish-German invasion of Russia. Had not the imperial
family been murdered by 'Magyar-Germans', acting on instructions from Jews, who in turn were acting on instructions
from 'the Red Kaiser' of Germany? And had not a monument
been erected in Moscow to that well-known Jewish hero,
Judas Iscariot? Such was the source on which the most
authoritative of British newspapers chiefly depended for its
understanding of the Russian Revolution.

Meanwhile the *Protocols* was being put into circulation, with
the object in the first instance of persuading the Government
to persevere with its policy of intervention in Russia. 'It is
incredible,' wrote an observer in 1920, 'but it is nevertheless a
fact, that these crazy forgeries have played a part behind the

---

[1] *Russia No. 1 (1919). A collection of reports on Bolshevism in Russia*,
p. 56. (Report from the Rev. B. S. Lombard to Earl Curzon.) For Lord
Kilmarnock's report, ibid., p. 32.

scenes in the international combinations for assisting the anti-
Bolshevist reaction in Russia, which has filled so much of the
public mind during the last two years, and which have cost
this country close on £100,000,000. . . . Russian intelligence
officers, armed with doctored typewritten translations of the
Nilus *Protocols*, with the anti-British passages carefully ex-
punged, were sent to London . . . where they circulated this
precious literature confidentially among cabinet ministers,
heads of public departments, and persons of influence in
society and journalism. That this campaign was not fruitless is
attested by many curious facts. . . .'[1] The campaign culminated
in the publication of an anonymous English translation of the
Protocols, with the title *The Jewish Peril*; this took place in
January or February 1920, to coincide with the appearance of
the first German translation. The book bore the imprint of
Eyre & Spottiswoode Ltd, and this was in itself a great
triumph: Eyre & Spottiswoode, the publishers of the Authorised Version of the Bible and of the Prayer Book, carry the
title of His (or Her) Majesty's Printers – and this enabled
antisemites all over the Continent to proclaim, probably with
more malevolence than ignorance, that the *Protocols* had been
published with the authority of His Majesty's Government.[2]

The same circles were delighted by the reaction of *The Times*,
which on 8 May devoted a long article to the book. On the
matter of authenticity *The Times* remained non-committal –
but it did note that nobody had yet shown the *Protocols* to be
spurious. Here was a work published in 1905, which foretold
in an uncanny way the situation of the world, and particularly
of Russia, in 1920. An impartial investigation was necessary,
for without it how could such a work fail to arouse the worst
suspicions? A sombre paragraph reveals what suspicions were
already afflicting *The Times* itself:

What are these 'Protocols'? Are they authentic? If so, what
malevolent assembly concocted these plans, and gloated over their
exposition? Are they a forgery? If so, whence comes the uncanny

[1] L. Wolf, *The Jewish Bogey*, London, 1920, pp. 34–5.
[2] It seems that this edition of the *Protocols* was printed to private
commission and therefore bears the imprint of the printers, Eyre &
Spottiswoode Ltd, instead of a publisher's imprint. The firm of Eyre &
Spottiswoode (Publishers) Ltd was not founded until April 1929.

note of prophecy, prophecy in parts fulfilled, in parts far gone in the way of fulfilment? Have we been struggling these tragic years to blow up and extirpate the secret organization of German world dominion only to find beneath it another, more dangerous because more secret? Have we, by straining every fibre of our national body, escaped a 'Pax Germanica' only to fall into a 'Pax Judæica'? The 'Elders of Zion', as represented in their 'Protocols', are by no means kinder taskmasters than William II and his henchmen would have been.

The Times was not the only responsible journal to express grave perturbation. The following week *The Spectator* devoted not only a long review but also an editorial to *The Jewish Peril*; and though it did not altogether exclude the possibility of forgery, it had little doubt that the *Protocols* were a genuine document of Jewish origin. And what a document! Anyone who has spent long hours trying to make some sense of their nonsense can only feel baffled to read, in what was one of the most sophisticated of British weeklies, that 'the "Protocols" are of very great ability', 'brilliant in (their) moral perversity and intellectual depravity' and indeed 'one of the most remarkable productions of their kind'.[1]

Yet in the first months after the publication of the *Protocols* there were hesitations and misgivings. Both *The Times* and *The Spectator* were inclined to acquit the majority of Jews of collaborating with the horrible Elders of Zion; and both published letters – not all of them from Jews – arguing against the genuineness of the *Protocols*. The right-wing newspaper *The Morning Post*, on the other hand, showed no such restraint. Just as *The Times* was influenced by its correspondent in Russia, Robert Wilton, so *The Morning Post* accepted everything it was told by its correspondent in Russia, Victor Marsden. Like Wilton, Marsden was an Englishman who had lived many years in Russia and had adopted, with passion, the outlook of Russian right-wingers. And if Wilton could by imagination conjure up a Soviet monument to Judas Iscariot, Marsden went further and produced a new translation of the *Protocols* (it is still on sale in London today). It is not therefore surprising that in the summer of 1920 *The Morning Post* should have published a series of eighteen articles expounding

[1] *The Spectator*, issue of 15 May 1920.

the full myth of the Judeo-Masonic conspiracy, with of course
due reference to the *Protocols*.

If the productions of Wichtl and 'Wilhelm Meister' reflect
the resentment of German ultra-nationalists when confronted
with defeat and revolution, these articles reflect the resentment of British ultra-nationalists at the stirrings of independence among the colonial peoples of the Empire. And just like
Auf Vorposten, The Morning Post recognizes quite clearly that
tales which before the war would have been dismissed with a
shrug could find believers now: 'The war has produced a
complete change of mentality, because we have had concrete
proof of close connection between rebellion in Ireland, trouble
in Egypt, disaffection in India, revolution in Russia, to mention only a few of the disorders brought about by Germany.
. . . But it is becoming every day more evident that the conspiracy against civilization did not finish with the defeat of
Germany. . . . Behind the scenes was a 'formidable sect' using
the Germans for their own ends instead of being used by them,
and when Germany fell and German money disappeared, the
conspiracy still went on unimpeded.' Signs of the conspiracy
at work were not hard to find. Who could doubt, for instance,
that the assassination in 1909 of an eminent member of the
Indian Civil Service, though carried out in London by an
Indian, had really been engineered from Paris by a German
woman and a handsome Jewess who, owing to the combined
support of Jewry and of Continental Freemasonry, wielded
immense power? For of course at the heart of the whole world-
conspiracy were Jews, and religious Jews at that: 'The fundamental notion of the "formidable sect" is the destruction
of Christianity and all religion except the Jewish'.[1]

It might be thought that such stuff would scarcely penetrate
beyond the lunatic fringe on the extreme Right, but this was
by no means the case. When in the autumn of 1920 these
articles were reprinted as a book with the title *The Cause of
World Unrest*, and with a preface by the editor of *The Morning
Post* himself, they produced a noticeable heightening of ten-
sion. In October the staid *Spectator*, shedding all caution,
produced an editorial which showed how things were changing. 'There are nations,' it stated, 'who will avoid, if possible,

[1] *The Cause of World Unrest*, London, 1920, pp. 190–4.

submitting their political status to a searching diagnosis. *The Morning Post*, greatly to its honour, realizes that the function of a newspaper is that of the watchdog. . . . The evidence that the paper brings to support its plea of conspiracy is clearly of enough substance and of enough importance to justify its action. . . . We hold that a case for inquiry has been made out, and we most sincerely wish that some body of the nature of a Royal Commission could be appointed to inquire into the whole subject.' The commission would investigate whether there existed a world-wide conspiracy under Jewish leadership and whether it was supported by the mass of religious Jews as a means of destroying Christianity. Should the answer be in the affirmative 'we shall be justified in moving with great caution in our admission of Jews to the fullest rank of citizenship. . . . We must drag the conspirators into the open, tear off their ugly masks, and show the world how ridiculous as well as how evil and dangerous are such pests of society.'[1]

The Spectator was seconded by *Blackwood's Magazine*, which insisted that if the country was to be saved from Bolshevism Jews must be immediately excluded from all influence, public or private, on government. A new weekly called *Plain English* was founded by Lord Alfred Douglas for the express purpose of antisemitic propaganda; it swore to the genuineness of the *Protocols* and even asserted that, on instructions from Jewish financiers, Winston Churchill had forged a telegram from Admiral Beatty, so as to enable the German fleet to escape after the battle of Jutland. Another journal, *The Hidden Hand*, was published by a group of professional antisemites called The Britons; it printed not only long commentaries on the *Protocols* but also the Zunder document, and proclaimed that the miners' strikes were all the work of Jews.

For a moment it looked as though antisemitism of the kind that was at work in Germany might become a political factor in Britain also, but in the end nothing came of it. In August 1921 *The Times* published on its centre page, on three consecutive days, the proofs that the *Protocols* were a forgery based on the *Dialogue aux Enfers*, and for good measure added a resounding leader entitled 'The End of the Protocols'. So far as Britain was concerned it was in effect their end. Eyre &

[1] *The Spectator*, issue of 16 October 1920.

Spottiswoode had already declined to reprint them, and now the reputable press stopped talking about them. They continued (and still continue) to circulate, but with the imprint only of that obscure body, The Britons. Lord Alfred Douglas argued that Maurice Joly was really Moses Joël, so the *Protocols* were Jewish after all; Baron Sydenham continued to proclaim that the *Protocols* proved the identity of Judaism, Pan-Germanism, and Bolshevism and to lament 'the failure of western minds to fathom the depths of eastern intrigue'; but these were isolated eccentrics.[1] Even Nesta Webster's well-known books, which interpret all modern history in terms of a conspiracy of Illuminati and Freemasons, are rather non-committal about the *Protocols*. And when, in the 1930s, the British Union of Fascists came into being, it too found the forgery too thoroughly discredited to be much use. By British standards the triumphs of 1920 had been impressive, but they were never repeated.

2

Things were different in the United States, where the *Protocols* enjoyed a limited but lasting vogue. There too they were first put into circulation, in typescript, by Russian right-wingers who were concerned to influence government departments. Then, in October 1919, extracts from the *Protocols* were printed in a series of articles in *The Public Ledger*, of Philadelphia. The articles, with headings like 'Red Bible Counsels Appeal to Violence' and 'Reds Plot to Smash World in 1919', were sensational enough – but all references to Jews had been removed, so that the plot seemed a purely Bolshevik affair. By the spring of 1920, following the publication of *The Jewish Peril* in Britain, this interpretation of the matter was being discarded. 'Trotsky Leads Jew-Radicals to World Rule. Bolshevism only a Tool for His Scheme', proclaimed the *Chicago Tribune* on 19 June; and it continued:

[1] Lord Alfred Douglas in his paper *Plain English*, issue of 27 August 1921; Baron Sydenham in an article in *The Nineteenth Century and After*, issue of November 1921, later reprinted by The Britons as a pamphlet, *The Jewish World Problem*.

For the last two years army intelligence officers, members of the various secret organizations of the Entente, have been bringing in reports of a world revolutionary movement other than Bolshevism. At first these reports confused the two, but latterly the lines they have taken have begun to be more and more clear.

Bolshevism aims for the overthrow of existing society and the establishment of an international brotherhood of men who work with their hands as rulers of the world. The second movement aims for the establishment of a new racial domination of the world. So far as the British, French and our own department's inquiry have been able to trace, the moving spirits in the second scheme are Jewish radicals. . . .

Within the ranks of Communism is a group of this party, but it does not stop there. To its leaders, Communism is only an incident. . . .

They are ready to use the Islamic revolt, hatred by the central empires for England, Japan's designs on India, and commercial rivalry between America and Japan. . . .

As any movement of world revolution must be, this is primarily anti-Anglo-Saxon.

For the United States antisemitic propaganda of this kind was something new, but it came at the right moment. Although the war had brought incomparably less suffering to the United States than to the European belligerents, it had proved a very disorientating experience – not least because of the abruptness with which it ended. Just when the nation was at last thoroughly roused to fight, when it had suffered no great losses and was in fact only beginning to feel its strength – suddenly there was no enemy left. It was not a state of affairs that could be easily accepted. The American Defense Society hastened to warn the public not to buy German products, on the grounds that they might be poisoned or deliberately infected with deadly bacteria. The Ku-Klux-Klan underwent a dramatic revival. Soon, however, fear and rage became concentrated on one foe: Bolshevism, along with every group that, rightly or wrongly, was suspected of sympathizing with it.

People who shortly before had accused one another of being pro-German now bandied charges of pro-Bolshevism. The Department of Justice reported that it had a card-index of 60,000 suspects; and the figure was surprisingly modest, for it was common knowledge that Bolshevism was stalking the country. Even the debate about prohibition tended to be

conducted in these terms, so that while the state superinten-
dent of the Anti-Saloon League of New York declared that
'the main centres of anarchistic activities have been wet
centres', the Association Opposed to National Prohibition
pointed out that 'all radical elements . . . are earnest advocates
of prohibition, as they assert that it is driving into the radical
groups many men who in normal times are law-abiding men'.[1]
No category of citizens was exempt from the suspicion of
subversion – the Senate committee investigating Bolshevism
was even asked to investigate the suffragettes. How could the
Jews have remained untouched?

The time was indeed ripe for full editions of the *Protocols*,
and they duly appeared – one in New York, with the title
Praemonitus Praemunitus (i.e. 'Forewarned is forearmed'), and
another in Boston, as part of a volume called *The Protocols and
World Revolution*. Above all from May to October 1920 Henry
Ford's newspaper *The Dearborn Independent* published a long
series of articles which forms an American counterpart to the
effort of *The Morning Post*; and in November these too were
republished as a book, *The International Jew: the world's
foremost problem*. *The Dearborn Independent* had a circulation
of some 300,000. As for *The International Jew*, thanks to a big
publicity campaign and the prestige of Ford's name it made a
powerful impact, particularly among the rural population –
for, just as in Europe, the myth of the Jewish world-conspiracy proved most attractive to people who were deeply
attached to the traditional ways and values of the countryside
and deeply disoriented by modern civilization.[2] Half a million
copies of the book were put into circulation in the United
States.[3] Moreover it was translated into German, Russian, and

[1] Quoted in C. Merz, *And Then Came Ford*, New York, 1929, p. 177.

[2] On the connexion between the American agrarian tradition and
antisemitism see J. Higham, *Strangers in the Land: patterns of American
nativism 1860–1925*, revised edition, New York, 1963 (p. 285 for Ford);
S. Lipset, 'Three decades of the Radical Right', in D. Bell (ed.), *The
Radical Right*, revised edition, New York, 1964; and cf. A. Nevins and
F. E. Hill, *Ford, Expansion and Challenge, 1915–1933*, New York, 1957,
p. 323.

[3] It is true that many of these were given away, and it is also true that
the circulation of the *Dearborn Independent* depended partly on semi-
compulsory buying by Ford agencies and dealers.

Spanish; in due course a shortened version of it was to become a stock item in Nazi propaganda. All in all *The International Jew* probably did more than any other work to make the *Protocols* world-famous.

The *Protocols* are indeed all things to all men. As interpreted here for an American public the world-conspiracy is a matter of Jew-Bolsheviks but certainly not of Freemasons; and the most horrible thing about it is that it undermines puritan morality. The ways in which the Elders seduce American youth are both unexpected and ingenious: 'Every influence that leads to lightness and looseness in Gentile youth today heads up in a Jewish source. Did the young people of the world devise the "sport clothes" which have had so deleterious an effect on the youth of the times?' But the rot starts earlier still: under the cover of such socialistic pretences as public safety 'children are hardly free to play nowadays except under play-masters appointed by the State, among whom, curiously enough, an astonishing proportion of Jews manage to find a place. . . . All this focuses up to the World Plan for the subjugation of the Gentiles. . . .'[1] Where this kind of thing can lead is seen in Soviet Russia; there sex knowledge is taught in schools, which means that the young are 'compulsorily drawn through sloughs of filth . . . with consequences that are too pitiable to relate'. In this way the Jewish rulers are destroying the moral fibre of Russia. For all Bolsheviks are Jews: and we are given a picture of Lenin and his wife, who in reality were childless and had not a drop of Jewish blood between them, chatting away in Yiddish with their little ones.[2]

It is a very strange book indeed; and one of the strangest things about it, considering how recently the United States had been at war with Germany, is that it adopts the German interpretation of the *Protocols*. Jewry, imagined as a closely organized, world-wide political power, is referred to as 'All-Judaan', which is a nonsensical name coined by German anti-semites. And the secret government of 'All-Judaan' – in other words, the Elders of Zion – is supposed to be allied not with Germany but with Britain. The war was really a war of 'All-Judaan' against Germany; it was a triumph for the Elders

---

[1] *The International Jew*, London edition, 1920, pp. 135–6.
[2] Ibid., pp. 214, 217.

that, by their control of the press, they had been able to drive
whole nations to hate Germany; and the final victory was
theirs alone. At the same time there is no doubt where the
Elders found their most whole-hearted support: London was
their 'first capital' and Paris their second. With Britain in
particular the secret Jewish government has a most useful
agreement: 'its fleet is the British fleet which guards from
hindrance the progress of all-Jewish world-economy.... In
return, All-Judaan assures Britain an undisturbed political
and territorial world rule.'[1]

At present the Elders are intent on obtaining dominion over
the United States, and they are making astonishingly rapid
progress. In the United States a few decades have sufficed for a
campaign which in Europe lasted 1,500 years, and it is clear
why: 'certain mistaken *ideas* of liberalism, certain flabby *ideas*
of tolerance' have been put about by the Elders and are
rapidly undermining the American will to resist.[2] The United
States would do well to study the cases of Russia and Germany; both countries have been brought low but both are now
rising in revolt. Germany is already bestirring herself to bring
Jewish power under control; as for Russia – 'when Russia
turns, a shudder will run through the earth'. The United
States must summon up the same ruthlessness; and quickly
too, for with the subjugation of the United States the great
conspiracy will reach its culmination, the establishment of the
Davidic monarch as ruler of the world: 'As the Jew is a past
master of symbolism, it may not be without significance that
the Bolshevik Star has one point less than the Star of David.'
For there is still one point to be fulfilled in the World Programme
as outlined in the Protocols – and that is the enthronement of
'our leader'. When he comes, the World Autocrat for whom
the whole programme is framed, 'the sixth point may be
added'.[3]

Some facts are known about the origins of this extraordinary
work. A Dr Edward A. Rumely, who had been a very active
member of a German propaganda ring in the United States
during the First World War, was a close friend of Henry Ford.
This enabled him to find a place on the staff of *The Dearborn*

[1] *The International Jew*, p. 30.
[2] Ibid., p. 141.
[3] Ibid., p. 233.

Independent for a German, Dr August Müller; and it seems to have been Dr Müller who wrote most of *The International Jew*. Also associated with the undertaking was a Russian refugee, Boris Brasol. In Russia this man had served under the fanatically antisemitic Minister of Justice Shchegolitov, who organized the Beiliss murder trial, and he himself believed passionately in stories of ritual murder. In 1918 he was employed by the United States Government on secret service work, and this enabled him to introduce American intelligence officers to the *Protocols*. He did much to promote the Boston edition of the *Protocols*, which was the work of the daughter of a tsarist general, Natalie de Bogory; and he also established contact with Ford's secretary and passed him materials on the *Protocols*. From all this it emerges that *The International Jew* was far more a Russo-German than an American product.[1, 2]

The publication of this book and of the *Protocols* produced some sharp reactions in the United States. President Wilson, the former Secretary of State Lansing, the Cardinal Archbishop of Boston, were among those who protested most vigorously. American Jews themselves refused to submit passively to these slanders and launched a campaign against *The Dearborn Independent*. Particularly active was the American diplomat Herman Bernstein, whose book *The History of a Lie* (1921) is one of the earliest studies of the forging of the *Protocols*; some years later, despite the legal difficulties involved, he even brought a libel action against Ford for publishing such tales. And in the end the great industrialist did recant. In June 1927 he wrote to the president of the American Jewish Committee, Louis Marshall, disclaiming all responsibility for the articles in *The Dearborn Independent* and for the book they had become. Although he owned both publications, he had no idea what was published in them; and in this whole matter he had been deceived by men

[1] Later Rumely became executive secretary of the so-called Committee for Constitutional Government, which between 1937 and 1944 spent some $2,000,000 on fighting Roosevelt; while Brasol was active in Nazi intrigues up to 1939.

[2] On the intrigues around Ford's campaign see Norman Hapgood, 'The inside story of Henry Ford's Jew-mania', six articles in *Hearst's International*, from June to November 1922.

on whom he had relied implicitly. Shocked to discover what had been done in his name, he solemnly retracted the accusations contained in *The International Jew* and undertook to withdraw the book from circulation.

So far so good – but it was not in Ford's power to abolish *The International Jew*. Especially in Germany its influence was great and lasting. Because of it, Hitler kept a photograph of Ford beside his desk for years; and when he heard, in 1923, that Ford might be running for President of the United States, he commented: 'I wish that I could send some of my shock troops to Chicago and other big American cities to help in the elections. . . . We look to Heinrich Ford as the leader of the growing Fascist movement in America. . . . We have just had his anti-Jewish articles translated and published. The book is being circulated in millions throughout Germany.'[1] What is more, the political antisemites in Germany refused to take the book out of circulation even when Ford asked them to, and were still distributing and advertising it at the outbreak of the Second World War.

But the harm was not confined to Germany, for in the end *The International Jew* was translated into sixteen languages. Ford's recantation can have reached only a few of the hundreds of thousands, or millions, who had been encouraged by his reputation as a man of affairs to accept the *Protocols* as genuine – and one may fairly wonder how many of those few took it seriously. For there is no real doubt that Ford knew perfectly well what he was sponsoring. He founded *The Dearborn Independent* in 1919 as a vehicle for his own 'philosophy' and he took a keen and constant interest in it; much of the contents consisted simply of edited versions of his talk. It is not conceivable that when, on 20 May 1920, the paper suddenly changed its format and began its attacks on the Jews, he should have failed to notice. But apart from this, Ford did in fact commit himself publicly on the subject of the Jewish world-conspiracy, in two books published in 1922 – *The Amazing Story of Henry Ford*, by James M. Miller, and *My Life and Work*, by Henry Ford in collaboration with S. Crowther. Nobody who studies certain passages written at his

[1] *Chicago Tribune*, quoted in J. R. Carlson, *Under Cover*, New York, 1943 edition, p. 210.

dictation can doubt that at least by that time he knew the *Protocols* and was determined that people should believe in them.[1]

Did he himself believe? At first sight it seems incredible that a man who could build up a huge industrial empire from scratch could be as naïve as that. Yet some of the things Ford did can be explained in no other way. When *The International Jew* began to make its impact a prominent American Jew, Isaac Landman, offered to provide enough money to enable the world's leading detectives to establish once and for all whether a secret Jewish government did or did not exist; whatever the results might be, they were to be printed in at least a hundred leading newspapers. Ford rejected the offer – but instead of leaving the matter at that, he himself put a squad of agents into New York to unmask the operations of the secret government. These agents – some of them fanatics and others mere crooks – shadowed prominent Jews, investigated such improbable bodies as the Shipping Board, and above all carried on a melodramatic correspondence with headquarters at Detroit, using code names as signatures. In the end they heard of the official New York Jewish community organization, which under the name Kehilla (Yiddish for 'kahal') was chiefly concerned with protecting and educating Jewish immigrants. This, they announced, was the secret government in whose hands President Wilson, Herbert Hoover, and Colonel House were willing tools.[2,3]

That Ford lent himself to such a performance strongly suggests that in this matter at least he was no cynic but a true believer. And one can see what could have made him so.

[1] E.g. pp. 240–2 in *The 'New Era Philosophy'*, by Henry Ford, which forms Part II of *The Amazing Story of Henry Ford*; and pp. 250–2 in *My Life and Work*. Both books were published in 1922.

[2] The detectives spent much energy in trying to trace a private telephone-line from the home of one particular Jew, Justice Brandeis of the United States Supreme Court, to the room in the White House where President Wilson lay gravely ill. They failed – not surprisingly, as Justice Brandeis had no private telephone at all. Two former senior members of the secret service joined Ford's detective service; they were both completely taken in by the 'White' Russian Rodionov, who claimed to have access to thirteen additional 'Protocols' 'in the original Hebrew'.

[3] Cf. J. N. Leonard, *The Tragedy of Henry Ford*, New York, 1932, pp. 203–4.

Paradoxically, this man who did so much to create the modern world of mass production and cheap travel detested modernity. He abominated cities, especially New York, and was convinced that the only true Americans were those in the farms and small towns of the Middle West; he cherished a sentimental nostalgia for the pre-industrial past. We have seen how easily such attitudes can lead to the most virulent form of political antisemitism. Moreover, Ford had absolutely no understanding of the complex ways in which societies operate and history is made. 'All the world needs for the guidance of its life could be written on two pages of a child's copybook,' he wrote in *The Dearborn Independent*. A man who could believe that could also believe that all the transformations and upheavals and torments of the modern world have a single explanation, enshrined in the few dozen pages of the *Protocols*. All in all the *Protocols* probably owe their most influential backing less to Ford's Machiavellianism than to his astounding innocence.[1]

After Germany, Britain, and the United States, the countries which gave the *Protocols* the warmest welcome and did most to make them a force in world affairs were Poland and France. The first Polish edition appeared early in 1920 and was sold out by 1921; whereupon the same translation was republished, with an introduction and a conclusion, by the antisemitic organization Rozwój ('Development'). Poland, of course, included a large part of what in the Tsar's empire had been the Pale of Jewish Settlement, and antisemitism was a well-established tradition; so it is not surprising that the *Protocols* should have had a considerable impact in the newly created state. The Roman Catholic clergy did much to encourage belief in them. In the summer of 1920, when Poland seemed likely to be overrun by the Red Army, the Polish episcopate sent to Roman Catholic bishops throughout the world a 'cry for help and rescue for Poland' which was clearly inspired by the *Protocols*. It reads as follows:

The real object of Bolshevism is world-conquest. The race which has the leadership of Bolshevism in its hands, has already in the

[1] Ford's naïvety emerges clearly in the conversation recorded in W. C. Richards, *The Last Billionnaire: Henry Ford*, New York, 1949, pp. 89–90.

past subjugated the whole world by means of gold and the banks, and now, driven by the everlasting imperialistic greed which flows in its veins, is already aiming at the final subjugation of the nations under the yoke of its rule. . . . The hatred of Bolshevism is directed against Christ and his Church, especially because those who are the leaders of Bolshevism bear in their blood the traditional hatred for Christianity. Bolshevism is in truth the embodiment and incarnation of the spirit of Antichrist on earth.[1]

This document was particularly misguided, because the overwhelming majority of Polish Jews, including those in the Jewish working-class party, the Bund, were in fact staunch opponents of Bolshevism. But the appeal, which was signed by two cardinals, two archbishops, and three bishops, was none the less potent for that. It did nothing to bring help to Poland but, read out in churches all over the world, it certainly impelled many Catholics to accept the myth of the Jewish world-conspiracy. And in Poland itself it must have helped to provoke the many murders of Jews which occurred during the Russian invasion.

In France the *Protocols* also enjoyed widespread and continuous favour. Interest was aroused by the first English translation and the notice which this received in *The Times*. Royalist journals associated with the Action Française reviewed the book, while the independent weekly *L'Opinion* produced an abbreviated version of it in three articles on 'The origins of Bolshevism'. This was in June 1920, and in the following three months there appeared no less than three complete translations. The daily newspaper *La Libre Parole*, faithful to the spirit in which Edouard Drumont had founded it twenty-eight years before, printed the first French translation of the entire *Protocols*, extending over nearly a month of issues. The review *La Vieille France*, edited by Urbain Gohier, also printed the whole text; and both these translations were reissued as popular pamphlets. More successful still was the translation dignified by the name of Mgr Jouin, *curé* of the church of St Augustine in Paris. This venerable ecclesiastic (he was born in 1844) had begun his campaign against the Judeo-Masonic conspiracy in 1909, by founding the *Revue Internationale des Sociétés secrètes*; he even established contact

---

[1] B. Segel, *Die Protokolle der Weisen von Zion*, p. 171.

before the war with the *pogromshchik* Butmi. After publishing a new translation of the *Protocols* in his review he republished it, in the autumn of 1920, as the first volume in a series entitled *Le Péril judéo-maçonnique*. As it turned out, this series was to run to five volumes in which the principal early versions of the *Protocols*, Russian, German, and Polish, were subjected to minute comparison and elaborated in long commentaries. The industrious author devoted seven years to this rewarding task, which he completed at the age of eighty-two. Elevated to the prelacy by Benedict XV, when he was already editor of the *Revue Internationale des Sociétés secrètes*, he was appointed apostolic prothonotary by Pius XI, when he was known as a leading sponsor of the *Protocols*; and these distinctions must certainly have added to the prestige of his publications.

A fourth translation appeared early in 1921 and it was to be the most popular of all. The only French version to be translated direct from the Russian, it was the work of Roger Lambelin, a life-long royalist who, after heading the political office of the Duke of Orleans, had left the old-style royalists in favour of the demagogic and antisemitic Action Française. This translation was outstandingly successful – it ran to sixteen editions within a year; by 1925 the figure had risen to twenty-five, and sales continued excellent right down to the Second World War. Today it is Lambelin's introduction that claims attention, as a historical document to set alongside the lucubrations of *Auf Vorposten* and *The Morning Post*. All, of course, are agreed that Bolshevism is the work of the Elders – but there agreements stops. Müller von Hausen might argue that the British and French Governments enjoyed the special protection of the Elders, and *The Morning Post* that the German Government and the Elders were indissolubly allied – Roger Lambelin achieved a new and ingenious synthesis: 'The British Government, under the premiership of Mr David Lloyd George, is completely bound to the policies of world Jewry. . . . In the United States, under President Wilson, the Jewish conquest was as obvious as in England.' But the Elders cared for Germany too: 'At the moment of the armistice and the first international negotiations the Jews rendered Germany a decisive service by camouflaging her states as democratic or socialist countries.' In fact France was the only sufferer from

'this strange peace, more favourable to the vanquished than
to the victors – except for the Anglo-Saxons. . . .'[1]

Alongside the editions of the *Protocols* produced by Frenchmen there appeared a number of works by right-wing Russians
who had taken refuge in France. Two of these give the complete
text of the *Protocols*, with long and fantastic commentaries:
L'Empereur Nicolas II et les Juifs, by General Nechvolodov,
published in 1924; and a work which became a standard
manual for adepts of the *Protocols: Le Juif notre maître* (1931),
by 'Mrs. L. Fry', who was the wife of a Russian called Shishmarev. From the point of view of the public all this formed a
single body of writing. Representatives of the extreme right
wing of French politics combined with the defeated supporters
of the Russian autocracy to make the *Protocols* known in
France.

It is a familiar picture, and one which was repeated in
country after country. Vinberg, Shabelsky-Bork, and somewhat later Schwarz-Bostunitsch in Germany, Brasol and
Cherep-Spiridovich in the United States, Zhevakhov and
Schwarz-Bostunitsch in Yugoslavia, Subbotin in South
America, Rodzayevsky in the Far East – these and many
other former tsarist generals, officers and right-wing politicians
played a decisive part in the dissemination of the *Protocols*.
These people collaborated with all kinds of right-wing bodies
for the furtherance of their own aim, which was restoration of
the autocracy in Russia; and these different bodies used them
for *their* aims, which varied from country to country. Out of
this collaboration came the finance and the organization which
were required to carry the *Protocols* across the world.

Save in Britain the unmasking of the forgery in 1921 seems
to have made little difference. Some editors and sponsors of
the *Protocols* copied Lord Alfred Douglas and pretended that
Joly was really a Jewish revolutionary called Moses Joël; but
most of them avoided the whole matter and simply maintained
that the *Protocols* must be genuine if the processes and events
they foretold were taking place. And who could deny that the
age was indeed one of wars and revolutions, slumps and inflation?

[1] Lambelin's introduction to his translation of the *Protocols*, pp. vi,
x–xii in the edition of 1935.

So the *Protocols* proceeded unchecked on their triumphant way. A whole international network of sponsors and 'students' of the *Protocols* came into existence. Journals all over the world collaborated in expounding them and exchanged 'information' and 'documents' – *The Dearborn Independent* in the United States, *The Patriot* and *The British Guardian* in Britain, *La Vieille France* and *La Libre Parole* in France, the *National Tidsskrift* in Norway, the *Dansk National Tidsskrift* in Denmark, *Dwa Grosze* and *Pro Patria* in Poland, and of course many journals in Germany. To the various German, English, and French translations there were soon added translations into Swedish, Danish, Norwegian, Finnish, Rumanian, Hungarian, Lithuanian, Polish, Bulgarian, Italian, Greek, Japanese, and Chinese. And meanwhile in Germany the *Protocols* were being incorporated into the ideology of a rising and ruthless political party.

CHAPTER VIII

Germanic Racism transforms the Myth

1

WHEN the judge at Techow's trial referred to Rathenau's 'sacrificial death' he spoke truer than he knew; for Rathenau was not simply assassinated as an Elder of Zion, he was offered up as a human sacrifice to the sun-god of ancient Germanic religion. The murder was timed to coincide with the summer solstice; and when the news was published, young Germans gathered on hilltops to celebrate simultaneously the turning of the year and the destruction of one who symbolized the powers of darkness.[1] What are we to make of these extraordinary facts?

The *Protocols* had indeed acquired a new dimension when they came into contact with that peculiar outlook which is known as *völkisch*[2] or sometimes as 'the Germanic ideology'.[3] The beginnings of this outlook – which was really a pseudo-religion – go back to the Napoleonic Wars. Germany is by no means the only country which first began to develop a national consciousness as a result of being invaded – but it so happened that in this case the invading power was itself the standard-bearer of the modern age, the champion of democracy, liberalism, rationalism. It is normal to reject the values of the invader and to affirm their opposites – and this meant that German nationalism was from the start partly backward-looking, partly inspired by a repudiation of modernity and a

---

[1] *Mitteilungen aus dem Verein zur Abwehr des Antisemitismus*, issue of 29 September 1922, p. 98.   [2] From *das Volk*, the people.

[3] On the *völkisch* outlook from the 1860s to Hitler see G. L. Mosse, *The Crisis of German Ideology*, New York, 1964; and for its beginnings, from the Napoleonic wars to 1850, see Eleonore Sterling, *Er ist wie Du*, Munich, 1956.

nostalgia for a past which was imagined as in every way unlike the modern world. And this attitude not only persisted but was intensified when economic developments pitchforked Germany into that same modern world. At the very time when Germany was turning into a great industrial power, a land of factories and cities, technology and bureaucracy, many Germans were dreaming of an archaic world of Germanic peasants, bound together by bonds of blood in a 'natural', 'organic' community.

Such a view of the world requires an anti-figure, and this was supplied partly by the liberal West but also, and more effectively, by the Jews. As we have seen, it is characteristic of latter-day, political antisemites that they see 'the Jew' not only as an uncanny, demonic being but also as an embodiment of modernity, a symbol of all those forces in the modern world which they themselves fear and hate. This was the case also with German antisemites of the *völkisch* variety – but with a difference. When these people looked to the past, to the ideal state which they supposed to have preceded the modern age, they looked far beyond throne and altar, back to an infinitely remote and almost entirely mythical world. For them 'the Jew' was not only, or mainly, the destroyer of kings and the enemy of the Church – he was above all the age-old antagonist of the Germanic peasant, he was the force which for two thousand years had been undermining the true, original German way of life. Historical Christianity itself was a Jewish creation which had helped to destroy the archaic Germanic world. Now capitalism, liberalism, democracy, socialism, and the urban way of life were continuing the process; together they made up 'the Jew's' world, the modern age which was his creation and in which he flourished.

The first major proponent of this outlook was an eccentric scholar, Paul Bötticher, usually known by his adopted name of Paul de Lagarde.[1] In his major work, *Deutsche Schriften* (*German Writings*), published in 1878, Lagarde expressed his disillusionment with the united Germany which had just come into being. He demanded a higher unity: that of the German

[1] On Paul de Lagarde, see F. Stern, *The Politics of Cultural Despair*, Berkeley and Los Angeles, 1961; and for a brieter account G. L. Mosse, op. cit., Chapter 2.

Volk, living once more as it had lived in the remote past and thereby realizing the divine intention for the world. But he recognized that this new order could not easily be achieved, and this he attributed to the Jews. Though he really knew nothing of Jewish religion he was convinced that it was at the heart of that modernity which was so fatal to the *Volk*. He foresaw a mortal struggle between the Jewish and the German ways of life – and when he talked of struggle, he meant physical violence: the Jews, he proclaimed, must be exterminated like bacilli. It was not for nothing that in 1944, when the Nazis were completing their vast massacres, an anthology of Lagarde's work was distributed to the troops on the eastern front.[1]

Yet at other times Lagarde could advocate the total assimilation of the German Jews into the German people. This was because for him Jews still meant simply the adherents of the Jewish religion, or what he imagined as that religion; he did not think of them as a 'race'. But at that very time the pseudo-science of German racism was coming into being. In 1873 Wilhelm Marr – the probable inventor of the word 'anti-semitism' – published a book with the significant title *Der Sieg des Judenthums über das Germanenthum . . . (The Victory of Jewry over Germandom, considered from a non-denominational point of view)*, and in 1881 Eugen Dühring, a lecturer in economics and philosophy at Berlin University, published *Die Judenfrage als Rassen-, Sitten- und Kulturfrage (The Jewish Question as a Question of Race, Morals and Civilization)*. In these works the Jews are shown not simply as evil but as irremediably evil, the source of their depravity lies no longer simply in their religion but in their very blood. In the 1890s this view of the matter was adopted and popularized by that tireless propagandist Theodor Fritsch – the same who, a generation later, was to publish the *Protocols*. In the innumerable pamphlets and periodicals put out by the Hammer publishing house, Fritsch proclaimed that by proving 'scientically' the depravity of the Jewish and the sublimity of the German 'race', German racists were inaugurating not only a prodigious advance in human knowledge but a new epoch of human history. The fact that there is no such thing as a

[1] F. Stern, op. cit., p. 63, footnote.

'German race' or a 'Jewish race' was of course ignored by all these writers.

Finally, in 1900, Houston Stewart Chamberlain – an Englishman by birth and the son of a British admiral, but a German by choice and eventually by nationality – published his two-volume work *Die Grundlagen des neunzehnten Jahrhunderts* (*Foundations of the Nineteenth Century*), which thanks to its eloquence and its appearance of learning became the Bible of the whole *völkisch*-racist movement. Here all human history was presented as a bitter struggle between spirituality, embodied in the German 'race', and materialism, embodied in the Jewish 'race' – the only two pure races, for all the others were but a 'chaos of peoples'. In Chamberlain's view the Jewish 'race' had been relentlessly striving, down the ages, to secure absolute dominion over all other nations. If once this 'race' were decisively defeated, the Germanic 'race' would be free to realize its own divinely appointed destiny – which was to create a new, radiant world, transfused with a noble spirituality and mysteriously combining modern technology and science with the rural, hierarchical culture of earlier times.[1]

This *völkisch*-racist view of the world was not by any means shared by all Germans. The nobility and the great industrialists disdained it; and so, at the other end of the social scale, did the industrial working class organized in the Social-Democratic movement. The reason was that these strata of German society were relatively secure in their self-esteem – the nobility and the industrialists because they enjoyed the reality of social and political dominance, the workers because their Marxist indoctrination – unrivalled for its thoroughness in any other country – inspired them with a sense of historic mission. More surprisingly, the peasantry too was uninterested. When peasants became actively antisemitic, as they did at various times in various places, it was always for specific economic reasons directly affecting themselves; the *völkisch* glorification of a mythical peasantry left them cold. But the *völkisch*-racist outlook did make a great appeal to certain

---

[1] On the exponents of racism see, in addition to G. L. Mosse, G. J. Pulzer, *The Rise of Political Anti-semitism in Germany and Austria*, New York and London, 1964.

sections of the middle class. The explanation for this lies in the curious history of the German middle class in the nineteenth and early twentieth centuries.[1] Two strata of the middle class were involved: on the one hand artisans and small retailers, on the other hand university students and graduates. It has often been remarked that artisans and small retailers were peculiarly prone to anti-semitism and in due course provided the bulk of the votes which brought Hitler to power. There is nothing mysterious about this. These sections of the population were survivals from an earlier age and they were gravely threatened by the development of modern capitalism. Though the Marxist prophecy that they would inevitably be proletarianized proved wrong, they did indeed live in a state of almost perpetual crisis. Barely able to cope with the new world of giant industrial and commercial undertakings, lacking even that rudimentary understanding of it which industrial workers received from their Marxist training, struggling frantically to preserve their status, these people felt an overwhelming need for a scapegoat.

The Jews were perfectly suited for the role – though not, as was commonly said, because they 'created' modern capitalism, or because they occupied the commanding heights in the German economy, or because they were mostly well-to-do, or because they were obviously foreign. In reality German Jews constituted a tiny minority with a falling birthrate, so that left to themselves they would in any case probably have disappeared by the end of the century. They mostly identified themselves passionately with the German fatherland, and they had gone very far on the road to total assimilation. A large proportion of them belonged to the lower middle class and shared all the hazards which that implied. Jews had no place among the giants of industry and their role in banking was a very limited one. And yet in spite of all this, German Jewry

[1] For the sociology of the *völkisch*-racist outlook see, in addition to Pulzer and Mosse, the penetrating article by H. P. Bahrdt, 'Gesellschaftliche Voraussetzungen des Antisemitismus', in the symposium *Entscheidungsjahr 1932* (ed. W. E. Mosse), Tübingen, 1965; and the works by P. W. Massing, Eva G. Reichmann and A. Leschnitzer, listed in the Bibliographical Note.

was the obvious scapegoat for the resentments of the lower middle class.

There were various reasons for this. There were the concentrations of well-to-do Jews in certain areas of Berlin and Hamburg, which could lead the unthinking to suppose that all Jews were rich, even that all rich people were Jews. There was the typical Jewish zeal in getting the sons to universities and thence into the liberal professions, which brought them into direct conflict with the more aspiring members of the lower middle class. Above all, Jews really did revolutionize certain trades, such as the clothing trade; and though the scale of their enterprises benefited the public, it threatened innumerable small firms. At the same time Jews in general were still just sufficiently different and exclusive to constitute a recognizable minority. And so, however unjustly, it came about that in the eyes of the lower-middle-class antisemite, harassed, frustrated, disorientated, the Jews were above all the symbol of modern capitalism, the beneficiaries of the system under which he himself was suffering.[1]

But though many members of the lower middle class were attracted by the *völkisch*-racist outlook, its creators, propagators, and most fanatical adherents were to be found elsewhere – in that rather higher stratum of the middle class to which many of the Jews themselves belonged. Irrational, unscientific, and demonstrably nonsensical as this outlook was, it was nevertheless the speciality of the educated – or rather, of those with a university degree. Lagarde was an orientalist of real distinction and latterly a university professor, Dühring was a university lecturer, Chamberlain was very widely read; while the main body of believers was to be found among university students and university graduates – the two being linked, often quite closely, in the *Burschenschaften* (fraternities).

This too can be understood only in terms of the peculiar history of the German middle class. In Germany the first section of the middle class to attain prestige consisted of writers, scholars, thinkers. Already early in the nineteenth century, at a time when Germany consisted simply of a mass

[1] Cf. E. Bennathan, 'Die demographische und wirtschaftliche Struktur der Juden', in *Entscheidungsjahr 1932*, pp. 87–131.

of petty principalities, as backward economically as politically, German intellectual achievements commanded respect throughout Europe. At that time many German intellectuals were liberal nationalists, equally devoted to liberal principles and to the cause of German unification. But their attempt at creating a united Germany in 1848 was a failure, and when unification came in 1871 it was imposed by the Prussian Junker Bismarck. Meanwhile the industrial bourgeoisie had appeared and together with the nobility monopolized political power. The writers and scholars and thinkers, once the spearhead of the bourgeoisie, found themselves pushed down the social scale. Excluded not only from political influence but from all contact with politics, accustomed to dealing with abstractions but not with real people in real situations, wounded in their self-esteem and seething with resentment, many of these people consoled themselves with constructing vast philosophies of history.

The *völkisch*-racist view of the world was one of these philosophies. It had the enormous advantage that it made any German who accepted it feel not only important but enormously, supremely important. For men with some pretensions to education but irked by their political impotence and social insignificance it had great attractions. To feel oneself the bearer of a divine mission, a paladin in the vast struggle of 'German spirituality' against the dark forces of 'Jewish materialism' – this was a most gratifying experience, especially as it carried with it no concrete political responsibilities whatsoever.

The appeal of the *völkisch*-racist outlook was perhaps even stronger among the German element in the Habsburg empire than it was in the Hohenzollern empire.[1] On this periphery of the German-speaking world, where ever since the war of 1866 the German element had felt isolated and threatened by the preponderant Slav element, the aggressive affirmation of German superiority had particular attractions. Moreover, the Jews were far more conspicuous in Austria than in Germany, and at both ends of the social scale: while the great majority lived in appalling poverty, a minority made up a large part of

[1] Pulzer's book deals with the (commonly neglected) Austrian contribution to the antisemitic tradition.

the professional class and a few were bankers of great wealth. That Austrian Jews did not regard themselves as forming one of the national groups within the Habsburg empire, but as belonging to the German group, did not help at all: the Germans rejected them. And here as in Germany the most militant antisemites were to be found, on the one hand, in a lower middle class which had failed to adapt itself to the demands of a rapidly developing industrial economy, and on the other hand among students and professional men. When Hitler came to power in 1933, a joke circulated in Germany: Hitler was Austria's revenge for Königgrätz, i.e. for Austria's defeat at the hands of Prussia in 1866. And there was a good deal in it, for the petty bourgeois Hitler did indeed embody a whole century of frustration, disappointment, and insecurity, and the boundless lust for revenge which possessed him was a magnified version of something which possessed a whole stratum of Austrian society.

Before the First World War the *völkisch*-racist outlook had relatively little impact on politics, whether in the Habsburg or the Hohenzollern empire. From 1880 onwards various anti-semitic parties appeared, and they had some success; but these organizations were seldom committed to any such high-flown ideology.[1] In the years immediately preceding the war racist fanatics tended to avoid day-to-day politics and to deal solely in 'ideas'. Austrian racists developed the cult of the swastika, and foretold that some day Jews would be castrated and killed under the aegis of that ancient sun-symbol. In Austria too Georg von Schönerer, after an unsuccessful career as a politician, set out to revive antique Germanic customs, including the solstice festival which a generation later was to play such a curious part in the Rathenau murder. In Germany there appeared a multitude of more or less esoteric bodies, such as the Germanen- und Walsungsorden (Order of Teutons and Volsungs), which also used the swastika as its emblem; and the Kulturbund für Politik (Cultural League for Politics),

---

[1] An exception was a party which came into existence in 1903 in the Sudetenland, that ancient outpost of Germandom on the Slav frontier: the German Workers' party, later the National Socialist German Workers' party, which after the war co-operated closely with the Nazi party in Germany.

which combined virulent racism with enthusiasm for a new kind of whole-meal loaf.[1]

At the time there were probably few who imagined that the *völkisch*-racist outlook would ever impinge much on practical politics. Yet even then, well before 1914, it influenced many schoolteachers and above all the famous Youth Movement, in which multitudes of young Germans sought escape from bourgeois stuffiness; it even touched at least one important and respectable political organization, the Pan-German Association. But above all, in its purest form, where a fanatical race-consciousness blended with teetotalism, vegetarianism, and occultism, it formed the outlook of many of the most sinister of the future Nazi leaders – including Hitler himself, vegetarian and teetotaler, much addicted to horoscopes and clairvoyants, and full of admiration for his countryman, von Schönerer.

It was the outcome of the war that enabled the *völkisch*-racist outlook to penetrate into the field of practical politics. The humiliation of defeat and the sufferings that followed it, the mortification felt over the peace treaties of Versailles and St Germain, the utter disorientation and widespread financial ruin which accompanied the collapse of the currency – these things produced an entirely new atmosphere. Moreover both Germany and Austria had lost the national minorities on which, formerly, nationalist arrogance and rancour had vented itself; while Germany seemed in addition to have lost any prospect of imperialist expansion. All this gave added appeal to the fantasy of an age-old, mortal struggle between the German and Jewish 'races'. Among university students it flourished with particular vigour. Jewish students had long been excluded from the student fraternities, but it was a significant innovation when, in 1919, this exclusion was extended to non-Jews who were married to Jews.

In the ideology of the political Right *völkisch*-racist ideas began to figure to an extent quite unknown before the war. In election campaigns from 1920 onwards the German National People's party (DNVP) used racist propaganda of great ferocity – and this party, at the peak of its success, polled six million votes. Admittedly the DNVP appealed to many

[1] Pulzer, op. cit., pp. 208, 231, 244.

different interests and for many different reasons; but on the
extreme Right there were various smaller organizations which
existed only to further racist antisemitism. Already before the
war the leader of the Pan-German Association, Heinrich Class,
had demanded that German Jews should be deprived of
citizenship, debarred from all official positions and from
teaching and the law, forbidden to own land, and taxed twice
as high as other Germans. Now he managed to lead his association in the same direction; in the last days of the war it
officially extended its work to embrace 'the Jewish question',
and a year later it created a special body to deal with these
matters: the Deutsch-völkischer Schutz- und Trutzbund
(Defensive and Offensive Alliance).[1]

The Alliance, which had the swastika as its emblem, quickly
acquired a membership of 300,000. After the Rathenau murder
it was suppressed – but to no effect, as its members promptly
joined the Nazi party. Meanwhile the old Order of Teutons
and Volsungs continued to exist, also using the swastika. In
November 1918 it produced, as a cover-organization, a body
called the Thule Bund; and it was a couple of members of this
short-lived organization who, early in 1919, founded the
German Workers' party, shortly to become the Nazi party:
Karl Harrer, Anton Drexler, and probably also Dietrich
Eckart, who has been called the spiritual father of the Hitler
movement and to whom Hitler dedicated *Mein Kampf*.[2]

These organizations were indoctrinated with the *völkisch*-
racist outlook in its most fanatical form, and when the *Protocols* came into their hands they reinterpreted them accordingly. In their eyes the machinations of the Elders of Zion
were the supreme expression of the characteristics which they
attributed to the Jewish 'race'. The Jewish world-conspiracy
was seen as the product of an ineradicable destructiveness, a
will to evil which was believed to be inborn in every Jew. A
peculiar breed of sub-human beings, dark, earthbound, was

[1] D. Frymann (pseudonym of Heinrich Class), *Wenn ich der Kaiser
wär*, Leipzig, 1912; and cf. A. Kruck, *Geschichte des Alldeutschen Ver-
bandes*, 1890–1939, Wiesbaden, 1954, pp. 130 seq.

[2] G. Franz-Willing, *Die Hitlerbewegung*, Vol. I; *Der Ursprung 1919–
1922*, Hamburg and Berlin, 1962, p. 127; and H. Phelps, 'Hitler and the
Deutsche Arbeiterpartei', in *American Historical Review*, vol. 68, No. 4
(July 1963), pp. 974–86.

working conspiratorially to destroy those sons of light, the
'Aryan' or Germanic 'race', and the *Protocols* contained their
plan of campaign. To that plan there could be only one
response – extermination, carried out under the symbol of the
sun-god, the swastika. Walther Rathenau fell as the first
victim in a massacre which was to begin in earnest a generation
later.

2

When the *Protocols* came into contact with the *völkisch*-racist
outlook the result was an apocalyptic vision not only of contemporary politics but of all history and indeed of all human
existence on this planet. And it was in the name of this quasi-
religious world-view that the Nazis and their accomplices
undertook the extermination of the Jews of Europe, as a prelude to the extermination of Jews throughout the world. This
is seldom realized even today, and as a blunt statement of
fact it does seem almost incredible. But the evidence is there,
in the pronouncements of the Nazi leaders and of the organizers of the exterminations, and it is incontrovertible.

One may start with the astonishing statement of Dieter
Wisliceny, a SS captain who was a close associate of Eichmann
and was executed in 1947 for his part in the attempt to exterminate Slovak, Greek, and Hungarian Jews. On 18 November 1946, in preparation for his trial in Czechoslovakia, he
described at length how the great massacre came about. Before
describing how the policy of genocide was formulated and
implemented, he had something to say about a matter 'without which it is impossible to obtain a clear view of the situation: the reasons which led Hitler and Himmler to undertake
the extermination of European Jewry'. What he had in mind
was the world-view which obsessed these men, and which he
pictured as follows:

Antisemitism constituted one of the main bases of the programme
of the Nazi party. Essentially it was the product of two ideas:
　　(1) the pseudo-scientific biological theories of Professor
Günther,[1] and

[1] Professor Hans K. Günther was the official theorist of racism in the
Third Reich.

(2) a mystical and religious view which sees the world as ruled by good and bad powers.

According to this view the Jews represented the evil principle, with, as auxiliaries, the Church (the Jesuit Order), Freemasonry and Bolshevism. The literature of this outlook is well known, the former writings of the Nazi party teem with such ideas. A straight line leads from the *Protocols of the Elders of Zion* to Rosenberg's *Myth*.[1] It is absolutely impossible to make any impression on this outlook by means of logical or rational argument, it is a sort of religiosity, and it impels people to form themselves into a sect. Under the influence of this literature millions of people believed these things – an event which can only be compared with similar phenomena in the Middle Ages, such as the witch-mania.

Against this world of evil the race-mystics set the world of good, of light, incarnated in blond, blue-eyed people, who were supposed to be the source of all capacity for creating civilization or building a state. Now these two worlds were alleged to be locked in a perpetual struggle, and the war of 1939, which Hitler unleashed, represented only the final battle between these two powers.

The usual view of Himmler is that he was an ice-cold, cynical politician. This view is certainly wrong. In his whole attitude Himmler was a mystic, who embraced this 'world-view' with religious fanaticism.[2]

From other sources we know that the same world-view obsessed Hitler himself throughout his political career. There are signs of the obsession already in the very first of his political utterances. In 1919 Hitler was employed by the army district command in Munich as 'education officer', with the job of immunizing the troops against the infection of democracy and socialism. On 16 September 1919 he wrote a letter to a certain Gemlich which shows clearly enough how he conceived of his assignment. Already the opening words concern 'the danger which Jewry today represents for our people' – and he promptly goes on to complain that ordinary German antisemitism still lacks the ideological coherence which would make it an effective political movement. It is not, he protests, enough to dislike Jews; Germans must realize that Jewry

---

[1] Rosenberg's *Mythus des 20. Jahrhunderts* (*The Myth of the Twentieth Century*) was one of the basic scriptures of Nazism.

[2] Text in L. Poliakov and J. Wulf, *Das Dritte Reich und die Juden*, Berlin-Grunewald, 1955, pp. 91–2.

forms a racial entity with very strongly marked racial characteristics, of which the passion for material gain is the most
dominant. This is what makes Jewry 'the racial tuberculosis
of the peoples'. Mere pogroms are inadequate to cope with such
a dangerous foe – 'there must be a rebirth of the moral and
spiritual forces of the nation' through 'the ruthless effort of
born leaders with a nationalist outlook and an inner sense of
responsibility'. A government formed of such men will
restrict the legal rights of the Jews, but it will not stop there:
its ultimate aim must be 'the removal (*Entfernung*) of the
Jews altogether'.[1] Thus the unknown ex-corporal who a
couple of days before had attended his first meeting with the
tiny German Workers' party, the nucleus of the future Nazi
party.

Probably Hitler knew of the *Protocols* already then, for they
had been advertised in *Auf Vorposten* and were being discussed among professional antisemites. Certainly by the time
he emerged into the political limelight, in 1923, his thinking
was permeated by them. As Germany passed through the
inferno of the great inflation, in which the savings of the
middle and working classes were wiped out and wages and
salaries became meaningless, Hitler offered his explanation of
the catastrophe: 'According to the *Protocols of Zion* the peoples
are to be reduced to submission by hunger. The second revolution under the Star of David is the aim of the Jews in our
time' – the first revolution being the establishment of the
Weimar Republic itself.[2] The following year, in the comfortable
prison where he was lodged after the abortive *putsch* in
Munich, Hitler dictated *Mein Kampf* – and much of that
dreary but revealing work is devoted to the manoeuvres by
which Jewry is supposed to be pursuing world-domination.
Freemasonry, we are told, is the trick by which the Jews make
the governing class serve their purpose, while the lower classes
are captured by means of the press. Capitalism, liberalism,
democracy, are the devices by which the Jews induced the
bourgeoisie to overthrow the aristocracy and the proletariat

---

[1] Printed in full in E. Deuerlein, 'Hitlers Eintritt in die Politik und
die Reichswehr', in *Vierteljahreshefte für Zeitgeschichte*, Munich, Vol. VII
(1959), Document 12, pp. 203–5.
[2] *Adolf Hitlers Reden*, ed. E. Boepple, Munich, 1933, p. 71.

to overthrow the bourgeoisie. This accomplished, the Jews are now introducing Bolshevism as a way of dominating the masses who brought them to power.

The source of all this is obvious enough, and Hitler had at least the grace to acknowledge it – even though Philip Graves had long since shown the *Protocols* to be a forgery. 'The extent to which the whole existence of (the Jewish) people is based on a continual lie,' he writes in *Mein Kampf*, 'is shown in an incomparable manner in the *Protocols of the Elders of Zion*, which the Jews hate so tremendously. The *Frankfurter Zeitung*[1] is for ever moaning to the public that they are supposed to be based on a forgery; which is the surest proof that they are genuine. What many Jews do perhaps unconsciously is here consciously exposed. But that is what matters. It is a matter of indifference which Jewish brain produced these revelations. What matters is that they uncover, with really horrifying reliability, the nature and activity of the Jewish people, and expose them in their inner logic and their final aims. But reality provides the best commentary. Whoever examines the historical development of the last hundred years from the standpoint of this book will at once understand why the Jewish press makes such an uproar. For when once this book becomes generally familiar to a people, the Jewish menace can be regarded as already vanquished.'[2]

Years later, when Germany was in the throes of the great slump, Hitler explained this world-wide disaster in precisely the same way as he had explained the German inflation. Hermann Rauschning has recorded his comments:

'It was the Jews, of course, who invented the economic system of constant fluctuation and expansion that we call capitalism – that invention of genius, with its subtle and yet simple self-acting mechanism. Let us make no mistake about it – it is an invention of genius, of the devil's own ingenuity.

'The economic system of our day is the creation of the Jews. It is under their exclusive control. It is their super-state, planted by them above all the states of the world in all their glory. But now we have challenged them, with the system of permanent revolution. . . .

[1] A leading German liberal newspaper.
[2] *Mein Kampf*, 11th edition, Munich, 1942, p. 337.

'I have read the *Protocols of the Elders of Zion* – it simply appalled me. The stealthiness of the enemy, and his ubiquity! I saw at once that we must copy it – in our own way, of course. . . . It is in truth the critical battle for the fate of the world.'

'Don't you think,' I objected, 'that you are attributing rather too much importance to the Jews?'

'No, no, no!' exclaimed Hitler. 'It is impossible to exaggerate the formidable quality of the Jew as enemy.'

'But,' I said, 'the *Protocols* are a manifest forgery. . . . It is evident to me that they can't possibly be genuine.'

'Why not?' grunted Hitler.

He did not care two straws, he said, whether the story was historically true. If it was not, its intrinsic truth was all the more convincing to him. . . .[1]

These are all more or less public statements by an outstandingly unscrupulous politician, and if one had no other evidence one might wonder how far Hitler the politician spoke for Hitler the man. But in fact there is plenty of other evidence – and what Hitler has to say about the Jewish world-conspiracy when chatting with friends, or in writings which he did not publish, is much stranger still. The earliest of these sources dates from before the Munich *putsch* of 1923 and consists of a little book by the bohemian poet and journalist Dietrich Eckart, called *Bolshevism from Moses to Lenin: a dialogue between Adolf Hitler and myself*, and published posthumously in 1924.[2] It is a reliable source, for Eckart was not only one of the founding members of the Nazi party, he was one of the very few real friends Hitler ever had (*Mein Kampf*, incidentally, ends with an invocation of his memory). It is quite inconceivable that such a man should have distorted his friend's views in a book intended for publication.[3]

The booklet contains references to earlier works and these are what one would expect: the *Protocols*,[4] Ford's *International*

---

[1] H. Rauschning, *Hitler Speaks*, London, 1939, pp. 235–6.

[2] *Der Bolschewismus von Moses bis Lenin – Zwiegespräch zwischen Adolf Hitler und mir*, Munich, 1924, is analysed in E. Nolte, 'Eine frühe Quelle zu Hitlers Antisemitismus', in *Historische Zeitschrift*, June 1961, pp. 584–606.

[3] Nazi propaganda kept quiet about the book precisely because it was too revealing.

[4] Hitler reveals that he knows 'the Kaiser's Dream', which, as we have seen, figures in the zur Beek edition of the *Protocols*.

Jew, Gougenot des Mousseaux, Fritsch's *Handbook of the Jewish Question*. But by combining these with *völkisch*-racist speculations, Hitler arrives at a whole 'philosophy of history', an interpretation of human existence from the beginning onwards, which has a certain crazy originality. As Hitler sees it, human history forms part of nature and follows the same laws as the rest of nature. If it has gone wrong, that shows that some force is at work to frustrate nature's intention; and that has in fact been the case for thousands of years. There follows an outline of history which portrays it as one long degeneration. Nature demands inequality, hierarchy, subordination of the inferior to the superior – but human history has consisted of a series of revolts against this natural order, leading to ever greater egalitarianism. This process is compared with disease, with the work of a bacillus: 'A proliferation right across the world, now slow, now leaping ahead. Everywhere it sucks and sucks. At first there is teeming abundance, in the end only dried-up sap.'

The force behind this disastrous process is the Jewish spirit, 'which has been there from the beginning'. Already in ancient Egypt the Children of Israel undermined a healthy, 'natural' society. They did this by introducing capitalism – Joseph being the first capitalist – but above all by inciting the lower orders to revolt, until nationally minded Egyptians rose in their wrath and chased the trouble-makers from the land – this is the true meaning of Exodus. Moses therefore is the first Bolshevik and a true precursor of Lenin, whom Hitler and Eckart both assumed to be a Jew. And so a process began which has been repeated over and over again ever since. In Hitler's eyes the lower social strata consist, all over the world, of similar, racially mixed and therefore inferior human material. The essence of the Jewish world-conspiracy is that it uses this racial hotchpotch to overthrow the racially pure upper classes and thereby to further its own drive for world-domination.

In conversation with his friend Hitler said frankly what he was careful never to say in public – that Christianity itself was part of the Jewish plot. Jesus was of course no Jew but an 'Aryan' – but then it was not Jesus but Paul who created Christianity. By extolling pacifism and the egalitarian spirit,

Paul deprived the Roman Empire of the hierarchical, military outlook which was its mainstay, and thereby ensured its doom – and all so that the Jews could move one step nearer their goal of world-domination. In modern times the Jews have repeated the same manoeuvre again and again, and the results have been the French Revolution, liberalism, democracy, and finally Bolshevism; the Russian Revolution with its millions of victims is nothing but the latest episode in the eternal war of Jewry against the other peoples of the world. But Hitler does not stop there – every historical episode that comes to his mind is evalued from the same point of view, how ever little connexion it may have with Jews and their affairs. Thus Luther made a disastrous mistake in attacking the Roman Catholic Church, for by doing so he weakened the Germans in their struggle against the Jews; he ought to have realized that Catholicism was being used by the Jews for their own pv :poses and have directed his attacks against these hidden manipulators. Indeed, if Luther had any merit it was that in his latter years he did attack the Jews; and when Hitler talked of the spirit of Luther he meant one thing only – Luther's hostility to the Jews.

In this little book, then, one comes to the very heart of Hitler's interpretation of history and of human existence. He was utterly convinced that everywhere and at all times the Jews strive for world-domination; that everywhere and at all times they aim to overthrow those who are actually dominant, the pure-blooded élites which nature has set as the governing class in all nations; and that everywhere and at all times they use the lower strata, the masses with impure blood, to carry out this work for them. And what Eckart recorded in 1923 or earlier, Hitler confirmed in his own writings soon afterwards – not so much in *Mein Kampf* as in that other book which he wrote in 1928 and which remained unpublished and unknown until 1961, when it appeared in English translation under the title *Hitler's Second Book* (in Britain) and *Hitler's Secret Book* (in the United States).

In the main this work is simply a plea for an alliance between Germany and Fascist Italy, but even here Hitler feels obliged to append, as a sort of epilogue, some pages of antisemitic invective. And this epilogue carries the argument a stage further: we learn that the Jew does not merely use the racially impure masses for his purposes – he has a whole strategy to ensure that they become more and more racially impure and therefore more and more amenable. 'His ultimate goal is the denationalization, the promiscuous bastardization of other peoples, the lowering of the racial level of the highest peoples as well of the domination of this racial mish-mash through the extirpation of the folkish intelligentsia and its replacement by the members of his own people.'[1] That is why 'after the Bolshevik revolution he completely tore down the bonds of order, of morality, of custom etc, abolished marriage as a lofty institution and instead proclaimed a general copula-tion with the aim of breeding a general inferior human mish-mash, by way of a chaotic bastardization, which by itself would be incapable of leadership and which ultimately would no longer be able to do without the Jews as its only intellectual element. . . . At the moment, he exerts himself to lead the re-maining states toward the same condition'.[2] Appalled by 'this most terrible of all crimes against mankind', Hitler omitted to explain how promiscuity among Russians could alter the biological composition of the Russian population.

Hitler's mind was not one that developed or matured. His chatter over the dinner-table at headquarters when he was Commander-in-Chief of the German Armed Forces during the Second World War has been faithfully recorded. If one examines it to see what he has to say about the Jews one finds precisely the same ideas as he propounded in the 1920s – and often expressed in precisely the same words. The way he sees the course of history is the same – as a decline and decay, a falling away from an original hierarchical order. The cause he imagines is the same – the evil, anti-natural principle incar-nated in the Jews and operating on racially impure popula-tions. Even the images are the same – images of disease, in-fection, pestilence: Christianity and Bolshevism are compared with syphilis and plague, the Jews themselves are constantly referred to as bacilli. 'The discovery of the Jewish virus,' he said to Himmler in 1942, 'is one of the greatest revolutions that have taken place in the world. The battle in which we are

[1] *Hitler's Secret Book*, trans. S. Attanasio, New York, 1961, p. 212.
[2] Ibid., p. 215.

engaged today is of the same sort as the battle waged, during the last century, by Pasteur and Koch. How many diseases have their origin in the Jewish virus!... We shall regain our health only by eliminating the Jew.'[1]

This brings us to the core of this extraordinary fantasy. There is in *Mein Kampf* an astonishing passage which ought to have attracted more attention than it did: 'If the Jew, with the help of his Marxist catechism, triumphs over the peoples of this world, his crown will be the dance of death for mankind, and as once before, millions of years ago, this planet will again sail empty of all human life through the ether.... I believe that I am today acting according to the purposes of the almighty Creator. In resisting the Jew, I am fighting the Lord's battle.'[2] One is impelled to ask: What ever can the man have meant? What possible sense can there be in this talk of an earth empty of all human life? And the answer to these questions, when one faces up to it, goes a long way to explain the monstrous deeds perpetrated by the Germans during the Second World War. It has of course nothing to do with atomic warfare – Hitler wrote these words in 1924. What he means is that only a tiny part of what is usually regarded as mankind consists of human beings – notably those whom he imagined to be of Nordic descent, plus, for political reasons, the Japanese. The rest – what he called the racial mish-mash – belongs not to mankind but to an inferior species. In using these creatures to kill off the ruling strata – who in his view must *ipso facto* be Nordic – the Jew is therefore literally depriving the earth of its human population. What will be left will be simply animals disguised as human beings, under the leadership of Jews, who are demonic beings disguised as human beings.

Even by the crazy standards of German racism these ideas were eccentric and extreme. Unfortunately they were held by the man who became dictator of Germany – and this meant that instead of remaining the property of some obscure group of cranks they became the creed of the SS. It was in the name of these weird fantasies, disguised as scientific truth, that the SS at the height of their power terrorized and martyrized Europe from the English Channel to the Volga. How Hitler's

[1] *Hitler's Table Talk*, ed. H. R. Trevor-Roper, London, 1953, p. 332.
[2] *Mein Kampf*, p. 70.

special version of the Jewish world-conspiracy was presented to these men is shown by a tract issued by SS headquarters:

'Just as night rises up against the day, just as light and darkness are eternal enemies, so the greatest enemy of world-dominating man is man himself. The sub-man – that creature which looks as though biologically it were of absolutely the same kind, endowed by Nature with hands, feet and a sort of brain, with eyes and mouth – is nevertheless a totally different, a fearful creature, is only an attempt at a human being, with a quasi-human face, yet in mind and spirit lower than any animal. Inside this being a cruel chaos of wild, unchecked passions: a nameless will to destruction, the most primitive lusts, the most undisguised vileness. A sub-man – nothing else! . . . Never has the sub-man granted peace, never has he permitted rest. . . . To preserve himself he needed mud, he needed hell, but not the sun. And this underworld of sub-men found its leader: the eternal Jew!'[1]

Once such a creed was applied it could only lead to massacre. The victims were not only the six million Jews who were killed as bearers of an imaginary plague. As we have seen, in Hitler's eyes Russia was the country in which the Jews, through the revolution, had most completely 'infected' the population, and this certainly had much to do with the extraordinary ferocity of the SS in the occupied territories of the Soviet Union. When the German attack began, Himmler announced that it was intended to kill thirty million Russians. The number of Russian dead is in fact put at twenty million; and the way in which whole armies of prisoners of war were put behind barbed wire and left to starve, and whole villages of men and women herded into barns to be burned alive, is certainly connected with the fact that these people were regarded as sub-human beings, bastardized by the Jews and enlisted in their service.

As for the Jews, it is possible that Hitler always intended to exterminate them. In his very first political pronouncement, the Gemlich letter of 1919, he already talked of their 'removal altogether'; Dietrich Eckart records him as saying that it would be useless to destroy synagogues and Jewish schools, as the Jewish spirit is incarnate in every single Jew and will

[1] L. Poliakov and J. Wulf, *Das Dritte Reich und die Juden*, pp. 120–1.

operate so long as any Jews exist. Admittedly in those early days his public speeches avoided all reference to massacre, but even then he sometimes let fall some ominous phrases. 'What is preparing today will be greater than the world war. It will be fought out on German soil for the whole world! Only two possibilities exist: we will be either the sacrificial lamb or the victor.'[1] This comes from a speech of 1923 and the subject is the struggle against the Jews. More ominous still is a passage in *Mein Kampf* which clearly foreshadows what was to happen in the extermination camps twenty years later. Germany, says Hitler, lost the war only because Jewish Marxists sapped the will to fight; and he continues: 'If at the beginning of the war or during the war 12,000 or 15,000 of these corrupters of the people had been held under poison gas . . . the sacrifice of millions at the front would not have been in vain. On the contrary, the removal of 12,000 rascals at the right time would perhaps have saved the lives of a million decent Germans, so valuable for the future.'[2]

Elsewhere in *Mein Kampf* he speaks of the overthrow of 'world-Jewry' with a truly apocalyptic fervour. We have seen how in the popular Christianity of the Middle Ages, and also in the eccentric Christianity of Sergey Nilus, the Jews were regarded as servants of Antichrist and destined for the same fate – to be destroyed, in preparation for the millennium, by Christ returning in majesty. Now in the Book of Revelation Antichrist is shown as trying to storm heaven and being cast down to hell; and the curious thing is that Hitler, though he loathed Christianity, was quite capable of using these age-old Biblical images when speaking of the fate of the Jews. 'The Jew goes his fatal way,' he wrote, 'until the day when another power stands up against him and in a mighty struggle casts him, the heaven-stormer, back to Lucifer.'[3] The apocalyptic feeling is unmistakable, and something of this was taken over by Himmler and the SS. At least at certain moments these people regarded the extermination of the Jews as a necessary prelude to some kind of Germanic millennium. Again it is worth considering the inside evidence provided by Wisliceny: 'While [Himmler] took the advice of astrologers and inclined

[1] *Adolf Hitler, sein Leben und seine Reden*, ed. A. V. von Koerber, Munich, 1923, p. 106.   [2] *Mein Kampf*, p. 772.   [3] Ibid., p. 751.

towards all the occult arts, the SS gradually turned into a new kind of religious sect. . . .' It was less new than Wisliceny supposed: medieval Europe too had known apocalyptic sects which believed that they had a divinely ordained mission to purify the world by exterminating the Jews.[1]

Wisliceny also said that in Hitler's mind the war of 1939 was above all the final struggle against Jewry; and from 1939 onwards Hitler himself publicly talked of the war in just those terms. As we have seen, German editors of the *Protocols* had always insisted that the First World War was the work of the Jews; now Hitler blamed them for the war he was about to inflict on the world, and at the same time prophesied the genocide he was about to carry out. In a speech to the Reichstag on 30 January 1939 he declared: 'Today I will once more be a prophet: if the international Jewish financiers in and outside Europe should succeed in plunging the nations once more into a world war, then the result will not be the bolshevization of the earth, and thus the victory of Jewry, but the annihilation of the Jewish race in Europe.'[2]

This prophecy provided a theme on which Hitler continued to embroider throughout the war. He repeated his threat before the Reichstag on 1 September 1939, at the very moment of the invasion of Poland. On 30 January 1941 he repeated it in the Sportspalast in Berlin: 'And I should not like to forget the hint which I already gave once before, on 1 September 1939, in the German Reichstag – that should the other world be plunged into a general war, Jewry as a whole will have played out its role in Europe. They can laugh at this today, just as they laughed at my prophecies before. The coming months and years will prove that here too I saw correctly.'[3]

In June 1941 the invasion of the Soviet Union and with it the extermination of the Russian Jews began, and by 30 January 1942 Hitler was able to speak with even greater confidence: 'We fully realize that this war can end only either in the extermination of the Aryan peoples or in the disappearance of Jewry in Europe. I said it already in the German Reichstag on

[1] Cf. N. Cohn, *The Pursuit of the Millennium*, revised editions, London and New York, 1961–62, pp. 49–65, 92–4.

[2] M. Domarus, *Hitler, Reden und Proklamationen, 1932–1945*, Neustadt/Aisch, 1962–63, Vol. II, p. 30.   [3] Ibid., p. 1663.

1 September 1939 – and I am careful not to make rash prophecies – that this war will not end as the Jews imagine, namely, in the extermination of the European Aryan peoples, but
that its outcome will be the annihilation of Jewry.'[1] In the
course of 1942 extermination camps were set up in Poland, to
which Jews were deported from all over Europe. In the New
Year message for 1943 Hitler was able to announce: 'I said
that the hope of international Jewry, that it would destroy
the German and other European peoples in a new world war,
will be the biggest mistake Jewry has made in thousands of
years; that it will destroy not the German people but itself –
and about that there is today no doubt. . . .'[2]
These were all public statements, made by the Führer to the
German people at large – explanations, as it were, of the policy
adopted by the German Government to combat the latest
manoeuvres of 'the international Jewish financiers', alias the
Elders of Zion. Again one is bound to ask how far they re-
flected Hitler's own beliefs – and again one finds complete
identity. Speaking privately with Himmler in October 1941
Hitler said: 'By exterminating this pest, we shall do humanity
a service of which our soldiers can have no idea. . . . From the
rostrum of the Reichstag I prophesied to Jewry that, in the
event of war's proving inevitable, the Jew would disappear
from Europe. That race of criminals has on its conscience the
two million (German) dead of the first world war, and now
hundreds of thousands more. . . .'[3] In the last weeks before he
committed suicide he returned to the theme: 'I have played
straight with the Jews. On the eve of war I gave them a last
warning. I warned them that if they again plunged the world
into war, they would not be spared this time – that the vermin
would be finally exterminated in Europe. They replied to this
warning by a declaration of war. . . . We have pierced the
Jewish abscess. The world of the future will be eternally
grateful to us.'[4] In the political testament which he dictated

[1] Ibid., Vol. II, pp. 1828–9.
[2] *Deutschland im Kampf*, ed. A. I. Berndt and Oberst Wedel, No. 81
(January 1943), p. 45.
[3] *Hitler's Table Talk*, pp. 79, 87.
[4] *Le Testament Politique de Hitler. Notes recueillies par Martin Bor-
mann*, Paris, 1959, p. 86.

on the night of 28–29 April 1945 (he shot himself on the 30th) he again insisted: 'It is untrue that I, or anybody else in Germany, wanted war in 1939. It was wanted and provoked exclusively by those international politicians who either came of Jewish stock, or worked for Jewish interests. . . .' And in the closing words of the testament, the last words he ever wrote, he summoned the elite of the German nation 'to merciless opposition to the world-poisoner of all peoples, international Jewry'.[1]

What is one to make of these utterances? The circumstances in which they were made show that they were in a sense sincere – yet how can Hitler possibly have believed that the Jews had caused the war which he himself had brought about? The answer can only be that for Hitler anything which opposed his own limitless craving for domination was automatically felt as part of the Jewish world-conspiracy. And that does indeed seem to have been the case at every stage of his career, including the war. Any nation, large or small, that attempted to defend its territory or its interests against the insatiable claims of Nazi Germany showed by that very fact that it was a tool in the hands of the Elders of Zion.

As one reflects on the implications of this, further questions present themselves. It has sometimes been argued that Hitler was simply a super-Machiavellian, a man without convictions or loyalties, an utter cynic for whom the whole aim and value of life consisted in power and more power. There certainly was such a Hitler – but the other Hitler, the haunted man obsessed by fantasies about the Jewish world-conspiracy, was just as real.[2] What one would like to know is just how far the near-lunatic was active even in the calculating opportunist. How much of the dynamism behind that astonishing career – from the creation of the Nazi party, through the struggle for power and the establishment of the dictatorship and the terror – how much of all this came from a secret dream of overthrowing the Jewish world-conspiracy by exterminating the Jews? An unanswerable question, no doubt – but one that

[1] In H. R. Trevor-Roper, *The Last Days of Hitler*, London, 1950, pp. 195, 198.

[2] Cf. E. Faul, 'Hitlers Ueber-Machiavellismus', in *Vierteljahreshefte für Zeitgeschichte*, Vol. 2 (1954), and notably p. 368.

occurred even to some important Nazis, though of course they put it differently. 'For what else,' asked the supreme judge of the party, Walter Buch, writing in the party's legal journal during the war, 'for what else did we struggle, take upon us want and deprivation, for what else did the courageous men of the SA and the SS, the boys of the Hitler Youth fall, if not for the possibility that one day the German people might start its struggle for liberation against the Jewish oppressors? In this struggle we are now involved. . . . Victory will be attained by Adolf Hitler. . . .'[1]

And again: to what extent did Hitler and his immediate associates model themselves on the imaginary Elders of Zion? According to Rauschning he took the *Protocols* as his primer for politics; and in the 1930s three whole books were written to show how in almost every particular Nazi policy followed the plan laid down there.[2] The argument can be pushed too far, but that does not mean it is wholly false. It is worth reflecting on two more recent judgements. 'The Nazis,' writes Hannah Arendt, 'started with the fiction of a conspiracy and modelled themselves, more or less consciously, after the secret society of the Elders of Zion . . .';[3] while Léon Poliakov comments that the Nazi leaders began by drugging themselves with sensational sub-literature of the type of the *Protocols* and ended by translating these morbid fantasies into a reality terrible beyond imagining.[4] There is a good deal in this. The ruthless struggle of a band of conspirators to achieve world-domination – a world-empire based on a small but highly organized and regimented people – utter contempt for humanity at large – a glorying in destruction and mass misery – all these things are to be found in the *Protocols*, and they were of the very essence of the Nazi régime. To put it with all due caution: in this preposterous fabrication from the days of the Russian pogroms Hitler heard the call of a kindred spirit, and he responded to it·with all his being.

[1] Quoted in M. Weinreich, *Hitler's Professors*, New York, 1946, p. 89.
[2] See Bibliographical Note.
[3] Hannah Arendt, *The Origins of Totalitarianism* (2nd edition), London, 1958, p. 366.
[4] L. Poliakov, preface to *Le IIIe Reich et les Juifs* (French edition), Paris, 1959.

CHAPTER IX

The Myth in Nazi Propaganda

1

THE *Protocols* and the myth of the Jewish world-conspiracy were exploited in Nazi propaganda at every stage, from the first emergence of the party in the early 1920s to the collapse of the Third Reich in 1945. They were exploited first to help the party to power – then to justify a régime of terror – then to justify war – then to justify genocide – and finally to postpone surrender to the Allies. The history of the myth during those years, of the changing purposes it was made to serve, mirrors faithfully the rise and fall of the Third Reich itself.

In the early days the chief propagator of the myth and of the *Protocols* was Alfred Rosenberg, the official 'ideologist' of the party. Rosenberg was a Balt of less purely German descent than he liked to pretend (one of his grandfathers was a Lett). As he came from Reval his original nationality was Russian, and even after the revolution he still took his examination as an architect in Moscow. He was in his mid-twenties when the revolution roused his interest in politics and turned him into a fanatical anti-Bolshevik. In 1918 he attached himself to the German troops on their withdrawal from Russia – like Vinberg, whom he knew well and who influenced him deeply. In Germany he joined the newly founded Nazi party and became an intimate associate of Hitler's.

Although he was never taken very seriously by Hitler and was already losing influence before the party came to power, Rosenberg left a permanent mark on Nazi ideology. The party was rabidly antisemitic from the moment of its foundation in 1919, but it became obsessed with Russian communism only in 1921–22; and this seems to have been largely Rosenberg's doing. He provided the link between Russian antisemitism of

the Black Hundred type and the antisemitism of the German
racists; more precisely, he took over Vinberg's view of
Bolshevism as a Jewish conspiracy and reinterpreted it in
völkisch-racist terms. The resulting fantasy, as expounded in
innumerable articles and pamphlets, became an obsessive
theme in Hitler's thinking and in the outlook and propaganda
of the Nazi party.

Rosenberg was the most educated of the Nazi leaders, but
that is not saying much. Although he set himself up as an
expert on Bolshevism, he never read a word of Marx or
Engels, never studied the history or theory of socialism, knew
nothing at all about the Russian revolutionary movement. It
was enough to know that Kerensky was a Jew called Kirbis
[*sic*] and that Lenin was a 'Kalmuk-Tartar' (he should have
compared notes with Hitler who, as we have seen, had his own
ideas about this). Much of his information was undoubtedly
supplied by Vinberg and other right-wing Russian émigrés –
many of his articles in the party newspaper, the *Völkischer
Beobachter*, were almost entirely based on *Luch Sveta*, while
large parts of his *magnum opus*, the unreadable *Myth of the
Twentieth Century*, were lifted straight from Vinberg's writings.

Between 1919 and 1923 Rosenberg produced, in addition to
innumerable articles, five pamphlets on the world-conspiracy
of the Jews (with or without the Freemasons), an abbreviated
translation of that notable nineteenth-century forerunner,
Gougenot des Mousseaux, and a whole volume of commentary
on the *Protocols*. And whereas his bulky *Myth of the Twentieth
Century* was read by hardly anybody (and certainly not by the
Nazi leaders), these early pamphlets had considerable influence. Typical of them all is *Pest in Russland* (*Plague in
Russia*), published in 1922. Here we learn that tsarist Russia
earned the hostility of Jews not (as one might have supposed)
by pogroms and oppression but by its resistance to finance
capitalism. In order to overcome this obstacle and at the same
time to punish the recalcitrant Russians, the Jews used their
dialectic skill, developed in centuries of commenting on the
Talmud, upon the Russian masses, who were easily misled
into exterminating the national élite. This enabled Jewish
Bolsheviks to nationalize Russian industry – which meant
simply appropriating it for the enrichment of themselves and

of their friends and relatives abroad. It remained only to organize the Red Army around a core of Letts and (a startling novelty) former Chinese silk-merchants – and the Russian people could at last be forced to submit to capitalism.

In all this a special role was reserved for Walther Rathenau. As Rosenberg saw it, Rathenau was closely connected with those all-powerful Jewish Bolsheviks in the Soviet Union; they shared with him the wealth they derived from Russian industry, while in return he arranged, through the Treaty of Rapallo, for the German people to be exploited in the interest of 'stock exchange and Soviet Jews'. If he and his like had their way, Letts and Chinese under Jewish command would soon be shooting down German workers. And who could deny that such people were 'long since ripe for prison and gallows'? Shortly after the appearance of this booklet Rathenau was assassinated by young men holding precisely these views. It was an appropriate beginning to a career which was to end, a generation later, with Rosenberg's execution as a major war criminal.

These writings of Rosenberg's are of course political propaganda, designed to serve the Nazi party in its struggle for power – but their atmosphere is one, rather, of apocalyptic prophecy. As we have seen, Hitler himself had his apocalyptic moments; with Rosenberg, however, it was a matter not of moments but of a permanent cast of mind. 'The Jew stands in our history as our metaphysical opposite,' he wrote in 1923, at the end of his commentary on the *Protocols*. 'That was *never* clearly grasped by us. . . . *Today* at last it seems as if the eternally foreign and hostile, now that it has climbed to such monstrous power, is felt and hated as such. For the first time in history instinct and knowledge attain clear consciousness. The Jew stands at the very top of the peak of power which he has so eagerly climbed, and awaits his fall into the abyss. The last fall. After that, there will be no place for the Jew in Europe or America. Today there begins, in the midst of the collapse of a whole world, a new era, a fundamental rejection in all fields of many ideas inherited from the past. One of the advance signs of the coming struggle for the new organization of the world is this understanding of the very nature of the demon which has caused our present downfall. Then the way will be open for a new age.'[1] That is how Rosenberg felt about the *Protocols* in 1923; a decade later a new edition of his work carried a foreword – which he must have approved if not written – celebrating the advent of the Third Reich: 'The luminous people in the centre – Germany – struggles up out of the claws of the Jewish world-entanglement to a mighty rebirth, it tears the meshes of the net in which it was caught by Talmudic trappers, and like a phoenix rises from the ashes of a burnt-out materialistic philosophy. The German Reich stands in the focus of the world, and a purified nation reveals itself for those who can see, shining brightly, like a new dawn of creation. The spirits of the underworld shrink back appalled before this rising-up ... Jewry, the spirit of decay, the dark demon of creative peoples, feels itself smitten to the heart. The circle of the Jewish plans for world-domination was not yet quite closed, it was too soon to drive the peoples yet again into a bloody war with one another.... May the new edition of this book reveal yet again to the German people in what a delusion they were imprisoned, before the great German movement shattered it ... and how deeply this perception was rooted amongst the leaders of National-Socialism from the very beginning of the movement.'[2]

Rosenberg was a simple soul and he really believed the balderdash he wrote. Josef Goebbels, who became the party's propaganda chief in 1928, was much more of a cynic, and the propaganda he put out consisted mostly of deliberate lies. A fine example is the variation on the *Protocols* which he sponsored in December 1929. Under the heading 'Slave Market' there appeared, on placards and in party journals, the latest decision of the international Jewish financiers: since Germany was unable to pay reparations in full, she must make up the deficit by exporting young men and women. These would be specially selected by the Jewish masters of Germany; young Jews would of course be exempt. 'Translated from Yiddish into German, that means: Forced export of German people. Of that there can be no doubt.' The source of this tale was

---

[1] A. Rosenberg, *Die Protokolle der Weisen von Zion und die jüdische Weltpolitik*, Munich, 1923, p. 147.
[2] Preface to 1933 edition of Rosenberg's *Protokolle*.

given as the *Berliner Tageblatt* – a perfectly respectable newspaper where no word of all this had ever appeared.[1]

This story figured in the campaign preceding the Reichstag
election of 1930, which marked the beginning of the spec-
tacular rise of the Nazi party. Between 1928 and 1933 the
party soared from ninth place in the Reichstag, with less than
one million votes and only twelve seats, to an easy first, with
more than seventeen million votes and 288 seats. Each stage
in the rise was accompanied by further floods of antisemitic
propaganda. It would be easy to argue – and it often has been
argued – that the party's success was mainly due to its antisemitism, even that anyone who voted Nazi must have been a
fanatical antisemite. And yet . . .

Hitler would never have come to power without the world
depression, which at one time brought the number of regis-
tered unemployed in Germany to six million and plunged
almost the whole population – the middle classes and the
peasantry as well as the industrial workers – into chronic
misery and anxiety. In such an atmosphere – which was all
the more desperate because the country was only just re-
covering from the earlier shocks of military defeat and a
devastating inflation – Hitler could deploy the whole range of
his demagogy. He attacked the victorious Allies, especially the
French, for enslaving the German people; and the German
republican régime, for its failure to cope with the crisis; and
the parties of the Left, for dividing the nation; and the parties
of the Right, for their ineffectiveness; and the plutocrats and
monopolists, for exploiting everyone else. In fact he attacked
everybody, even if his most ferocious attacks were reserved
for the Jews. And above all he offered a show of iron determination, of readiness to act and act radically, in a society
unaccustomed to the uncertainties which are inseparable from
democracy – and especially from new and inexperienced
democracy. All these things helped Hitler to power – or rather,
helped him to the 37·3 per cent of the total vote which was the
most he ever obtained in a truly free election (July 1932). And
the one thing on which all witnesses seem to agree is that the
Germany in which Hitler came to power was not in fact a
country gripped in a frenzy of antisemitism, hypnotized by the

[1] *C. V. Zeitung*, Vol. VIII (1929), p. 561, and Vol. IX (1930), p. 15.

myth of the Jewish world-conspiracy and thirsting for the blood of the Jews. Admittedly the most popular edition of the *Protocols* had sold nearly 100,000 copies in a dozen years – but Remarque's famous anti-war and left-wing novel *All Quiet on the Western Front*, published in 1929, sold a quarter of a million copies in a single year, and plenty of other 'progressive' novels also enjoyed big sales.

Nor can it be taken for granted that even the whole of the Nazi party itself, with its relatively small membership of about one million, was fanatically antisemitic. In 1934 an enterprising American sociologist, Theodore Abel, advertised for life-histories by members of the party, showing what led them to join. Six hundred members voluntarily sent in their autobiographies. The astonishing fact is that 60 per cent of these Nazis never mentioned antisemitism at all. Some even expressly dissociated themselves from this aspect of party policy: 'It quickened my pulse to hear about the Fatherland, unity and the need for a supreme leader. I felt that I belonged to these people. Only their statements about the Jews I could not swallow. They gave me a headache even after I had joined the party.' Moreover, statistical analysis showed that whereas antisemitic sentiments figured in nearly half the life-histories supplied by members of the middle classes, including the liberal professions, they figured in less than 30 per cent of those supplied by industrial or agricultural workers.[1] If real commitment to the antisemitic cause was as exceptional inside the party as this survey suggests, it can hardly have been widespread in the mass of the population which did not join the party.

Yet when all qualifications are made, it remains true that very many of the seventeen million who voted Nazi in 1933 must have been willing to expose their Jewish fellow-citizens at least to some loss of civil liberties. And there can be no doubt, either, that there were plenty of fanatical anti-semites, for instance in the national student movement (which had been captured by the Nazis in 1931) and among the 400,000 members of the SA (Storm Troop) – some hundreds of thousands who would have agreed with the contributor to Abel's collection who said: 'The history of the world would

[1] T. Abel, *Why Hitler Came into Power*, New York, 1938, p. 164.

have lost its meaning if Judaism, with its corroding spirit, the embodiment of all evil, were to win the victory over the true and good encompassed in Adolf Hitler's idea. My belief is that our leader, Adolf Hitler, was given by fate to the German nation as our saviour, bringing light into darkness.'[1] Such were the fruits of fifty years of propaganda, culminating in fourteen years of intensive, virulent, unrelenting propaganda since the war, operating above all on the young. They were deadly fruits, for it was precisely this mixture of the fanaticism of a minority with the indifference of the many that made possible the whole development, from the first restrictions to the final extermination.[2]

In February 1933 Hitler became Chancellor, and on 1 April the persecution of the Jews began with a compulsory one-day boycott of Jewish shops. Already in justification of this first antisemitic measure the *Protocols* were invoked – notably by Julius Streicher in the *Völkischer Beobachter*. The 'Plan of Basel,'[3] he declared, had been on the point of fulfilment, but 'on Saturday, 1 April, at 10 a.m., the German people begins defensive action against the Jewish world-criminals! National-Socialists! Strike down the world-enemy!'[4] The boycott was a try-out; as nobody protested, the Government proceeded to introduce antisemitic legislation. Very soon Jews were excluded from the civil service and the liberal professions, and in

[1] Ibid., p. 243.
[2] The findings of W. S. Allen, in *The Nazi Seizure of Power: the experience of a single German town, 1930–1935*, Chicago 1965, pp. 77–8 and 209–12, suggest that the divergence between the fanatical Nazis and the bulk of the population was even greater than is indicated here. Whereas for the fanatics antisemitism was a deadly serious matter, most people regarded the antisemitic propaganda as so much talk, which was quite unrelated to the Jews they knew personally and would in any case not lead to serious persecution. Allen's study concerns a single middle-sized town in Hanover and his findings are not necessarily valid for the whole country. This much however seems certain: antisemitism played only a limited part in bringing Hitler to power, but indifference played an important part in facilitating the subsequent persecution. See below, pp. 210–13.
[3] 'Plan of Basel' because the *Protocols* were supposed to have originated at the first Zionist congress at Basel.
[4] Article by Streicher in the *Völkischer Beobachter*, issue of 31 March 1933.

September 1935 the Nuremberg Laws finally cast them out from the community of the German nation. And in the non-stop propaganda campaign which accompanied these measures the *Protocols* and the Jewish world-conspiracy bulked very large indeed. The *Völkischer Beobachter* invoked them constantly, while Streicher's weekly *Der Stürmer* alternated between elaborations of the *Protocols* and lurid stories of German maidens raped by Jews and German children ritually murdered. The efforts of *Der Stürmer* were particularly important, for this vile paper had a circulation of nearly half a million – one of the biggest of any German periodical – and it was also displayed on special notice-boards in towns and villages throughout the country; most sinister of all, it was used in schools.

The *Protocols* themselves were officially advertised. The new party edition of 1933 carried an urgent appeal to every citizen: 'It is the duty of every German to study the terrifying avowal of the Elders of Zion, and to compare them with the boundless misery of our people; and then to draw the necessary conclusions and to see to it that this book comes into the hands of every German. ... We, German racists, must be grateful to Providence for illumining our path precisely at the moment when all seemed lost. Difficult struggles await us. The first task is to disintoxicate the soul of the German people and to wake its understanding of the nobility of the Aryan race. With God, for the resurrection of Germany!'[1] The *Protocols* did in fact sell excellently – and, unlike that other sacred text of the Third Reich, *Mein Kampf*, they were not only purchased but read. And it is certain, too, that many of those who read them became fanatical believers.[2] In less than two years after Hitler's accession to power intellectual and moral standards in Germany had dropped to a point where a Minister of Education could prescribe the *Protocols* as one of the basic textbooks for schools.

These developments did not affect the Jews alone. In

[1] *Die Geheimnisse der Weisen von Zion*, Parteiverlag, Munich, 1933, p. 21.
[2] F. Bauer, 'Antinazistische Prozesse und politisches Bewusstsein', in *Antisemitismus: zur Pathologie der bürgerlichen Gesellschaft*, ed. H. Huss and A. Schröder, Frankfort/Main, 1965, p. 177.

tsarist Russia the myth of the Jewish world-conspiracy had been used as a means of discrediting the revolutionary movement; in the Weimar Republic it had been used by the Nazis as a means of discrediting the democratic régime; now in the Third Reich it was used as a means not only of discrediting possible opponents of the dictatorship but also of justifying the whole régime of terror. Writing in 1935 Reinhard Heydrich, Himmler's principal lieutenant, noted that all oppositional organizations had been smashed – but at the same time insisted that the Judeo-Masonic world-conspiracy was still pursuing its aim of undermining, poisoning, and destroying the German people. 'We must learn, from the history of the last few thousand years, to recognize the enemy. Then we shall suddenly see that we are today, for the first time, grasping the enemy at the very roots of his strength. Can one wonder that he defends himself all the more fiercely?' He admitted that this supposed activity of the great conspiracy was so little evident that it was almost impossible to detect: 'When after the seizure of power all visible opposition disappeared and the spiritual struggle began, many of our SS lacked the arms for this struggle because they failed to recognize the all-embracing nature of the enemy.' Nevertheless he insisted: 'We fighters must face it: We need years of bitter struggle to drive back the enemy finally in all fields, to destroy him and to make Germany secure, in its blood and its spirit, against new penetrations by the enemy.'[1]

What this meant in practice was that anyone whom the régime wished to persecute and destroy, for whatever reason, could be denounced as an agent of the perennial Jewish world-conspiracy. It also meant that to deny the reality of that world-conspiracy was to label oneself as an enemy of the régime and to expose oneself to persecution and destruction. So an anti-semitic myth originally concocted by a few eccentric priests in reaction against the French Revolution became in the 1930s a device by which a despotic government could consolidate its hold over a great European nation.

The myth of the Jewish world-conspiracy was also a means

---

[1] Quoted in H. Buchheim, *Die SS – Das Herrschaftsinstrument. Befehl und Gehorsam* (vol. I of *Anatomie des SS-Staates*), Olten and Freiburg im Breisgau, 1965, pp. 114–15.

by which the Government tried to make its foreign policy acceptable to the German people. That policy aimed at war, but that is an aim which no modern European government – not even Hitler's – could openly admit. From 1933 onwards German foreign policy was therefore presented as above all a defence against a deadly encirclement organized by the Jews. In particular the Soviet Union was portrayed as Hitler had always imagined it – as a land of sub-men ruled by Jews. Goebbels regularly distinguished himself by his outbursts on this subject at the annual party rallies at Nuremberg. In 1935 he declared that Bolshevism was a Satanic plot which could have been hatched only in the brain of a nomad; while Nazi Germany was a bulwark against which the Asiatic-Jewish flood would break in vain. A year later he announced that Bolshevism was pathological and criminal nonsense concocted and organized by the Jews for the purpose of destroying the European nations and establishing world-domination on their ruins.[1] Streicher also had some eloquent things to say. When the Soviet Union was at last admitted to the League of Nations, in 1935, he argued that the governments of the democracies which had supported this move must consist of those famous 300 men mentioned by Rathenau – 'and those 300 men are members of the Jewish race and conspirators of Freemasonry'.[2]

Meanwhile various diligent researchers were producing works with titles like *Jews Behind Stalin* to show that everyone of any importance in the Soviet Union was a Jew. As in reality almost all the Jews who were at all prominent in the Soviet Communist party were just then being liquidated by Stalin, this was no easy task – but it was accomplished just the same, by the simple device of ascribing Jewish descent to everyone with a Latvian, Armenian, or Tartar name and to a lot of ordinary Russians as well. It is true that this procedure was soon extended beyond the Soviet Union. Soon every politician anywhere who tried to thwart Hitler's plans – starting with Roosevelt – was declared to be a Jew, a half-Jew, or at least

[1] On Goebbels's antisemitic propaganda 1935–38 see E. K. Bramsted, *Goebbels and National Socialist Propaganda 1925–1945*, Michigan State U.P., 1965, and Z. A. B. Zeman, *Nazi Propaganda*, London, 1964.

[2] J. Streicher, 'Der Feind des Völkerfriedens', in *Der Judenkenner*, No. 5 (March 1935), p. 94.

married to a Jewess. Enormous quantities of propaganda along these lines were put out by Goebbels's Propaganda Ministry – where little of it was believed – and by various party offices under Rosenberg – where rather more was believed. Strange contortions were performed in 1939–40, to fit the needs of the German-Soviet non-aggression pact; it was even discovered that the Soviet Union was not ruled by Jews at all and that the whole idea had been a deception practised on simple Germans by a Judaised Britain. This, however, taxed the ingenuity even of Goebbels, and it must have been a relief when in 1941 the identification of Jews with Communists proved to have been right after all.

Yet whatever other targets this propaganda might be directed against and whatever other purposes it might be made to serve, its main target was always the Jews themselves, and its main purpose was to present these human beings as demonic beings. At the end of that path lies murder – and already before the war those who dealt in the *Protocols* were hinting at a possibility which was beginning to take shape in their imagination. By the end of 1936 *Der Stürmer* was looking forward to a world-wide cleansing operation: 'The mobilization of the German people's will to destroy the bacillus lodged in its body is a declaration of war on all Jews throughout the world. Its final result will decide the problem whether the world is to be redeemed by German virtues or to perish by the Jewish poison. . . . We believe in the final victory of the German people and thus in the liberation of all non-Jewish humanity. Those who vanquish the world-Jew will save the earth from the Devil.'[1] At the Nuremberg party rally of 1937 Goebbels excelled himself: 'Europe must see and recognize the danger. . . . We shall point fearlessly to the Jew as the inspirer and originator, the one who profits from these dreadful catastrophes. . . . Look, there is the world's enemy, the destroyer of civilizations, the parasite among the peoples, the son of Chaos, the incarnation of evil, the ferment of decomposition, the demon who brings about the degeneration of mankind.'[2]

---

[1] Quoted in L. W. Bondy, *Racketeers of Hatred. Julius Streicher and the Jew-baiters' International*, London, 1946, pp. 36–7.

[2] Text in *Der Parteitag der Arbeit* (i.e. proceedings of the 1937 congress), Zentralverlag der NSDAP, Munich, 1938, p. 157.

By October 1938 it was possible to be more precise, and *Der Stürmer* could write of the Jews: 'Bacteria, vermin and pests cannot be tolerated. For reasons of cleanliness and hygiene we must make them harmless by *killing them off*.'[1]

All this would have been mere rhetoric if it had not been for the war, which by 1941 placed the majority of European Jews in Hitler's power and gave him vast and remote spaces in which to carry out the exterminations.[2] As we have seen, Hitler defined his war as a war waged by 'world Jewry' against National-Socialist Germany; and once the exterminations began this became a constant theme in internal German propaganda. Not that the propaganda ever spoke unambiguously of mass executions and gassing (that was strictly forbidden), but it constantly hinted that the Jews were being made to pay for the war with their lives. It was a curious manoeuvre, as though the Nazi leaders were trying to involve the whole German people in their own guilt, yet without ever really admitting that guilt.

Very soon after the German forces invaded Russia a booklet appeared under the sponsorship of Goebbels and with the title *German Soldiers See the Soviet Union*. 'The Jewish question,' it reported, 'is being solved with imposing thoroughness. . . . As the Führer put it . . .: "Should Jewry succeed in inciting the European nations to a senseless war, this will mean the end of this race in Europe!" The Jew ought to have known that the Führer is accustomed to take his word seriously, and now he has to bear the consequences. They are inexorably hard but necessary if ultimately quiet and peace are to reign among nations.'[3] By November 1941 Goebbels himself was in effect publicly justifying the killing of Jews. 'In this historical contest,' he declared, 'each Jew is our enemy. . . . All Jews by virtue of their birth and race belong to an international conspiracy against National-Socialist Germany. . . . Each German soldier who falls in this war goes to the debt account of the

---

[1] Quoted in Bondy, op. cit., p. 61.

[2] Already before the war hundreds of German Jews were killed in the concentration camps; but the number of political prisoners who perished was far greater. It was the war that opened up the possibility of destroying the Jewish population of Europe.

[3] Quoted in M. Weinreich, *Hitler's Professors*, New York, 1946, p. 141.

Jews. He is on their conscience and they, therefore, must pay
for it.'[1] In a speech at Karlsruhe in May 1942 the head of the
German Labour Front, Robert Ley went further still: 'It is
not enough to isolate the Jewish enemy of mankind – the Jew
has got to be exterminated.'[2] In the same month the party
journal *Volk und Rasse* announced: 'A right understanding of
Jewry must require its complete annihilation.'[3]

By 1943 even the antiquated myth of Jewish ritual murder
was being revived. In the 1930s this theme had been practically
reserved for Streicher and *Der Stürmer*, but now men with
university doctorates began to produce solemn tomes to show
that ritual murder represented in miniature what the war
demonstrated on a grand scale – the Jewish plan to kill off all
Christians. Himmler was so enchanted by one of these books
that he distributed copies throughout the senior ranks of the
SS and sent hundreds more to be distributed to the extermination squads in Russia. And he had another bright idea:
'We must at once employ investigators in England[4] to follow
and check the reports of trials and police announcements concerning missing children, so that we can include short announcements in our broadcasts, that a child has disappeared in
such-and-such a place, and that this is probably the result of a
Jewish ritual murder. . . . I am of the opinion that we could
give antisemitism an incredible virulence by means of antisemitic propaganda in English, perhaps even in Russian,
giving special publicity to ritual murders.'[5]

It was a delusion shared by Hitler, Himmler, and Goebbels
that British and American morale could be undermined by
propaganda about the Jewish world-conspiracy. This propaganda did indeed have some effect in France and even in
Britain in the winter of 1939–40, when there was a good deal
of vague talk about 'the Jews' war'; but it had less and less
effect thereafter, and it was a fantastic miscalculation that led
Goebbels in 1943 to devote from 70 per cent to 80 per cent of

[1] Quoted in Weinreich, op. cit., pp. 144–5.
[2] Quoted in Bondy, op. cit., p. 157.
[3] Quoted in Weinreich, op. cit., p. 185.
[4] [sic] A novel use for spies in wartime!
[5] Text in L. Poliakov and J. Wulf, *Das Dritte Reich und die Juden*,
Berlin-Grunewald, 1955, p. 360.

all foreign broadcasts to antisemitic themes.[1] The Nazi leaders were however so firmly locked in their delusion that they really expected big antisemitic movements to arise in Britain and the United States, overthrow the democratic régimes, make peace with Germany and join in the work of exterminating the Jews. Some insight into their state of mind is provided by Johann von Leers,[2] whom Rosenberg had imposed on the University of Jena as a full professor and who specialized in the *Protocols*, *The Rabbi's Speech*, and tales of ritual murder. This is what he had to say in the foreword to his book *Die Verbrechernatur der Juden* (*The Criminal Nature of the Jews*), in 1942:

> If the hereditary criminal nature of Jewry can be demonstrated, then not only is each people morally justified in exterminating the hereditary criminals – but any people that still keeps and protects Jews is just as guilty of an offence against public safety as someone who cultivates cholera-germs without observing the proper precautions.

By this time the fortunes of war were turning against Germany, and so the Jewish world-conspiracy was invoked to reinforce the German will to fight on. In February 1943 the *Deutscher Wochendienst* (*German Weekly Service*), which consisted of confidential instructions issued by Goebbels for the benefit of writers and speakers on politics, made the following recommendation: 'Stress: If we lose the war, we do not fall into the hands of some other states, but will all be annihilated by world Jewry. Jewry is firmly decided to exterminate all Germans. International law and international custom will be no protection against the Jewish will for total annihilation.'[3] This of course was cynical and calculated propaganda, but it was something else as well: a barely disguised description of what Germans were at that moment doing to Jews. For as Germany's chances of winning the war diminished, the drive to exterminate the Jews took on a quality of fury and desperation – as though the Nazi leaders were resolved that this

---

[1] *The Goebbels Diaries*, ed. Louis P. Lochner, London, 1948, p. 287.

[2] After the war von Leers fled, became a Moslem and, under the name of Omar Amin, worked as an adviser to President Nasser on propaganda. He died in 1965.

[3] Quoted in R. Hilberg, *The Destruction of the European Jews*, Chicago, 1961, p. 655.

united in a passionate determination to defeat the Jewish
world-conspiracy. Confronted with the almost unbelievable
fact of five or six million murdered Jews, many in the outside
world found it easy enough, at the end of the war, to accept
this picture as accurate. But how accurate was it?

The picture that emerges from first-hand observations made
in Germany under the Nazi régime is more complex. It is
perfectly true that already by the time Hitler came to power
a large part of the German population was infected with
antisemitism – and in a form which went a good deal beyond
the rather vague prejudice current in the western democracies.
The typical German antisemite wanted to see German Jews
excluded from public office, subjected to disabilities in their
education and careers, pushed into a position of an under-
privileged minority. There, however, his demands stopped.
Unjust and uncivilized as they were, they were yet very
different from the aspirations of Hitler and his associates.

Within the first couple of years of the Nazi régime all these
demands were fulfilled and more than fulfilled. Jews disappeared from all positions of prominence and influence,
personal contacts between Jew and non-Jew practically
ceased, the mass emigration of Jews began. Now the question
was – what next? It was conceivable that the limited antisemitism of the many would expire because it no longer
had a real objective. It was also conceivable that it would be
whipped up to a higher level of intensity, transformed into a
murderous fanaticism. By exploiting the myth of the Jewish
world-conspiracy the Nazi leadership hoped to forestall the
first of these possibilities and to achieve the second. How far
did they succeed?

A very shrewd and experienced observer, Michael Müller-
Claudius, who had been studying the development of antisemitism for many years, carried out investigations in 1938
and again in 1942. After the officially organized pogrom of
9–10 November 1938, when squads of young Nazis destroyed
and looted synagogues and Jewish shops and houses throughout Germany and killed some scores of Jews, Müller-Claudius
had informal conversations with 41 party-members from all
social strata. To the casual comment, 'Well – so a start is being
made at last with carrying out the programme against the

Jews?' he got the following reactions: 26 persons, or 63 per cent of the total, expressed downright indignation at the outrages; a further 13 persons, or 32 per cent, answered non-committally; 2 persons (a student and a bank employee) approved – and they did so because they believed in the Jewish world-conspiracy. In the eyes of this 5 per cent physical violence against Jews was justified because 'terror must be met with terror'.[1]

Four years later Müller-Claudius carried out a further investigation. It was the autumn of 1942, when the remaining German Jews were being deported to an unknown destination in the east – ostensibly, to do manual labour as a contribution to the war effort. This time he put a series of skilfully designed questions to 61 party-members, again chosen from all social strata. The result was different in various respects. Only 16 persons, or 26 per cent, showed signs of concern for the Jews, while the proportion of the indifferent had risen to 69 per cent (42 persons). The proportion of fanatics, on the other hand, was unchanged: 3 persons, or 5 per cent of the total. And for this group, as before, the Jewish world-conspiracy was a self-evident fact and the extermination of the Jews an absolute necessity: 'It's obvious that the destruction of Jewry is a war-aim. Without it the final victory would not be secure.' – 'International Jewry provoked the war. . . . After the final victory the Jewish race must cease to exist.' – '(The Führer) owes it to mankind to liberate it from Jewry. . . . The Führer will order how they are to be exterminated.'[2]

These findings of Müller-Claudius, which have been sub-stantially confirmed by other careful observers, enable one to estimate with some objectivity what Hitler and Goebbels achieved and what they failed to achieve.[3] On the one hand the

[1] M. Müller-Claudius, *Der Antisemitismus und das deutsche Ver-hängnis*, Frankfort/Main, 1948, pp. 162–6.

[2] Ibid., pp. 166–72. The whole book is a most valuable study of anti-semitism in Germany from the 1920s to the end of the Third Reich, and it deserves to be much better known than it is.

[3] Expert examination of 1,000 German prisoners of war over the period 1942–44 showed 24 per cent to be more or less critical of the régime; 65 per cent to have the kind of attitude which suggests that, if they had been asked about the Jews, they would have reacted with in-difference; and 11 per cent to be fanatically Nazi. The rather higher

mass of the German population was never truly fanaticized against the Jews, it was never obsessed by the myth of the Jewish world-conspiracy, it could not really think of the war as an apocalyptic struggle against 'Eternal Jewry' – but on the other hand it dissociated itself from the Jews more and more completely as the years passed. By 1942 most people at least suspected that something dreadful was happening to the deported Jews, and an appreciable number must have known, for professional reasons, just what was happening – and few cared much. The contrast between 1938 and 1942 shows the extent to which the whole population had been conditioned not so much to positive hatred as to utter indifference.

Of course allowance has to be made for the traditional German subservience to authority; for the strain and harassment of war; for the increasingly ruthless terror which was being exercised against the population itself. Yet the fact remains that when it was realized that the inmates of lunatic asylums were being killed, there was such an outcry that the policy was promptly reversed; whereas hardly a voice was raised on behalf of the Jews. The reason seems plain enough. Anyone who spoke up for the Jews was at once labelled as a member of their conspiracy and fit only to share their fate; and very few were prepared to expose themselves and their families to such hazards. In such circumstances it is extremely tempting to disguise one's timidity by identifying oneself at least partly with the official attitude. There was no need to talk of the Elders of Zion – it was enough to agree that Jews were somehow sinister, in any case not deserving of anyone's concern. And this attitude at least the Nazi leadership managed to instil into the great majority of the population.

In the minds of most Germans, German Jews ceased altogether to be regarded as compatriots, the last traces of solidarity disappeared; as for the Jews in countries occupied

---

proportion of fanatics is not surprising, as the Müller-Claudius sample consisted entirely of people old enough to have belonged to the party by 1933 at the latest, whereas most of the prisoners of war had spent their adolescence under the Nazi régime. See Henry V. Dicks, 'Personality traits and National Socialist ideology', in *Human Relations*, Vol. III, No. 2 (June 1950), pp. 111–54, London and Ann Arbor, U.S.A.

by the Germans, hardly anyone gave them a thought. A mood of passive compliance became general. And meanwhile the fanatics, if no more numerous than before, acquired a new importance. Scattered through the civilian population and the armed forces were individuals, certainly numbering many hundreds of thousands, perhaps even a couple of million, who accepted the conspiracy-myth with all its murderous implications and who were prepared to denounce anyone who questioned it to the SD (security service). It was a state of affairs which, if it fell far short of Hitler's ideal, still enabled him to proceed unmolested with the extermination of European Jewry.[1]

The extermination itself was organized and in the main carried out by the professionals of the SD and the SS. These bodies did not by any means represent a typical cross-section of German society. They consisted mostly of volunteers who when joining already had a pretty good idea of what they might be called upon to do – and who in any case were accepted only if they had shown outstanding enthusiasm in the Hitler Youth. It would be an over-simplification to say that these men were all genuine fanatics. At the higher levels there were plenty of criminal opportunists for whom the whole murderous business was simply a chance for extortion, loot, and professional advancement. Among the camp guards there were also plenty of opportunists, who simply preferred a comfortable and privileged existence to the dangers and hardships of the front; and there were also some true sadists, hungry for the chance to beat and torture. Yet even these people needed a pretext for their activities, some excuse which would enable them to kill and kill with an easy conscience. And at every level of the SD and SS there were fanatics eager to provide just such a justification, in the form of the myth of the Jewish world-conspiracy.

So this old myth, as reinterpreted by Hitler, became part of the ideology of the most ruthless and efficient body of professional killers in all human history. The psychoanalyst Bruno Bettelheim found that the SS guards at Dachau and

[1] A subtle socio-psychological study of the German population under the Nazi régime is: Wanda von Baeyer-Katte, *Das Zerstörende in der Politik*, Heidelberg, 1958.

Buchenwald believed absolutely in the Jewish world-con-spiracy.[1] Rudolf Hoess, the commandant of Auschwitz, at the time regarded the extermination of the Jews as necessary 'so that Germany and our posterity might be freed for ever from their relentless adversaries'; and if he later decided that the extermination was wrong after all, that was only because by discrediting Germany it 'brought the Jews far closer to their ultimate objective' of world-domination.[2] For many of the SS the conspiracy-myth was in fact far more than an ideology or a world-view – it was something which took possession of their psyches, so that they were able, for instance, to burn small children alive without any conscious feelings of com-passion or of guilt.[3]

The leaders of these men expected no less of them. In October 1943, at Posen, Himmler said to a group of high-ranking SS: 'We had a moral duty towards our people, the duty to exterminate this people which wanted to exterminate us. . . . Most of you know what it means to see a pile of 100 corpses, or of 500, or of 1,000. To have gone through that, and still – with a few exceptions – to have remained decent people, that is what has toughened us. It is a glorious page of our history, which has never been written and never will be. . . .'[4] Others were less reticent still. In August 1942 Hitler and Himmler visited the Polish town of Lublin to discuss methods of extermination with the local head of the SS and SD, the Austrian, Odilo Globocnik. When a member of Hitler's suite asked whether the dead Jews should not be cremated rather than buried, 'as a future generation might think differently of these matters', General Globocnik replied: 'But, gentlemen, if after us such a cowardly and rotten generation should arise that it does not understand our work which is so good and so necessary, then, gentlemen, all National-Socialism will have been for nothing. On the contrary, bronze plaques should be put up with the inscription that it was we, we who had the

[1] B. Bettelheim, *The Informed Heart*, London, 1961, p. 226.
[2] R. Hoess, *Commandant of Auschwitz*, London, 1959, pp. 153, 178.
[3] Cf. Elie A. Cohen, *Human Behavior in the Concentration Camp*, trans. M. H. Braaksma, New York, 1953, pp. 273 seq.
[4] Text in L. Poliakov and J. Wulf, *Das Dritte Reich und die Juden*, p. 215.

courage to achieve this gigantic task.' Hitler agreed: 'Yes, my good Globocnik, that is the word, that is my opinion, too.'[1] One day the SS doctor Pfannenstiel (he was also Professor of Hygiene at the University of Marburg) visited the extermination camp of Treblinka. The camp SS gave a banquet in his honour and in his speech of thanks the doctor said: 'Your task is a great duty, a duty useful and necessary. . . . Looking at the bodies of the Jews, one understands the greatness of your good work.'[2]

These are extraordinary words and they point to an extraordinary phenomenon. In the middle of the twentieth century, in the heart of civilized Europe, there had appeared a large body of men in whom there was no trace of what traditionally had been known as conscience and humanity. These technicians of genocide went blithely about their business – and even today those of them who appear before the German courts appear quite unrepentant. No doubt many factors – of innate temperament and childhood experience and later training – combined to produce this result. It is still true that in order to do what they did these men needed an ideology, and that this was provided by the *Protocols* and the myth of the Jewish world-conspiracy.

---

[1] *Trials of War Criminals before the Nürnberg Military Tribunal under Control Council Law No. 10.* U.S. Government Printing Office, Washington. Vol. I, pp. 866 seq. (deposition of Kurt Gerstein).

[2] Ibid., p. 870.

CHAPTER X

Forgery Pushers on Trial

1

ALREADY in the 1890s Mgr Meurin called on the rulers of
Europe to league themselves against the Jewish conspiracy.
In 1906 Tsar Nicholas II and Count Lamsdorf tried, however
ineffectively, to build a system of alliances on just such a
basis. As conceived by these pioneers the Antisemitic International would have been an inter-governmental organization
for the suppression of revolutionary, radical, and even merely
liberal movements throughout Europe. The Nazis took over
the idea and gave it a new content. This seems to have been
the work above all of a German from the Baltic provinces of
Russia, Max Erwin von Scheubner-Richter, during the short
period when he was a leading theoretician of the Nazi Party
(he was shot dead in the Munich *putsch* of 1923, as he marched
arm in arm with Hitler). Reflecting on the fact that Jews are
to be found all over the world, Scheubner-Richter hit on the
notion that antisemitism might provide a means by which
German National-Socialism could find allies abroad.

Unlike his predecessors the Archbishop of Port-Louis and
the Russian Foreign Minister, Scheubner-Richter did not
think of these allies as being necessarily governments – they
could just as well be right-wing revolutionaries. Already at
that early stage in the party's history one comes across the
slogan, modelled on the famous ending of *The Communist
Manifesto:* 'Antisemites of all countries, unite!' Hitler himself
adopted the idea with enthusiasm – Hermann Rauschning
reports him as saying: 'Antisemitism is a useful revolutionary
expedient. ... Antisemitic propaganda in all countries is an
almost indispensable medium for the extension of our political
campaign. You will see how little time we shall need to upset

the ideas and criteria of the whole world, simply by attacking Judaism. It is beyond question the most important weapon in my propaganda arsenal. . . .'[1] The Nazis did in fact propagate the myth of the Jewish conspiracy throughout the world in the hope that it would undermine resistance to their own drive for world-domination. And in this campaign the *Protocols* played a vital part. Of the three books that made up the sacred scriptures of Nazism and which sold in millions – *Mein Kampf*, Rosenberg's *Myth of the Twentieth Century*, and the *Protocols* – only the last was exported for propaganda abroad.

The propagation and defence of the *Protocols* outside Germany was mainly the responsibility of an organization called the *Weltdienst* (World Service), headed by a retired colonel, Ulrich Fleischhauer. A disciple of Theodor Fritsch and a friend of Dietrich Eckart, Fleischhauer emerged from the First World War to found, already in 1919, a centre for the dissemination of antisemitic propaganda, the U. Bodung publishing house at Erfurt. The moment Hitler took power in 1933 he received a memorandum, ostensibly from 'a few undaunted nationalists from Holland, Belgium, Luxemburg, Switzerland, Austria and Hungary', urging that a 'technical assistance office' should be set up as the nucleus for an international antisemitic movement. This office would concern itself with establishing liaison between antisemites in various countries and with the dissemination of antisemitic 'enlightenment' throughout the 'Aryan-Christian' world. The appeal was successful: Fleischhauer's organization was officially encouraged to embark on a major expansion – which incidentally provided comfortable jobs for several of the 'dauntless nationalists'. Under the name of *Weltdienst* the Erfurt centre acquired a certain importance and notoriety in the years up to the outbreak of war. By 1937 it could boast that 'for the first time in world history, international Jewry was faced by an international counter-organization, the cell of a true League of Nations. . . . Our work reaches to the furthest corners of the earth.'[2]

[1] H. Rauschning, *Hitler Speaks*, London, 1939, p. 233.
[2] On the *Weltdienst* see L. W. Bondy, *Racketeers of Hatred*, pp. 66–105; Z. A. B. Zeman, *Nazi Propaganda*, pp. 72–3; and O. J. Rogge, *The Official German Report*, New York, 1961, notably pp. 76–8.

Fleischhauer consistently denied that the *Weltdienst* was connected with the German Government or with the Nazi party, but these statements, always inherently implausible, are now known to have been false. From 1933 to 1937 the *Weltdienst* was subsidized by the Propaganda Ministry and from 1937 onwards by the foreign policy office of the Nazi party under Rosenberg. This backing enabled it to carry on propaganda of various kinds. It published a fortnightly, also called *Weltdienst*, the aim of which was stated at the head of each copy: 'To enlighten ill-informed Gentiles, irrespective of the state or country to which they may belong. These information sheets, which deal with the machinations of the Jewish underworld, accordingly form a necessary part of the intellectual armoury of every Gentile.' This publication was translated into many languages,[1] and so were the various antisemitic brochures that supplemented it. The *Weltdienst* also organized international conferences – which, unlike those organized by Julius Streicher, were held in secret; at the conference at Erfurt in 1937 as many as twenty-two countries were represented. The object of all this activity was to build up an international network based on blind belief in the *Protocols* and the Jewish world-conspiracy.

As early as 1934–35 two sensational trials, one in South Africa and the other in Switzerland, drew attention to what was going on. In July and August 1934 a local division of the Supreme Court, sitting at Grahamstown, Eastern Province, South Africa, heard a civil action brought by the Rev. Abraham Levy, minister of the Western Road synagogue, Port Elizabeth, against three leaders of the Nazi-type organization known as the Grey Shirt Movement. The three men, Johannes von Strauss von Moltke, Harry Victor Inch, and David Hermannus Olivier, were sued for having published a scurrilous document on the lines of the *Protocols*. The trial created a great stir in South Africa. Its political significance was emphasized by the defendants themselves, who appeared in uniform – von Moltke in the uniform of the South African

---

[1] During the war the number rose from half a dozen to eighteen. But by then Fleischhauer had been ousted and his organization merged into the Institute of the NSDAP for Research into the Jewish Question, at Frankfort.

Gentile National-Socialists, the others in that of the Grey Shirt Movement; and just before the trial began the Grey Shirt newspaper *Die Waarheid* (i.e. *Truth*) published long extracts from the *Protocols*.[1]

The fabricated document had been read aloud at two political meetings and printed in the newspaper *Die Rapport*, edited by Olivier. Like the *Protocols*, it was supposed to be an outline of the Jewish plan for world-domination, but in crudity and sadism it surpasses all earlier antisemitic forgeries and faithfully mirrors the new age which began when the Nazis came to power.[2] The conclusion of the document gives a fair impression of its quality:

We will fool the public, so that their belief in *Live and Let Live* will be intensified a thousandfold. We will make them digest as much silly rot as their decayed and filthy minds are capable of understanding. Hitler, Lunatic Goering, Von Papen and their co-Lunatics, with the Asylum Contingent (namely the Brownshirts), are guilty of devastation, and crimes against Civilization, which we have built up. They raped our women, murdered our old men, bombarded and dynamited our Synagogues, Threw our children to their hunting dogs, – Made our little ones to dance on hot coals until they fried. Made our husbands run the gauntlets in the passage ways in our clubs while they themselves struck them as they passed. . . .

Brethren, although for countless centuries you have been despised and hated, in the near future the races of the Earth will kiss your feet and worship you, they shall bow down before thee and praise thee. They shall beg mercy of thee and *thou shalt refuse*. They shalt [*sic*] acknowledge that thou art the Chosen, the *Infallible*. Our elected leader will be the first Sovereign over all the Earth. The Communist World. And at last the Talmud Torah and Prophecies will be fulfilled. I may say that we are on the threshold.

---

[1] *Die Waarheid* called itself the 'official organ of the South African National Party with which is incorporated the S.A. Gentile National-Socialist Movement and the S.A. Grey Shirts'. Extracts from the *Protocols* were printed in the issue of 1 June 1934.

[2] The main features of the trial are recorded in the judgement read by Sir Thomas Graham and Mr Justice Gutsche in the Supreme Court on Tuesday, 21 August 1934. The judgement is printed in full in a 64-page pamphlet published by Grocott and Sherry, Grahamstown: *Judgment, Grey Shirt Libel Action at Grahamstown*. The fabricated document is given at pp. 5–8.

On your very life take care of these instructions, do not mention
a word to not even your own what is contained in these pages. You
know our law. You know the Result. . . .

ISSUED BY THE SELECT HIGH CIRCLE OF THE ANTI-NAZI PRO-
PAGANDA VIGILANCE COMMITTEE C.X.V.O. 3838 AND AUTHORIZED
FOR USE BY THE TRUSTEE AND THE SIX COUNCIL MEMBERS ONLY.

'RABBI.'

Victor Inch's account of how he came into possession of this
document also deserves to be recorded. He claimed that stolen
Jewish letters had been passed to him by two boys who had
since been 'spirited away' by the Jews; these letters had put
him on the track of the conspiracy and had inspired him to
break into the Western Road synagogue, where he duly found
the document lying on a table. The judges had of course no
difficulty in recognizing this tale as a fabrication. But if Inch
was a liar another of the defendants, David Olivier, was
genuinely deceived. This man was convinced that, with the
document in their possession, his colleagues Inch and von
Moltke went in danger of their lives; on one occasion he had
even collected a commando of 150 farmers to rescue von
Moltke, whom he believed to have been kidnapped by the
Jews. In fact the three defendants represented, in miniature,
that combination of knavery and gullibility which was the
very essence of the Antisemitic International. And that is also
how it looked to the judges at Grahamstown, who fined
Olivier a mere £25, while fining von Moltke £750 and Inch
£1,000. Inch had moreover to face a criminal trial on various
counts, including perjury and uttering a forged document;
and for him the outcome was, in addition to his fine, a sentence
of six years and three months' hard labour.

2

In the Berne trial of 1934–35, which attracted world-wide
attention, the *Weltdienst* was directly involved. Just what this
implied is revealed by correspondence preserved in the Wiener
Library. More surely than any amount of published propaganda, these confidential letters reveal the inner life of the
Antisemitic International – the genuine delusions as well

as the calculating dishonesty, the fierce internal conflicts as well as the underlying unity of purpose. It seems well worth while to rescue a few of these strange documents from oblivion.

The story opens within a few months of Hitler's accession to power. On 13 June 1933 a Swiss antisemitic organization, the National Front, held a demonstration in Berne; among the propaganda distributed were copies of the thirteenth edition of Theodor Fritsch's version of the *Protocols*. The Jewish community of Berne and the united Jewish communities of Switzerland took the opportunity to demonstrate in court the spuriousness of the *Protocols*. Five persons, some of them members of the National Front, others of the Union of Swiss National-Socialists, were cited under the Swiss law forbidding the printing, publication, or sale of indecent writings; the most prominent were Theodor Fischer, the editor of the antisemitic newspaper *Eidgenossen*, and a musician called Silvio Schnell. The Berne court nominated an expert on the *Protocols* and asked each of the parties to nominate an expert of its own. Not surprisingly, the defence was most unwilling to agree to the nomination of experts; and when its objection were overruled it still failed to produce an expert. At last it nominated a certain German pastor, but this gentleman could not be traced. When the court met in October 1934, after more than a year's delay, there were still only two experts instead of the stipulated three; nobody had been found who was willing seriously to defend the authenticity of the *Protocols*.

There was also the matter of the witnesses. The plaintiffs produced an impressive array of these, ranging from Chaim Weizmann, who spoke on the aims of Zionism, to the Frenchman du Chayla and such non-Jewish Russians as Burtsev, Svatikov, and Nicolaevsky, who between them did a good deal to illumine the dark and tortuous story of the *Protocols*. In answer to all this the defence was able to produce only one solitary witness, whose contribution was limited to saying that the *Protocols* were not the only document of their kind – was there not also *The Rabbi's Speech*? – and so they must be genuine. All in all the defence found itself at such a disadvantage that it decided to look around, however belatedly, for expert support. An adjournment was requested for this purpose and proceedings were suspended until the end of April 1935.

From this point the leading roles were played not by the defendants themselves nor by their counsel but by one Ulrich von Roll, a prominent member of the National Front who bore the title of *Gauleiter* for the Canton Berne, and above all by a sinister individual called Boris Toedtli. Some two years later, in November 1936, the Swiss police raided Toedtli's house in Berne. The letters found there, which led to the arrest of Toedtli on a charge of espionage, afford a vivid glimpse of the manoeuvres which were practised behind the scenes at the Berne trial, on the one hand by the Swiss Nazis, on the other by the *Weltdienst*.

The trial was adjourned on 31 October. On 19 November Ulrich von Roll took a foolhardy and irretrievable step – he sent to the headquarters of the Nazi party at the Brown House, Munich, the following appeal for help:

... I turn to you to enquire, courteously, whether and to what extent you are able and willing to place yourselves at our disposal. ... Could you possibly supply us with an expert, who at first would simply assist us but later perhaps might act as a proper witness on our side? ... Do you not think that your cooperation will be of interest or even of importance from your own point and from the point of view of the ideas for the which the NSDAP stands?[1]

Von Roll's initiative brought results: within a couple of weeks contact had been established with Fleischhauer at Erfurt. At once the correspondence takes on an air of clandestinity – all the persons involved, German, Swiss, and Russian, are referred to by cover-names only. This conspiratorial procedure becomes understandable when one realizes that the Swiss Nazis were not asking simply for expert advice. On 16 January 1935 Ulrich von Roll wrote to Fleischhauer:

Either you receive an official permit to export currency – and then you can just as well send the money direct to us in Berne as via Basel or Solothurn; or else somebody brings the money across the border – and then it can be paid into our account in Basel or elsewhere just as well as into any other account. ...

But soon von Roll had come to regret this arrangement. On

[1] Photostats of the von Roll correspondence printed here are in File 83 in the Wiener Library archives.

21 February he expressed his exasperation in a letter to one of the defendants in the trial:

> In my view it's deplorable that we are all so dependent on Erfurt – specially in financial respects. They would certainly be rather more modest and approachable over there, if they didn't know just how very dependent we are on them. . . .

The *Weltdienst* did its best to disguise its interference in the internal affairs of Switzerland: the money was sent in the name of an 'international committee'. Von Roll must have suspected – quite rightly – that the committee did not really exist, and he must have voiced his suspicions.[1] The answer he received shows Fleischhauer at his most pompous and arrogant:

> I am absolutely astonished and speechless at your demand that I should first tell you the names of the gentlemen who are responsible for the committee.
>
> I have had all kinds of experiences, but such a . . . – I can find no parliamentary expression for it – has never yet come my way.
>
> What do you want with the names of the people responsible for the committee? Be content that the committee exists! . . .
>
> You write moreover: '. . . it may be that Herr Farmer[2] plays this part . . .' To this I reply:
>
> 1. in our organization nobody plays at all;
> 2. in our organization nobody plays a 'part';
> 3. in our organization we work for the great cause;
> 4. in our organization there is no place for prying and unheard-of demands;
> 5. in our organization there is only honest, purposeful work;
> 6. we shall not in future let ourselves be disturbed by questions like yours and shall not answer any more letters;
> 7. Farmer does not belong to the committee.

Von Roll was learning the cost of accepting help from Nazi Germany. According to his lights he was a Swiss patriot and, unlike some of the more extreme Swiss Nazis, he could not easily accept the total subservience demanded by Erfurt. In

---

[1] After the war it was established that the German Propaganda Ministry, operating through the *Weltdienst*, spent 30,000 marks on the Berne trial. (See Rogge, *The Official German Report*, p. 77.)

[2] Farmer is a cover-name for Pottere, a leading member of the Erfurt organization.

desperation he turned for help to Princess Karadja, resident in Locarno-Monti. The princess, who was the mother of the Rumanian consul-general in Berlin, was quite wealthy herself and above all had wealthy friends whose support she enlisted for various antisemitic projects. The Aryan Protection League, which was supposed to be an Anglo-American undertaking, was her creation. On 8 February she sent von Roll an account of the league which, in its blend of inflated idealism and wilful blindness, expresses perfectly the political attitude of countless Nazis:

I do not work for the trial, but for the *movement* in general. My intention is, before I die, (if God grants me this favour), to establish contact between people in all countries with which I am in contact, so that they can cooperate *with one another* when I am gone.

I wish to build a 'façade', all white and bright and shining. There must be nothing suspicious about it. *Nothing secret.* I ask for no oaths and show no distrust . . . *BUT nobody will* penetrate further than the vestibule!!! (I do not wish at all to know what goes on in the back rooms. Dear people like *you* and some others must arrange that after your own ideas! I am 'the left hand' and do not want to know what 'the right hand' does.) You will, I think, agree with this policy? I really think it is important for our cause to have a beautiful façade and vestibule, don't you think so?

So I don't feel that I have anything to do with 'destruction'. Those who concern themselves with that, must of course keep their intentions secret. But they must know one another and assure themselves of the reliability of their collaborators. Each committee that is connected with the league must have *full autonomy*. The façade can take no responsibility for the various groups.

I must confess that I am really happy and proud at what I have already achieved in this short time.

On 1 March von Roll wrote to the princess in the vain hope of finding in the Aryan Protection League an alternative source of funds:

My position is of course so difficult because I have received no money except from Erfurt. . . . In my view it is really stupid of Erfurt simply to want to dictate everything, which is clearly the aim. In this way our Swiss trial becomes a German affair and that is simply impossible for Switzerland. But it's remarkable – in

Germany they simply don't see this. There they pretend there is
an international committee that has nothing at all to do with
Germany and is therefore qualified to conduct the trial in whatever
way it pleases. . . . My collaborators here completely agree with
me about all this, but are of the opinion that, being the weaker
party, we must yield to the stronger, namely Erfurt, because we
are dependent on them. For this reason I can nowhere find the
necessary support. . . . I want to prevent us here from becoming a
branch office of Erfurt, of National-Socialism or of Germany.

Hampered by such scruples, von Roll was no match at all
for his colleague, Boris Toedtli. What Toedtli thought of von
Roll emerges from a letter which he wrote to the defendant
Silvio Schnell on 9 March:

As for v. R., I've seldom seen anything so low. Yesterday G.
showed me his statement of account. An absolute swindle! . . .
Let him write! In your place I wouldn't even answer him, it's a
pity to waste money on the postage! He keeps on meddling in our
affairs, one ought to be able to shake him off at last, for good and
all. He only causes more and more confusion with his chatter.

Unlike von Roll, Toedtli was not inhibited by any feelings of
loyalty towards Switzerland and was more ready to put himself wholly at the disposal of Erfurt. After the Berne trial was
over, and while an appeal was pending, he wrote two singularly
frank letters to Fleischhauer. The first, dated 6 October 1935,
reads as follows:

Schnell writes that he and I are being accused on all sides of
being in the service of Germany, and opinions and circumstances
being what they are in Switzerland, that means that one is morally
dead. If these accusations are not literally true – still, we are fighting in the first place to support Germany in the struggle against the
powers of darkness.

The other letter, dated 5 July 1936, contains the following
passage:

Herr Ruef[1] advised me to write to you and ask for a recompense
for my work. He considers that the German currency control will
understand that we have been fighting for Germany in the first
place and are therefore entitled to claim something in return.

---

[1] Counsel for the defence.

Strange sentiments, coming from a man who was Swiss by birth and ancestry. They became more understandable (though not more laudable) when one learns what kind of life Boris Toedtli had behind him.[1] Though his parents were both Swiss, they lived for many years in Russia, and he himself was born in Kiev in 1896. As a young man he fought in the World War and then in the civil war, of course on the side of the 'Whites', and was made an officer. He lost his hearing in an explosion, was captured by the Bolsheviks, nearly died of typhus, and meanwhile his father's factory was confiscated. The family was allowed to emigrate to Switzerland but never recovered financially. Boris Toedtli became a photographer but failed to keep himself. His attempts at other careers were even less successful and at the time of his arrest he was still dependent on his parents and parents-in-law. In 1933, when Nazi-type movements appeared in Switzerland, he joined first one and then another. In the National Front he became deputy to the *Gauleiter* von Roll – whom we have seen him trying to oust.

It is a familiar picture. Like so many Nazis, Toedtli was a déclassé with unfulfilled ambitions for a middle-class career. And like so many 'White' Russians, he lived for the day when Russia would cast off what he saw as a Judeo-Masonic tyranny. 'I am antisemitic from personal experience,' he said. 'This is the explanation for my whole behaviour. . . . My family and I lost everything in Russia. The Jew alone was to blame, not at all the Russian people.' Frustrated, resentful, politically illiterate, he was indeed ideally qualified to become a champion of the *Protocols*.

It was a year after the end of the Berne trial that the head of the All-Russian Fascist Party, Rodzaevsky, sent from the headquarters at Kharbin a document appointing Toedtli his deputy in Europe, with responsibility for directing the regional leaders in France, Belgium, England, Italy, Algeria, Morocco, and the Congo, and with special powers to negotiate with the German authorities. This step, which gave Toedtli some scope as an organizer of espionage and terrorism, also proved his

---

[1] Information concerning Toedtli, including the account of his career which he gave to the Swiss police, are in File 77 in the Wiener Library archives.

undoing, for it led to his arrest by the Swiss police.[1] But long
before that Toedtli had been in touch with 'White' Russians
in Paris and Jugoslavia. In the winter of 1934–35, while von
Roll was carrying on his painful dealings with Erfurt, Toedtli
was corresponding with former tsarist generals and colonels,
members of the Black Hundreds and the like. His aim was to
produce these people as witnesses for the defence when the
Berne trial was resumed. In fact the financial dependence of
the Swiss Nazis on German funds, which so distressed von
Roll, was mainly caused by these manoeuvres of his rival,
Toedtli. The 'White' Russians had to be provided with visas,
passports, accommodation, train-fares, in some cases also with
fees; and for all this the *Weltdienst*, or rather the German
Propaganda Ministry, paid.

The replies which Toedtli received from the various 'White'
Russians were preserved by a collaborator of the *Weltdienst*,
Jonak von Freyenwald, and are now in the Wiener Library.[2]
Some of them are of interest even today, for not being intended
for publication they reveal with great directness and naïvety
the extraordinary delusions which prevailed in those circles.
Some of the 'White' Russians knew perfectly well that the
Elders of Zion did not exist – but that made no difference, for
they still believed in the conspiracy unfolded in the *Protocols*.
Thus on 4 November 1934 General Krasnov wrote to Toedtli
as follows:

I must tell you that your affair is of unusual difficulty, for the
following reason. The *Protocols of Zion* are apocryphal so far as
their form is concerned, i.e. they were composed by Nilus, but on
the basis of precise Jewish decisions. Therefore the Yids will
always, from a formal point of view, be right, for strictly speaking
there were no 'protocols', there were single decisions which the
Yids published at various times and in various places and which
Nilus brought together in a single whole with the title *Protocols of
Zion*. I cannot tell why Nilus chose this way of publishing them.

[1] Toedtli was arrested before he could do much harm and his sentence
was correspondingly light: two months' imprisonment and nine-tenths
of the costs. He fled to Germany to avoid serving his sentence, but in
December 1939 the German-Russian pact compelled him to leave
Germany and return to Switzerland, where he was promptly arrested.
He died during the war.

[2] In File 1 of the Freyenwald Collection.

Perhaps he did it to give them a bigger circulation, to get wider circles of readers interested in them. But in this way he provided the Jews with a perpetual loophole – they can deny not only the genuineness of the *Protocols* but also the genuineness of what is written in them. The court does not bother about the essence of the *Protocols*, it takes cognisance simply of the naked fact – 'protocols' of this kind did not exist, and that suffices.

On 5 November the notorious Markov II – Nikolai Yevgenevich Markov, a former right-wing deputy in the Duma and a leading figure in the Union of the Russian People – produced an even more tortuous argument:

. . . all the questions in court turned on who wrote the *Protocols* and when. Nobody wrote them, for they are the result of the work of a thousand-year-old world-conspiracy, a programme which has been unmasked again and again, which constantly changes in the methods adopted for its realization, but which was constant in its essence: messianism, the struggle to dominate the world and sub-jugate mankind.

On New Year's Day, a letter from Belgrade, signed I. Lanskoy, offered a startling suggestion:

It is *very* important to investigate exactly the journey which Nahum Sokolov[1] made on the way back from the Basel congress in 1897. It is essential to check his route: what railway-lines did he use, where did he stop and where was he going to? Did he cross the Russian frontier, and where?

I appreciate all the difficulty of such a task but I believe that an experienced detective would not consider it an impossible one.

No wonder that von Roll, confronted with offerings such as these, and harassed at the same time by Toedtli's intrigues, began to develop a hearty dislike of 'White' Russians. On 28 January he wrote as follows to Markov II (of all people!):

. . . the Russians are the worst of all . . . they exaggerate things to such an extent that sometimes one would like to drop the whole business. No, it's really no fun at all – our struggle with our

---

[1] Nahum Sokolov (1861–1936), a Polish Jew, was one of the leading figures in the early history of Zionism. From 1920 he was president of the executive of the Zionist organization and from 1921 chairman of all the Zionist congresses. He went from Russian Poland to attend the first Zionist congress in 1897: whence this communication.

opponents is less difficult than our struggle with our collaborators. One really needs to be young and to have good nerves.[1]

All this activity did however produce one result: the defence was able at long last to produce an 'expert', as required by the court. It produced Ulrich Fleischhauer, and despite his career as a publisher and distributor of antisemitic literature he was accepted by the court. He distinguished himself, if not by his scholarship, at least by his zeal. The 'experts' were of course expected to avoid all contact with the witnesses; but this did not prevent Fleischhauer from inviting a selection of 'White' Russians to Erfurt, where he rehearsed them in the evidence they were supposed to give. It was sheer waste of time,[2] for in the end the court declined to summon any of the 'White' Russians as witnesses – perhaps unfortunately, as it has enabled later editors of the *Protocols*, right down to the present day, to complain that the evidence for the authenticity of the *Protocols* was never properly presented at Berne. In reality this 'evidence' was presented at enormous length by Fleischhauer, who submitted a written opinion of 416 printed pages and oral evidence which lasted for six days.[3]

To appreciate the level at which Fleischhauer conducted his argument one has only to study his comments on Maurice Joly and the *Dialogue aux Enfers*. He could not deny that the *Protocols* were largely copied from the *Dialogue* – so he adopted the argument, first put forward by Lord Alfred Douglas in 1921, that Maurice Joly was a Jew and his book, whatever its overt meaning, a coded version of the Jewish plan for world-domination. Joly might have been baptized a Catholic, there might be no known trace of Jewish ancestry on either side – but had not the Freemason Gambetta spoken the funeral sermon beside his grave, and was that not proof enough? But in case it was not, Fleischhauer had a further proof to offer. He had discovered that a character in the novel *Alt-Neuland* by the founder of Zionism, Theodor Herzl, was called Joe

[1] Copy in File 18 of the Freyenwald Collection.

[2] Except for Markov II, who was given a permanent job as head of the Russian section of the *Weltdienst*. Other 'White' Russians were less fortunate; in view of the revelations which accompanied Toedtli's arrest many of them were expelled from France.

[3] Documents captured after the war show that the opinion was mostly written for Fleischhauer by other people, notably Pottere.

Levy. Now to obtain the name 'Joly' one has only to remove the 'e' from Joe and the 'ev' from Levy – a procedure which, he felt, 'probably has some secret meaning for the Jews'.[1]

Not surprisingly the court was unable to make much sense of these speculations, but that did not prevent Fleischhauer from pursuing them long after the trial was over. Nor was he alone in this. It must have given him immense satisfaction to receive the following communication, dated 6 February 1937, from an Italian baron who was a subscriber to the *Weltdienst*:

You are quite right in saying that all Jolys were most zealous revolutionaries. And what revolutionaries! The Vatican State police used to regard them as a real plague and the devil's own emissaries.

It is true that the baron's information concerning these mysterious beings was limited. 'My material,' he admitted, 'is rather slight, and consists of family traditions and a few short studies.'

The Berne trial ended on 14 May 1935. Judge Meyer found that the *Protocols* were largely plagiarized from Joly's book and were indecent literature; and he imposed a fine on the two main defendants. His comment could hardly have been sharper. 'I hope,' he said, 'that there will come a time when nobody will any longer understand how in the year 1935 almost a dozen fully sane and reasonable men could for fourteen days torment their brains before a court at Berne over the authenticity or lack of authenticity of these so-called "protocols", these *Protocols* that, despite all the harm they have caused and may yet cause, are nothing but ridiculous nonsense.'[2] And when Fleischhauer asked for a fee of 80,000 Swiss francs for his services as expert, the court promptly reduced the sum by nine-tenths.

That however was not the end of the matter. The defendants appealed and the case was heard by the Court of Appeal in Berne in the autumn of 1937. On 1 November the court ruled that as the *Protocols* were not salacious, the law concerning indecent literature could not be applied to them; the sentence

[1] Bulletin No. 6 in *Der Berner Prozess um die 'Protokolle der Weisen von Zion'*. (This is a collection of bulletins on the progress of the second part of the trial, in April–May 1935. A copy is in the Wiener Library.)

[2] Ibid., Bulletin No. 23.

was therefore quashed. This has enabled later editors of the *Protocols* to claim that the Court of Appeal refused to commit itself on the authenticity of the *Protocols*. In reality the court ruled that 'this scurrilous work contains unheard-of and un-justified attacks against the Jews and must without reserva-tion to be judged to be immoral literature', and it added a re-commendation: 'It will be for other authorities to forbid, for reasons of state, the propagation of writings of this kind.' The court also refused to award damages to the defendants, on the grounds that 'whoever disseminates libellous and insulting writings of the greatest possible coarseness, runs the risk of being summoned before the courts and must take the con-sequences'.[1]

The Berne trial, then, achieved all it could reasonably have been expected to achieve: the proceedings had revealed the *Protocols* as a fabrication designed to cause persecution and massacre, and they had been reported at length in hundreds of newspapers throughout the world. It is hardly necessary to add that this made not the slightest difference to the Nazis and their accomplices. The *Weltdienst* conference of 1937, consisting of 'many experts, authors and political leaders from more than twenty countries', passed a solemn resolution re-affirming the authenticity of the *Protocols*. Fleischhauer found himself suddenly famous and much in demand as a lecturer; when he lectured at Munich the rectors of the city's two universities did not disdain to appear as guests of honour. After all – as the German press insisted – who could doubt that the trial had been initiated and stage-managed, and the judges suborned, by the ever-resourceful Elders of Zion?

[1] A mimeographed copy of the 1937 judgement is in the Wiener Library. The passage quoted is at pp. 49–50.

CHAPTER XI

The Antisemitic International

1

As soon as Hitler came to power in Germany the myth of the Jewish world-conspiracy began to be propagated throughout the American continent. In Canada its most ardent champions were the Blue Shirts, who were recruited from French Canadians. The Blue Shirts, otherwise known as the Parti National Social Chrétien, had much in common with the South African Grey Shirts, and there was in fact a living link between the two organizations: Henry Hamilton Beamish, an Englishman who was also the founder of The Britons and who had done more than anyone, ever since 1920, to propagate the *Protocols* in Britain. In the 1930s Beamish established contact with the *Weltdienst* and became a sort of travelling salesman for the most virulent form of antisemitism. Resident in Rhodesia and at one time a member of the Rhodesian Parliament, Beamish appeared as a voluntary witness for the defence at the Grahamstown trial; and he also visited Canada and put himself at the service of Adrien Arcand, the leader of the Blue Shirts. The pamphlet *The Key of the Mystery*, which consisted of forged and distorted texts illustrating the Jewish world-conspiracy, was published in Montreal by Arcand – and in South Africa it was pushed with great vigour, in English and Afrikaans versions. On his side Beamish looked forward to a career as Propaganda Minister in a Canada dominated by Arcand. History decided otherwise, and when war came both Beamish and Arcand were interned; but even then a secret society, the Order of Jacques Cartier, continued to distribute *The Key of the Mystery* and similar material in the hope of weakening the Canadian war-effort.[1]

[1] L. W. Bondy's *Racketeers of Hatred* remains a valuable source of

In the United States little had been heard of the *Protocols* or of the Jewish world-conspiracy since Henry Ford's recantation in 1927 – but here too the situation changed immediately Hitler came to power.[1] At once Nazi propaganda concentrated on reinforcing the already very powerful and widespread isolationism, compounded of fear of war, a general dislike of European entanglements, and a particular suspicion of Britain. And naturally enough the propaganda was first directed towards the German-speaking community in the United States. By the outbreak of war the members of the German-American Bund (at first called Friends of the New Germany) numbered some 25,000, almost all of them of German birth and half of them still German by nationality. These people, most of whom belonged to that same lower middle class which predominated in the German Nazi movement itself, were deluged with literature sent direct from Germany, including countless tons of copies of the *Protocols* in the zur Beek edition, of Wichtl's old book on the Jewish conspiracy and the First World War, and of the German translation of Ford's *International Jew*. But soon there appeared purely American agencies which dealt in the same kind of propaganda; by 1939 there were some 120 of these. Mostly they were insignificant in membership and influence,[2] but there were two exceptions, run by a Roman Catholic priest and a Protestant Fundamentalist minister respectively: Father Charles E. Coughlin's organization, The National Union for Social Justice and the Christian Front, and the Rev. Gerald B. Winrod's Defenders of the Christian Faith.

Father Coughlin, 'the radio priest', was a belated convert to antisemitism.[3] In the early 1930s he already had a national reputation as a broadcaster on religion and politics, but he was

---

information concerning the personalities in the Antisemitic International, including Beamish and Arcand.

[1] For the United States see: D. Strong, *Organized Anti-Semitism in America*, Washington, 1941, Copyright Public Affairs Press; J. R. Carlson, *Under Cover*, New York, 1943 edition; and O. J. Rogge, *The Official German Report*.

[2] William Dudley Pelley's Silver Shirts acquired 15,000 members in one year (1933–34), but quickly waned when in 1935 Pelley was indicted and convicted for selling worthless stock.

[3] On Coughlin see C. J. Tull, *Father Coughlin and the New Deal*, Syracuse University Press, New York, 1965.

quite uninterested in Jews. When Roosevelt launched the New Deal Coughlin supported him; but by 1935 he had turned against the President and was furiously attacking the New Deal as not radical enough. Sincerely concerned, it would seem, about the mass misery caused by the great depression and impatient with Roosevelt's moderation, Coughlin created a new political party, the National Union for Social Justice, which soon had a membership of at least four million. But the Union suffered a disastrous defeat when it ran a candidate for President in 1936 and failed to win the electoral vote in a single State. After two years of relative neglect, in 1938 Coughlin suddenly began to broadcast in favour of an authoritarian corporate state. At the same time he founded a new organisation, the Christian Front, as an alliance of Christians of all denominations against communism and against plutocracy – and he made it plain that he regarded Roosevelt as a servant of both those powers.

Coughlin was nearing the brink of the antisemitic morass, but in the end it was considerations of foreign policy that pushed him over. In 1938 his newspaper *Social Justice* was increasingly concerned with foreign affairs, and its standpoint was that of the most extreme isolationism of the period. Moreover, like many Irish-Americans, Coughlin hated Britain. It was therefore only to be expected that Coughlin and *Social Justice* would end by echoing German propaganda about the Jewish world-conspiracy. This final step was in fact taken in the summer of 1938, at the height of the crisis over the Sudetenland. At the same time as it was justifying Hitler's onslaught on Czechoslovakia and raging against Churchill, *Social Justice* printed a series of articles by the leading propagandist for Nazi Germany, George S. Viereck; and it followed them up by printing the *Protocols* themselves. It was the biggest campaign of its kind since the days of *The Dearborn Independent*, for *Social Justice* had a circulation of a million. Moreover, by November Coughlin was expounding the *Protocols* in his Sunday broadcasts – he even revived the old story that a Jewish firm in New York had financed the Bolshevik revolution. According to the American Institute of Public Opinion his usual audience was 3,500,000, and over two million of these found him convincing. In the end he even involved his own church at Royal Oak, Michigan, in his antisemitic campaign. His Shrine of the Little Flower, conveniently situated on the Detroit highway and equipped with souvenir shops, hot-dog stands, a Shrine inn, and a Shrine garage, attracted multitudes of tourists and became a major distribution centre for the *Protocols*. 'Christ Himself sponsored this little leaflet for your protection,' he wrote on brochures listing stores which employed no Jews – though the more immediate sponsor is known to have been the German-American Business League.

Coughlin was not of course representative of Roman Catholicism in the United States. Cardinal Mundelein of Chicago answered his antisemitic campaign with the forthright statement that he 'is not authorised to speak for the Catholic Church, nor does he represent the doctrine or sentiment of the Church'. Another outspoken Catholic critic was Frank Hogan, the president of the American Bar Association. Nevertheless the turbulent priest was not censured by his immediate superiors, and this made it easier for him to convince vast numbers of Roman Catholics that his voice was indeed the voice of the Church. Particularly among the less prosperous and less educated of the Roman Catholics of Irish descent he built up a devoted following. Over 400 members of the New York police belonged to his Christian Front. The inner circle of his followers even included some priests, among them the president of the International Catholic Truth Society, the Rev. Edward Lodge Curran.[1] Some 2,000 churches were willing to sell copies of *Social Justice*. All in all there is no doubt that Coughlin did manage to introduce into the Roman Catholic population of the United States a more virulent type of antisemitism than it had known in the past.

There is no doubt, either, that his movement did in effect serve Nazi interests, even though he himself had no links with the German Government or with Nazi organizations in the United States. It was not for nothing that the German-American Bund was a major distributor of *Social Justice*, or that Streicher's *Stürmer* reprinted extracts from it, for *Social Justice* in turn mirrored very closely the short-wave broadcasts put out by Goebbels' propagandists. Indeed on one

---

[1] It also included the inevitable 'White' Russian – George Agayeff.

occasion Coughlin reprinted a large part of one of Goebbels's own major speeches – and attached his own signature to it: identification could scarcely go further. And nothing changed when the European war began in 1939, or even when the United States entered the war two years later. As late as March 1942 *Social Justice* was accusing the Jews of having started the war. In fact this proved the undoing of the newspaper and of Coughlin, for at this point the Government intervened: *Social Justice* was suppressed, and in response to a government initiative the Archbishop of Detroit at last imposed silence on Coughlin.

Like Coughlin, the Protestant Fundamentalist Gerald B. Winrod, of Wichita, Kansas, came late to antisemitism. A self-appointed preacher with no formal theological training, he founded the Defenders of the Christian Faith in 1925 for the purpose of combating modernism in religion. It was only when Hitler was about to take power that Winrod suddenly realized that the true cause of modernism, and indeed of all other evils, was 'Jewish Bolshevism'. He at once set about producing a series of writings in which the reality of the Jewish world-conspiracy would be demonstrated from the Book of Revelation. Already in 1932 he produced a book about the *Protocols*, called *The Hidden Hand*. In 1933 his pamphlet *The Protocols and the Coming Super Man* sold some 22,000 copies, and it was soon followed by *The Truth about the Protocols* and *The Anti-Christ and the Tribe of Dan*. By 1936 nearly 100,000 copies of his antisemitic pamphlets had been printed, while the circulation of his leaflets – brochures of a dozen pages or less, distributed free – ran into millions; in one month alone 75,000 of these productions were given away, largely in jails and hospitals. The monthly magazine, the *Defender*, had 100,000 regular subscribers and sprouted a Spanish edition, *El Defensor Hispano*, for the benefit of Puerto Rico, Cuba, and Mexico. Winrod also became a major distributor of the *Protocols* themselves. And as a broadcaster, lecturer, and organizer of meetings about the *Protocols* he was indefatigable.

If Coughlin called himself 'the sole unbiased source of truth', Winrod too maintained that he was acting under divine guidance; 'beyond all doubt,' he wrote of one of his pamphlets, 'this is one of the most important books the Holy Spirit has

ever prompted me to write'.[1] Mixing his attacks on Jewry with
almost equally virulent attacks on the Roman Catholic Church,
he found the bulk of his following where, traditionally, anti-
Catholic feeling was strongest – in the 'Bible Belt' running
from Texas to Missouri, and above all in Kansas. His supporters consisted of small-town and rural folk, mostly poor and
ill-educated – people who had seldom if ever seen a Jew but
who were convinced that the great cities, with their labour
organizations, their complex ways of life, their polyglot popu-
lations of recent immigrants, were somehow centres of a
Jewish plot against 'fundamental Americanism'. Among such
people Winrod had a real appeal: when he stood for senator
for Kansas it was found necessary to launch a campaign to
'keep Fascism out of Kansas' – and even then he polled
54,000 votes in a four-sided contest.

How far did Winrod in fact support the Nazis? It might be
thought that a man whose mental horizon was prescribed by
the Book of Revelation would have little sympathy with the
neo-mysticism of blood and soil, but this was not the case.
From the very beginning of the Nazi régime Winrod praised
Hitler and Goebbels, quoted the *Stürmer* and announced that
'the Hitler revolution has saved Germany and perhaps all
Europe, from an invasion of Jewish communism, directed
from Moscow';[2] in return his book *The Hidden Hand* was
translated into German. When the Berne trial began he went
to Germany and established contact with Fleischhauer and
the *Weltdienst*. Back in the United States he discussed the trial
at length in a series of articles which embellished the *Defender*
from February to July 1935 and presented the defendants as
'fine Swiss patriots', Fleischhauer as a brilliant champion of
truth, the judge as criminally biased. Soon the *Defender* was
comparing Adolf Hitler with Martin Luther and announcing:
'Germany Stands Alone. Of all the countries of Europe,
Germany is the only one that has had the courage to defy
Jewish Masonic Occultism, Jewish Communism, and the
international Jewish Money Power.'[3] Although Winrod represented less of a threat to American democracy than did

[1] Quoted in Strong, op. cit., p. 72.
[2] Quoted in Rogge, op. cit., p. 213.
[3] Ibid., p. 214.

Coughlin, and never even began to organize a political movement – yet within his limits this ultra-Protestant preacher
served the Nazi cause more truly than the Catholic priest. 'The
American Streicher' he was called in the German press, and he
did his best to deserve the title.

There is no point in exaggerating the importance of the
innumerable antisemitic groups which appeared in the United
States in the 1930s; none of them had the slightest chance of
causing a major upheaval, let alone the revolution they talked
of. Nevertheless they are not altogether without historical
significance. Through their books and pamphlets, broadcasts
and lectures, they hammered at a public of several millions
that the New Deal was a reign of terror imposed by Jews on
the population of the United States. 'Minnesota Close to Red
Abyss as Murder Terrorizes Voters' – 'Dictator for America
Looms; Reds Concentrating Energies behind Pro-Jewish
Despot' – 'A Death List of the Enemies of Jewish Bolshevism
Exists in the United States' – these were typical headlines.
Even the anti-syphilis campaign was presented as part of the
conspiracy: ' . . . this entire scheme is one leading up to the
wholesale inoculation of Gentiles with vaccine syphilitic
germs'.[1] Although wholehearted believers in the Jewish world-
conspiracy were few, there is no doubt that many people were
more or less disorientated by this constant stirring-up of deep
and barely conscious anxieties.

Among the people who did the stirring-up were some who
longed for physical violence. William Dudley Pelley, the leader
of the Silver Shirts, looked forward to 'a bath of violence' and
'history's greatest pogrom'; his lieutenant, William Zachery,
shouted at a public meeting: 'I want all of you to go out and
get guns, and I want each of you to get plenty of ammunition.'
Another antisemitic propagandist, James B. True, wrote in
his paper *Industrial Control Report*: 'Urge your congressional
representatives to oppose all anti-gun and registration legislation. Remember that the Constitution gives all United States
citizens the right to bear arms, and unless all signs fail we shall
need that right.'[2] An interview which the same man gave to the

[1] Quoted in Strong, op. cit., p. 160.
[2] The remarks by Pelley, Zachery, and True are quoted from Strong,
op. cit., pp. 152–7.

Rev. Dr L. M. Birkhead, National Director of the Friends of Democracy, reveals with complete naïvety a state of mind which, as we now know, was that of many of the Nazi leaders themselves:

I found True to have the look and determination of a fanatic. Spread out on his desk were a half-dozen wooden pieces which looked like the lower ends of an axe handle. On examination I found that they had straps running through one end much the same as a policeman's billy. When Mr True began to explain to me that he had a militant organization in the South which he was equipping with arms in order to kill off the Jews, I began to understand what these hip-pocket-flask billies were for. They were Mr True's 'Kike Killers'.

'What are you trying to do through your organization?' I asked Mr True.

Quick as a flash he replied, 'To defeat the only real enemy that America has today.' That enemy, it appears, is the Jew Communism which the New Deal is trying to force on America.

'We may have to do something more militant than vote,' Mr True said with the emphasis of a man who believed that bullets might have to be substituted for ballots.

I asked him just what he meant by being more militant.

'What I mean is that the thing has possibly gone too far for us to save the country by political methods,' True replied. '. . . I don't see any way out except a pogrom. We have got to kill the Jews. Ballots don't mean anything to them.'

'May I ask, Mr True, if you aren't oversimplifying the problem?' I said by way of interruption. 'Suppose we could line up the fifteen million Jews up against a wall and shoot them, that wouldn't solve our problems. We'd still have them with us – the same old problems.'

True speaking: 'That's just where you're wrong. Our problem is very simple. Get rid of the Jews and we'd be on the way to Utopia tomorrow. The Jews are the source of all our troubles. That's plain to anyone who makes a study of this problem, and I have studied it deeply.'

'Who is it that is trying to destroy our Constitution and the American form of government? The Jew.

'You take the hiring of "big, buck niggers" by the Jews to attack white women in the South. That's right in the Talmud. The Talmud teaches the Jew that it's right to do that. . . .

'Communism is the major part of the Jewish conspiracy today. Why, just look at Russia where the Jews run the country.

'I want to leave you with a thought,' said Mr True as I arose to leave. 'I predict a pogrom in America. I don't see how it can be avoided.'[1]

The groups headed by Pelley and True were, admittedly, insignificant – but one finds the same attitude even among some elements in Coughlin's Christian Front. In the spring and summer of 1939, while Hitler was preparing to launch his war, Coughlin's henchmen were warning big audiences in New York that a Jewish-Communist coup was imminent – that any day now they could wake up to see the gutters flowing with blood – 'Christian blood, your blood, the blood of Christian boys and Christian leaders!'[2] This imaginary danger was used to justify massacre. One of Coughlin's organizers, George Van Nosdall, told a Christian Front meeting, 'Boys, we are going to work. I am ready to line the God-damned Jews right up against the wall.' At another meeting he shouted: 'When we get through with the Jews in America they will think the treatment they received in Germany was nothing. . . . Judaistic gore will soon flow in the streets of New York City.' Another organizer even instructed his audience: 'When you are in a crowd yell "Kill the Jew".'[3]

All this talk, in a country like the United States, was of course mere wind. But it is worth noting nevertheless, for it shows that even in the United States many of those who dealt in the *Protocols* were just the kind of people who under the Nazi régime became the organizers and executants of genocide.

The operations of the *Weltdienst* extended also to South America, particularly Argentina. A commission for the investigation of anti-Argentinian activities was alarmed to find, in 1943, the extent to which resident Germans had allowed themselves to be used by Erfurt as distributors of the *Protocols*. A future Minister of Justice under Peron, Martinez Zuviria, wrote two books, *Oro* and *Kahal*, about the Jewish world-conspiracy, and was duly honoured by the German community. Some Roman Catholic clerics cooperated happily in this propaganda, which once more took on the religious colouring it had possessed in the days of Mgr Meurin. The

[1] Strong, op. cit., pp. 124 seq.
[2] Quoted in Carlson, op. cit., p. 60.
[3] Strong, op. cit., p. 158.

monthly *Clarinada* wrote in August 1937; '*Clarinada* fights the Jews because they are the inventors, leaders and henchmen of communism throughout the world. *Clarinada* fights the Jews because – following the directives of the Elders of Zion – they corrupt Christian morality and stimulate human vices and defects in order to annihilate the spiritual conquest of humanity brought about by Jesus Christ, the first victim of the God-destroyers.' A year later *Clarinada* earned quotation in *Der Stürmer* by suggesting a remedy: 'It is a great pity that all Jews without distinction are not being buried alive so that peace could at last reign within the great Argentinian family.'[1]

2

By the eve of the Second World War the *Protocols* were enjoying a greater vogue than they had enjoyed even in 1920, before they were first unmasked. In the countries of eastern Europe where there were large Jewish minorities and important Fascist movements, the myth of the Jewish world-conspiracy provided a constant theme for propaganda and for political argument. In Poland Piasecki's Falanga even tried in October 1937 to arrest President Moscicki and massacre his more or less liberal associates, on the grounds that they were agents of international Judeo-Masonry.[2] But above all these fantasies were invoked by governments which were allied to or dependent on Nazi Germany – and this happened even in countries which had no Jews.

In Spain there had been no Jews for more than four centuries, but that did not prevent the Nationalists from presenting the civil war as a struggle against Judeo-Masonry.[3] Nationalist newspapers carried headlines saying 'Our war is a war against Judaism', and amazed their readers with tales of the prodigious power, wealth, and cunning of a Jewish government which had never been mentioned before. Outside Spain this propaganda enjoyed a marvellous success in quarters

---

[1] Quoted in Bondy, op. cit., pp. 242–3.

[2] See L. Blit, *The Eastern Pretender*, London, 1965, pp. 70–2.

[3] It is true that after the great expulsion of 1492 dwindling numbers of crypto-Jews (Marranos) lingered on in Spain. But the Nationalists were certainly not thinking of them.

sympathetic to General Franco; among Father Coughlin's followers, for instance, it was a commonplace that the forces of the Spanish Republic represented the embattled might of the Elders of Zion. And years later, in October 1944, when the majority of the Jews on the European Continent had already been killed, the official Spanish radio station Radio Falange could still proclaim: 'The Jewish danger is no unfounded fantasy. . . . Nothing is more urgent than to fight against the Communist and the Jew'.[1]

The case of Japan was strangest of all, for there Jews were so completely unknown that nobody could imagine what kind of creatures they could be. However, Hitler had said in *Mein Kampf* that Jewry 'fears the presence of a national Japanese state in its millennial Jewish kingdom and desires that the ruin of that state shall precede the establishment of its own dictatorship';[2] and the hint was sufficient. The Japanese Government needed some excuses which might seem in the eyes of the world to justify its attack on China, and the myth of the Judeo-Masonic conspiracy provided one such excuse. According to the Japanese delegate to the *Weltdienst* congress of 1938, Fujivara, 'Judeo-Masonry is forcing the Chinese to turn China into a spearhead for an attack on Japan, and thereby forcing Japan to defend herself against this threat. Japan is at war not with China but with Freemasonry, represented by General Chiang-Kai-shek, the successor of his master, the Freemason Sun-Yat-Sen.' The war in China bore 'the sacred mark of sacrifice'; Japanese soldiers were dying not for any narrow national interest but for the sake of the whole world, which they were struggling to 'save from the Judeo-Masonic-Bolshevik claws'. The conclusion was obvious: 'Do not abandon us, the isolated bulwark in the Far East!'[3] Meanwhile the Japanese General Shioden was also visiting the Third Reich, establishing contact with Streicher and the *Weltdienst* and visiting the anti-Masonic museum at Nuremberg. He proved an apt pupil, for by July 1939 the *Stürmer* was proud to print a letter from him: 'I am pleased to inform you that the copious information and material collected dur-

---

[1] Quoted in Bondy, op. cit., p. 211.
[2] Hitler, *Mein Kampf*, p. 724.
[3] Quoted in H. Rollin, *L'Apocalypse de notre temps*, p. 514.

THE ANTISEMITIC INTERNATIONAL

ing my journey in Germany has now been translated into Japanese by experts. This will contribute to the enlightenment of the Japanese about the Jewish plan for world-domination. . . .'[1]

Here we are in the world of farce, but it is characteristic of the story of the *Protocols* that it keeps jerking one out of farce into the starkest tragedy. We have seen how the men who propagated the *Protocols* were often *pogromshchiki* at heart, waiting hungrily for the chance to organize massacre.[2] Whether they ever got that chance or not depended entirely on what happened to their countries during the Second World War. In the embattled democracies such people lapsed into obscurity, when they did not disappear into jail – but in those parts of Europe where the Nazi leaders were able to implement their plans for genocide various dingy figures, hitherto known only as editors or publishers of the *Protocols*, were suddenly transformed into important administrators, with responsibility for drafting and implementing antisemitic legislation. As often before, but on a far more massive scale, dealing in the *Protocols* led to dealing in murder. It is worth looking briefly at a few such cases.

In France the most active champion of the *Protocols* in the years immediately before the war was one Darquier de Pellepoix. As plain Monsieur Darquier this man had behind him a whole career of failure before he took to antisemitic politics. He held a good position with a French firm in Antwerp but was dismissed for speculating against the franc. Reinstated, he was sent to London but got himself arrested for being drunk and disorderly. Next he emigrated to Australia, married money, and bought a sheep-ranch – but it failed. Back in France, he was accidentally involved in the right-

---

[1] Quoted in Bondy, op. cit., p. 246.

[2] This was the tendency even in England. Mosley's British Union of Fascists was rather non-committal about the *Protocols* – and its antisemitism, though real, was never of the exterminatory kind. But the *Protocols* provided the ideological basis for the much more extreme (and numerically insignificant) Imperial Fascist League, headed by Arnold Leese, which had close links with the Nazis and openly favoured the gassing of all Jews. Leese, incidentally, also propagated the ritual murder myth. (C. Cross, *The Fascists in Britain*, London, 1961, pp. 153–4.)

wing demonstration of 6 February 1934 and had the good luck
to be wounded in the rioting. This gave him the happy idea of
founding an 'Association of the Wounded of 6 February'. He
added 'de Pellepoix' to his name, took to wearing a monocle,
and embarked on an antisemitic campaign which in violence
far surpassed anything offered by the Action Française. This
brought him some success, for in 1935 he was elected to the
municipal council of Paris as representative for the fashionable
district of Ternes.

Next Darquier founded a new movement, the Rassemblement Antijuif de France, with a programme modelled on the
antisemitic legislation which had been introduced in the Third
Reich. French Jews were to be disfranchised and were to be
excluded from the civil service and the armed forces, the
property of Jewish organizations was to be confiscated for the
benefit of 'the French community ruined by Judeo-Masonic
policy'. But the programme also contained a vaguer and still
more menacing item: 'Expulsion of all Jews likely to con-
taminate the moral or physical health of the nation.'[1] What
this really meant was revealed in a public statement which
Darquier made in May 1937: 'The Jewish question must be
solved, and very urgently: either the Jews must be expelled
or they must be massacred.'[2]

At the time few could take such a remark seriously – but
one of those few was Darquier himself, and he did his best to
prepare the way. In the last couple of years of peace the
Rassemblement Antijuif de France concentrated on publishing
and distributing literature about the Jewish world-conspiracy.
It was at Darquier's meetings in 1937 that the Canadian booklet *The Key of the Mystery* was distributed for the first time in
France. Above all the movement's fortnightly paper, *La
France enchaînée*, regularly carried advertisements for the
Protocols – 'a prophetic book which every Frenchman ought
to read'. Anyone who secured five subscriptions for the paper
received, as a reward, five free copies of the *Protocols*. And in
1938 there appeared the proud announcement: 'The Rassemblement Antijuif has just published an annotated edition of
the *Protocols of the Elders of Zion*, price 2 francs. This very low

[1] The programme is given in Rollin, op. cit., p. 556.
[2] As reported in the Paris newspaper *La Lumière* on 22 May 1937.

price is intended to enable all Frenchmen to recognize the machinations of Enemy No. 1: the Jew. . . . In publishing this new edition, we appeal to all Frenchmen who are not completely chloroformed or emasculated. France must awake!'[1]

It was no coincidence that this advertisement appeared at the height of the Munich crisis. Throughout August and September 1938 *La France enchaînée* produced articles with such headings as 'War Danger: Jewish-Russian plot in Czechoslovakia' – 'War comes nearer, the Jews' war' – 'Will Jewry dare to unleash world war?' The publication of the new edition of the *Protocols* was accompanied by the announcement: 'It is Jewry that has created the democratic front. It is Jewry that has brought the United States out of their splendid isolation. It is Jewry that wants war. France, soldier of the Jew! No! Everyone must proclaim the truth.'[2] Under a mask of patriotism Darquier was in fact serving the interests of the Third Reich, and the Nazis knew it well enough: his immediate reward was to be applauded in the *Völkischer Beobachter*. The French authorities knew it too. The effects of Darquier's propaganda were so considerable, especially in Alsace, that the French Government had to take the step, which at that time was an extraordinary one, of restricting the liberty of the press. On 25 April 1939 a decree was promulgated which forebade, under penalty of fine or imprisonment, all antisemitic propaganda. Darquier was prosecuted and sentenced to three months in prison. In court he cried: 'I have striven to fight the Jewish invasion which is submerging France.'

It was the war that gave Darquier his chance. As a captain in the army he was again imprisoned for subversive propaganda; but he was released in time to be captured by the Germans, who had the good sense to set him free at once. In the new conditions he quickly made a political career, and in Laval's second cabinet (May 1942) he was appointed Commissioner-General for Jewish Affairs, in succession to Xavier Vallat. In this capacity he supervised the deportation of the 9,000 foreign Jews who were handed over to the Germans.[3]

---

[1] Quoted in Rollin, op. cit., p. 556.　　　　[2] Ibid., p. 555.

[3] Laval in the end refused to hand over the French Jews. The French Jews who perished (probably about 85,000) were mostly taken by the Germans themselves in the Occupied Zone.

At the end of the war he was tried *in absentia* and sentenced to death; but he was able to make his way to Spain.

In Italy the history of the *Protocols* is indissolubly linked with the name of Giovanni Preziosi.[1] Political antisemitism was unknown in Italy before the First World War;[2] and when the ex-priest Preziosi took to political propaganda during the war, he too was concerned not with Jewish but with German machinations. In a book he published in 1916, *La Germania alla conquista dell' Italia*, he argued that Germany was dominating Italy through the great bank the Banca Commerciale. It was only after the war that he decided that the same bank was really Jewish and the instrument of a Jewish conspiracy. From 1920 onwards Preziosi's journal *La vita italiana* was arguing that the western democracies, Freemasonry, international socialism, and Bolshevism were all means by which a hidden Jewish power was seeking to subordinate the world, but especially the poorer and more dynamic nations, to Jewish interests. Who could deny that of the three statesmen who had opposed Italian claims at Versailles two – Wilson and Clemenceau – were in the hands of the Jews, while one – Lloyd George (!) – was himself a Jew? And what were all these manoeuvres but the latest manifestations of a conspiracy which dated at least from the destruction of the Temple in 70 A.D.?

But in 1921 Preziosi published a translation of the *Protocols* and from 1922 onwards he and his journal were firmly integrated into the international network. Thus the August 1922 issue of *La vita italiana* contained an article by Preziosi himself, justifying the murder of Rathenau; another article signed P. Praemunitus, which was the title of the first American edition of the *Protocols*; and above all an article entitled 'The Jews, the passion and the resurrection of Germany (Thoughts of a German)', which was signed 'A Bavarian' and is now known to be by Adolf Hitler himself. Preziosi was in fact the one publicist in Italy who from the start fully accepted Hitler and Nazism. Even the Fascists had as a whole considerable

[1] On Preziosi see R. De Felice, *Storia degli ebrei italiani sotto il fascismo*, Turin, 1961, pp. 54–64, 502–18.
[2] The clerical antisemitism associated above all with *La civiltà cattolica* had no influence on nationalist politics.

reservations about the kindred but infinitely more ruthless movement which was extending its power to the north of the Alps. In particular they were not antisemitic, and they were mostly shocked when in 1933 the Nazis began to reveal the full extent of their brutality. Preziosi on the other hand proved quite unshockable.

For some eighteen years Preziosi and the little group around *La vita italiana* remained isolated and ineffective. Even when the *Protocols* were republished in 1937, bookshops refused to stock them and the press to review them. Then, in 1938, Mussolini decided that to make the alliance with Germany really solid, it was indispensable to launch an antisemitic campaign – and for Preziosi things changed overnight. Now several important newspapers gave favourable attention to the *Protocols*; and soon the work was officially sponsored by the Italian service for propaganda abroad, the Committee of Action for the Universality of Rome. Before the end of the year Preziosi was appointed Minister of State.

But it was the Italian armistice of September 1943 that brought Preziosi to the peak of his career. With Mussolini a prisoner of the Allies, the Germans were trying to find a new government for the part of Italy they had occupied. Preziosi went to Germany and so impressed Rosenberg that he chose him as his candidate to head the new government. These hopes vanished with Mussolini's liberation, but Preziosi had other resources. He began to broadcast to Italy, blaming the Judeo-Masonic conspiracy for the capitulation and demanding a 'purge' of Freemasonry and an 'integral solution of the Jewish question'. He also sent to Mussolini a letter such as the Duce can seldom have received, warning him of the consequences of failing to cope with the 'conspiracy'; and he sent a copy to Hitler. Mussolini gave way and in March 1944 appointed this man – whom he had always despised and detested – Inspector General of Race. Later in the year Preziosi was given the rank of ambassador as well.

At first Preziosi concentrated his efforts on introducing into the Italian Social Republic – as Mussolini's régime in north Italy was called – laws confiscating Jewish property, debarring Jews and half-Jews from public office, and forbidding mixed marriages. In this he was unsuccessful, and he retorted by complaining in *La vita italiana* that the Republic was in the hands of Freemasons acting for the Jews. But in fact all this was only preparatory to a far more sinister plan. In June 1944 Preziosi submitted to Mussolini a memorandum urging that his inspectorate should be turned into an Italian version of the Gestapo, with unlimited powers to carry out police activities throughout the Republic and to exact collaboration from all public authorities and military formations. This, he announced, was made necessary by the 'injustices' which were occurring each day in the Republic. What he had in mind was that the Italian population was helping Jews to evade deportation and extermination by the Germans. If he had had his way, the number of Italian Jews killed would no doubt have been greater than it was (the number is put at about 10,000, out of a total Jewish population of 25,000); but in the end Mussolini preferred to leave the Germans to their own devices. The Government of the Republic was still discussing these things in the spring of 1945, when it was overthrown by popular insurrection. To avoid being killed by the crowd Preziosi committed suicide.

Darquier and Preziosi were not free agents; both served governments which were not interested in killing Jews, and this severely limited their own activities. Their Hungarian counterpart Lászlo Endre found himself in a more fortunate position, after equally obscure beginnings.[1] Throughout the 1930s Endre was active as an antisemitic propagandist, and shortly before the outbreak of war he produced a whole book 'proving' the genuineness of the *Protocols*; but he never achieved the slightest political importance so long as Hungary remained independent. Even after Hungary entered the war as Germany's ally the Regent, Admiral Horthy, though willing to allow some harassing of Jews by Hungarians, refused absolutely to let the Germans deport and exterminate them. But in March 1944 Horthy took steps to withdraw the Hungarian troops from the Russian front, and this resulted in the immediate occupation of Hungary by the German army and the imposition of a new, wholly subservient government.

[1] On Endre see J. Weidlein, *Der ungarische Antisemitismus*, Schorndorf, 1962, pp. 166 seq.; and E. Levai, *Black Book on the Martyrdom of Hungarian Jewry*, Zurich and Vienna, 1948.

Eichmann arrived and hurled himself into the task of deport-
ing the 800,000 Hungarian Jews. His closest Hungarian
collaborator was Endre, now a Secretary of State and charged
by the new cabinet with this welcome task. On the day of the
first deportations, 15 May, Endre opened an Institute for
Race Research in Budapest; he took the opportunity to
announce that 'the Government has decided to settle the
Jewish question once and for all, in the shortest possible time'.
He did his best; and it was largely thanks to his energy that
within six weeks some 450,000 Jews had in fact been des-
patched by freight-train to the gas-chambers of Auschwitz – a
hundred in each wagon, without food or water for a journey of
three days and nights.

At the end of the war Endre was executed. According to a
Hungarian of similar outlook, on the night before his execution, 21 March 1946, he sent the following farewell message:
'The *Protocols of the Learned Elders of Zion* are true. . . . The
means to establish a world kingdom are in [the Jews'] hands
and they will destroy everything that might constitute an
obstacle to the new world state. . . . Jewish policy is *to
exterminate* not only those who did something but *even those
who might yet do something or could have done something.* . . .'[1]

Such was the Antisemitic International in the Nazi era. No
doubt the men we have been considering were impelled by all
kinds of motives. Some saw in the administration of massacre
a unique chance of wielding power and enjoying prestige;
others were keen to appropriate the belongings of the killed;
others were sadists who sought gratification in pursuing,
torturing, and killing defenceless people. All this is true – and
yet the fact is inescapable: behind the massacre as a whole
there was a blind fanaticism which was largely inspired by the
Protocols and the myth of the Jewish world-conspiracy. Again
and again one comes across the same weird, apocalyptic
atmosphere, hints of some gigantic final battle in which the
demonic hosts will be eliminated, the world released from the
strangling octopus, a new age brought to birth. This atmosphere is unmistakable in many of the political speeches and

[1] L. Marschalko, *The World Conquerors*, trans. A. Soranyi, London,
1958, p. 241.

writings of that period, and it is much the same in New York
as in Budapest. But for its supreme, most naïve expression one
has to turn from such utterances – which after all could never
be completely frank – to a novel published in 1937 by a French
writer who was later to abet the Nazis in France, Ferdinand
Céline. In *Bagatelles pour un massacre* Céline swears to the
genuineness of the *Protocols* and of *The Rabbi's Speech*; and he
goes on:

Let us recall, for our pleasure and to remind ourselves, the main
provisions of the *Protocols*. . . . For an Aryan, nothing is more
invigorating than to read them. . . . It does more for our salvation
than any number of prayers. . . .

Do you know that the executive power over the whole of world
Jewry is called the 'Kahal'? . . . Assembly of the Elders of Israel?
. . . Our fate . . . depends entirely on the good favour of the big
Jews, 'the big occult ones'. It's not stupid to think that our fate is
certainly still being discussed in the consistories of the Kahal, as
much as in the Masonic lodges, indeed much more.

In short, Frenchmen . . . you will go off to war at the moment
chosen by Baron de Rothschild . . . at the moment fixed in full
agreement with his sovereign cousins in London, New York and
Moscow. . . .

I want something solid! . . . Realities! . . . Those who really are
responsible! . . . I've got a hunger! . . . an enormous hunger! . . .
a world-wide hunger! a hunger for Revolution . . . a hunger for
planetary conflagration . . . for the mobilization of all the charnel-
houses in the world! An appetite which is surely divine, divine!
Biblical![1]

Céline was himself a near-paranoiac and for that very reason
saw perfectly clearly what would happen if once believers in
the *Protocols* had absolute power. In his eyes the *Protocols*
were a warrant for genocide; and that is precisely what they
became.

[1] F. Céline, *Bagatelles pour un massacre*, Paris, 1937, pp. 277–89. In
April 1938 France's most distinguished literary review, the *Nouvelle
Revue française*, published a review by Marcel Arland commending this
book as 'effective' and a fine example of French eloquence; it singled
out, for particular praise, a passage evoking ritual murder.

A Case-study in Collective Psychopathology[1]

IT is often said that wherever Jews have settled since the Dispersion, antisemitism has appeared in the local population. This belief is mistaken. It is true that traditionally the Jewish religion has encouraged a certain separateness and exclusiveness, notably by making it impossible for a strict Jew to marry a non-Jew and difficult for him even to eat together with non-Jews. Yet these circumstances have never in themselves prevented Jews from taking part in the life of the wider society, or from having cordial relations with non-Jews. For some two thousand years Jewish settlements existed in India and China without attracting any particular attention; to this day the Jewish artisans and peasants of India are regarded simply as one of the innumerable religious communities of the subcontinent, with nothing in the least odd about them. But there is no need to labour the point. There are after all many other minorities in the world which show traits of separateness in one way or another, and they are not always seen as enemies.

Even in those parts of the world where antisemitism is endemic it can have very different meanings. There is a kind of antisemitism which is fairly closely related to the role played by Jews, or at least by some Jews, in the society in question. For instance, it has happened again and again that Jews, because of their peculiar history, have been pioneers in trade and money-lending in predominantly agricultural societies, while at the same time living more or less segregated from the population around them. In such cases they have attracted the same kind of hostility as, say, Indian traders in southeastern Africa or Chinese traders in Java.[2] Again, the centuries

---

[1] An earlier version of this was published in *Commentary*, New York.

[2] Cf. S. Andreski, 'The economic interpretation of antisemitism in eastern Europe', in *The Jewish Journal of Sociology*, vol. V, No. 2 (December 1963), pp. 201–13.

in the ghetto inevitably fostered attitudes of inferiority and of compensatory superiority in many Jews, which did not automatically disappear the moment the ghetto walls fell; and this too helped to feed antisemitism. But in all this there is nothing that is not parallelled in many other forms of social antagonism the world over. And certainly, though these factors might have led to occasional outbreaks of violence, they would never by themselves have led to attempts at genocide. The antisemitism that leads to such results is of a different and very special kind.

Exterminatory antisemitism appears where Jews are imagined as a collective embodiment of evil, a conspiratorial body dedicated to the task of ruining and then dominating the rest of mankind. This kind of antisemitism can exist almost regardless of the real situation of Jews in society. It can prosper where Jews form a large, cohesive and clearly recognizable minority, but also where the only Jews are a few scattered individuals who hardly regard themselves as Jews at all. And if it thrives on the spectacle of rich and influential Jews, it does not necessarily wilt where all Jews are poor. Most striking of all, it can be found among people who have never set eyes on a Jew and in countries where there have been no Jews for centuries.

This kind of antisemitism is a matter of fantasy, and what it fantasies is the opposite of reality. In reality Jews are just as diverse as one would expect from their extraordinarily varied history. Even before the creation of the State of Israel introduced new complexities there was little enough to link, say, an assimilated, free-thinking Frenchman of Jewish descent with a rigorously orthodox rabbi in eastern Europe, or an artisan in Salonika with a doctor in Berlin, or any of these with the second or third generation of Jewish immigrants in the United States. No doubt a certain awareness of common origins and a common cultural heritage, an awareness also of repeated persecutions and migrations, colours the outlook of most Jews; but this is vastly different from the unity and uniformity which antisemites imagine. Again, since the Dispersion there has been no central Jewish authority of any kind. Though individual rabbis have at times attained great moral prestige, there has been nothing in the least like a government

– not even an ecclesiastical government – with authority over all Jews; even the chief rabbinate in the various countries is a modern invention which originated simply as an administrative convenience. Above all, the Jews of the world have never possessed, as a collectivity, any considerable power. In some countries and at some times individual Jews might achieve positions of influence, and individual Jewish communities might be able to defend their interests when these were threatened; it could even happen that prosperous and fortunate communities were able to assist persecuted Jews in other lands. The fact remains that Jews have not been able either to protect themselves or their fellows from wholesale massacre or to induce any great power to do so.

After the Second World War the Higher SS and Police Leader in Central Russia, Erich von dem Bach-Zelewski, made the following statement:

I am the only living witness but I must say the truth. Contrary to the opinion of the National-Socialists that the Jews were a highly organized group, the appalling fact was that they had no organization whatsoever. . . . It gives the lie to the old slogan that the Jews are conspiring to dominate the world and that they are so highly organized. . . . If they had had some sort of organization, these people could have been saved by the millions; but instead they were taken completely by surprise.[1]

The lack of congruence between the myth of the Jewish world-conspiracy and the realities of the Jewish situation has never been better expressed.

The myth of the Jewish world-conspiracy, then, has very little to do with real people and real situations and real conflicts in the modern world; and this seems natural enough when one considers how it originated. The fantasy of Jews as a brotherhood of evil was first conceived between the second and fourth centuries, as a device for immunizing Christians against the attractions of the parent religion; and seven or eight centuries later, in western Europe, it developed into a coherent and terrifying demonology. From the twelfth century onward Jews were seen as a conspiracy of sorcerers working

[1] Statement to Leo Alexander, quoted in R. Hilberg, *The Destruction of the European Jews*, pp. 662–3.

on orders from Satan for the spiritual and physical ruination of Christendom. This was the period when Jews began to be massacred on charges of killing Christian children, of torturing the consecrated wafer, of poisoning wells. And in the same period the mystery-plays taught people that Antichrist would be a Jew and would have the Jews as his most devoted followers.

Myths do not necessarily disappear with the circumstances that first produced them. They sometimes acquire an autonomy, a vitality of their own, that carries them across the continents and down the centuries. This was very much the case with the demonological view of Jewry and Judaism. In many parts of eastern and central Europe it was still widely believed right into the twentieth century that the blood of Christian children was used for making the unleavened Passover bread. Within the last twenty or thirty years it has happened to Jewish tourists in the remoter parts of Spain to be told that they could not possibly be Jews, as they had no horns.

Such facts are no mere curiosities, for the modern myth of the Jewish world-conspiracy grew straight out of these age-old superstitions. This is so true that certain individuals have dealt in both the medieval and the modern versions of the myth: the first editor of the *Protocols*, the *pogromshchik* Krushevan, also disseminated charges of ritual murder, and so did Streicher and von Leers; while Himmler himself, when once he heard the tales of ritual murder, found them immediately convincing. Even that profoundly medieval fantasy, the legend of Antichrist as the Messiah of the Jews, persisted into modern times. des Mousseaux was obsessed by the idea; while the first influential edition of the *Protocols* formed part of Nilus's prophecy of Antichrist, and in the *Protocols* themselves the future king of the Jews has all the traditional traits of Antichrist. And what after all are the Elders of Zion but sorcerers in the service of Satan – quite openly in Goedsche's novel, where the devil appears in person among the assembled rabbis, and still recognizably in the current editions of the *Protocols*?

But not even the Nazis could have constructed an effective ideology solely from archaic superstitions, from eschatological prophecies and tales of black magic. It is characteristic of antisemitic forgeries and fabrications of the type of the *Protocols* that they combine the medieval with the modern. While the basic assumptions and attitudes are those of an ancient demonology, the supposed conspiracy is a thoroughly modern affair. For one thing, it operates on a bigger scale; whereas ritual murder was imagined as happening from time to time, now here, now there, the Elders of Zion are imagined as an international government whose machinations constantly affect the whole world. And again, the means by which the Elders pursue their goal belong entirely to the nineteenth and twentieth centuries. Instead of muttering spells these sorcerers place articles in the press, instead of poisoning wells they plunge whole countries into slumps and wars and revolutions.

In all this the *Protocols* faithfully reflect the complex structure of latter-day antisemitism at its most virulent. For in the eyes of fanatical antisemites the Jew, while retaining all the mysterious, uncanny, supernatural attitudes that were wished upon him in the Middle Ages, is also the symbol of modernity, or rather of everything that is felt as frightening in the modern world. The modern age brought the emancipation of the Jews, first in France at the time of the French Revolution and then in one country after another during the nineteenth century. Everywhere Jews quickly became prominent in those fields for which they had been fitted by their previous history: banking, certain branches of commerce, journalism. And at the same time Jews became prominent in liberal, radical, and revolutionary movements – as was only to be expected in view of their own experience of oppression and their often very incomplete emancipation. There was nothing mysterious in any of this – but it did mean that those who for whatever reason suffered helplessly from the modern world, and could not adjust themselves so as to benefit from it, could easily see in the Jew the embodiment of the civilization they detested.

Even here, of course, the myth of the Jewish world-conspiracy remained grotesquely remote from reality. It is true that Jews benefited from the French Revolution, but totally untrue that they caused it. It is true that some Jews became prominent bankers, but utterly false that banking was invented by Jews as a means to securing world-domination. And while many Jews became important figures in journalism and in politics, the views they expressed and the interests they supported ranged over almost the entire political spectrum.

There is in fact a great irony in the myth of the Jewish world-conspiracy – which is, that it reached its most coherent and deadly formulation at the very time when Jews were in reality more divided than ever before – between orthodox and reformed, practising and indifferent, believing and agnostic, assimilationist and Zionist, not to mention the many who utterly rejected their Jewish origin. But all this had not the slightest effect on the myth or on those who propagated it; for they were in any case convinced that though the powers of darkness might put on many forms and wear many disguises, in their ultimate purposes they were at one.

In one form or another the myth of the Jewish world-conspiracy has survived for many centuries and has spread across the world from continent to continent. And it has always shown the same astonishing capacity both to turn certain individuals into blind fanatics, beyond the reach of rational argument and impervious to evidence, and to disturb and confuse in varying degrees large numbers of otherwise quite sensible people. This surely suggests that it answers to deep and enduring unconscious needs. I know that in advancing such a hypothesis one invites scepticism, and there is no denying that many attempts to apply the findings of dynamic psychology to social phenomena have been misguided. But one is dealing here with very bizarre phenomena indeed; and I do not think that one can account for these particular fantasies, nor for the fact that they are always attached to this particular group, unless one takes unconscious mechanisms into account.

Reflecting on these matters some ten years ago, I advanced the hypothesis that these notions about Jews are above all a matter of unconscious negative projections, i.e. of the mental mechanism by which human beings read into the behaviour of others the anarchic tendencies which they fear to recognize in themselves. More specifically, I argued that in this form of anti-semitism the Jews, as a collectivity, are unconsciously seen both as the 'bad' son, i.e. the rebellious son full of murderous wishes towards the father, and the 'bad' father, i.e. the potential torturer, castrator, and killer of the son. Later I discovered that several professional psychoanalysts had preceded me with precisely the same hypothesis; [1] and the present study has convinced me that it is indeed a fruitful one.

Half of the hypothesis is familiar enough. Following Sigmund Freud himself, various psychoanalysts have argued that the Jews, because they reject the Christian God, are unconsciously seen by some Christians as 'bad', rebellious sons – indeed, as parricides. This means that, traditionally, it has been easy and tempting for a Christian to make the Jew into a scapegoat for any unconscious resentment he may have against his father, or for that matter against his God.[2] But this is only one aspect of the matter, and not, it seems to me, the most important.

Unconsciously 'the Jew' is even more closely identified with the 'bad' father than he is with the 'bad' son. This is understandable enough, for the historical relationship of the Jewish people to Christianity and to Europe makes it almost inevitable that it should be seen as a kind of collective father-figure. As an identifiable people the Jews are of course very much older than most of the European peoples, but that is not all: the Jewish religion is the parent religion out of which, and in rivalry with which, Christianity developed. Most important of all, perhaps, is the fact that while the God of Christianity combines the attributes of father and son, the God of the Jews is father only – and, one may add, in the eyes of Christians who learn of him only from the Old Testament

---

[1] E.g. R. M. Loewenstein, *Christians and Jews: a psychoanalytic study*, New York, 1951 (translation of *Psychoanalyse de l'antisémitisme*, Paris, 1951); H. Loeblowitz-Lennard, 'The Jew as symbol', in *The Psychoanalytic Quarterly*, Vol. XVII (1948) and more recently B. Grunberger, 'Der Antisemit und der Oedipuskomplex', in *Psyche* (Stuttgart), August, 1962 (special issue on the psychological and social preconditions of antisemitism). Cf. N. Cohn, *The Pursuit of the Millennium*, London and New York, 1957, p. 72, and more fully in the revised editions 1961–62, pp. 72–3.

[2] S. Freud, *Moses and Monotheism*, London, 1939, pp. 145–7; Loewenstein, op. cit., pp. 37, 99.

and know nothing of the later development of Judaism, a singularly tyrannical and merciless father at that.

The Jews in Christendom, then, were ideally situated to receive the Oedipal projections associated with the 'bad' father. This was a terrible fate, for the fantasied 'bad' father is infinitely more hateful than any real father could ever be. This is inevitable, in view of the psychic processes by which this figure is produced. When a small boy both loves and hates his father with such intensity that the conflict becomes intolerable, he may split the father-image into a 'good' father and a 'bad' father. This enables him, by idealizing his real father or some father-surrogate, to acquire a father whom he can love unreservedly. Unfortunately the same process also produces a father-image which is utterly hateful – and this too can be projected on to any suitable father-surrogate that offers. To realize just what this implies one has to remember what infantile hatred is like – that where a small child hates, it wishes to kill, smash, utterly destroy the hated object. At the same time it feels intensely guilty. This feeling of guilt is quickly repressed into the unconscious, but it finds an outlet nevertheless. The hated object itself turns into a monster demanding retribution, an eye for an eye and a tooth for a tooth. The figure of the 'bad' father becomes a persecutor, endowed with all the merciless hatred and destructive fury which the child feels, but dare not fully recognize, in himself.

So it comes about that the small boy constructs out of his own destructive impulses and his own sense of guilt a father-figure of quite monstrous cruelty and murderousness – a castrating, torturing, cannibalistic, all-powerful being beside whom even the harshest of real parents would appear harmless. The trouble is that the many men who never cease to be small boys in their emotional lives continue to see these monsters around them, incarnated in other human beings. It was the tragedy of the Jews that from the later Middle Ages onwards they tended to be seen in just such a way. In popular art they commonly appeared as extremely old men who are also devils – creatures with enormous growths of hair and beard, but also with horns and tails and with expressions of horrible cruelty.

Viewed in these terms the worst of the traditional antisemitic accusations take on a new and still more disturbing meaning. One has only to look at any medieval picture illustrating a ritual murder story (for instance, that reproduced as Plate 19) to recognize the unconscious content of the fantasy. A small boy – it is, significantly, always a boy, never a girl – is surrounded by a group of elderly men with long beards, who are torturing and castrating him and drawing off and collecting his blood. The same unconscious content is clearly recognizable in the other constantly recurring accusation, which was of torturing the consecrated wafer. This of course was effective only where and when Christ was believed to be physically present in the host, that is to say in Roman Catholic countries; but there it was very effective indeed – in Poland it provoked massacres at late as the eighteenth century. Here too the illustrations show bearded Jews attacking the wafer with nails and pincers – and, as though to uncover the true meaning of these stories, we are sometimes told not only that the host gushed blood but that, at the height of the torture, Christ appeared in the wafer as a small child, bleeding and weeping.

All this helps to throw a new light on the oldest and deadliest charge of all, the charge of deicide, which was still a subject of such passionate debate at the Vatican Council in 1965. In Freud's eyes the idea of deicide had only one unconscious meaning, and that was parricide; but that is not its only possible meaning. For Christians the crucified Christ has the significance much more of a son than of a father. If, therefore, as is constantly asserted in Christian teaching, the Jews are collectively guilty of the death of Christ, they are not so much parricides as slayers of a son, the suppressors of a new generation, those who destroy fresh life and thwart its promise. And nobody who has ever watched a passion-play can doubt for a moment that that is how medieval people really did interpret the Jewish part in the crucifixion.

If one now turns from the medieval to the modern world one makes an astonishing discovery: the Jew has retained his symbolic value as simultaneously the 'bad' son and the 'bad' father. Again the first half of the hypothesis may seem more familiar than the second. Helped by the circumstance that numerous Jews have become prominent in the modern world as innovators, radicals, and revolutionaries, traditionalists have often seen all Jews as a sort of collective 'bad' son, a denier and destroyer of order and authority. But again it is the second part of the hypothesis that is the more important. Modern civilization is commonly experienced, by those who suffer under it, as incomprehensible, uncontrollable, omnipotent; and in so far as Jews were thought to be the creators of that civilization and the masters of its mysterious powers, this tended to perpetuate and reinforce their symbolic significance as 'bad' parents. And indeed it is obvious enough that the Elders of Zion are father-figures. Their very name shows it; and what they do to nations is strictly comparable with what the 'bad' father is imagined as doing to the son. They draw off the life's blood of the nations and divert it to their own sinister purposes, they drive the peoples to torment and death in wars, they deprive millions of food. Above all they have the monopoly of power. Mysterious, inscrutable, they manipulate and torment human beings who in their hands are as helpless and ignorant as children.

Now it is quite certain that this image of the Jew profoundly influenced Hitler himself. An American psychoanalyst has pointed out how mistaken it is to see Hitler as a father-figure: 'Hitler is the adolescent who never even aspired to become a father in any connotation, nor, for that matter, a Kaiser, a president. . . . He is the Führer: the glorified older brother, who replaces the father. . . . He is . . . a gang leader who keeps the boys together by demanding their admiration, by creating terror, and by shrewdly involving them in crimes from which there is no way back.'[1] The worst of these crimes were performed against the father, incarnated in the Jew. Another psychoanalyst, delving into Hitler's youth and family background, has found strong grounds for thinking that he unconsciously identified his own father with a particular Jewish doctor and so with Jews as a collectivity.[2] If this is true, one may be sure that the process was greatly facilitated

[1] E. H. Erikson, 'Hitler's imagery and German youth', in C. Kluckhohn and H. A. Murray, *Personality in Nature*, London, 1949, p. 493. (First published in *Psychiatry*, Vol. V (1942).)

[2] Gertrud M. Kurth, 'The Jew and Adolf Hitler', in *The Psychoanalytic Quarterly*, Vol. XVI (1947).

by the age-old unconscious identification of 'the Jew' with the 'bad' father.

It was often noted that the Jews whom the German troops in eastern Europe treated with the greatest cruelty were the orthodox Jewish men with their long beards. The photographs of youngsters mocking, humiliating, and killing these men of truly patriarchal appearance provide a counterpart to the old woodcuts of ritual murder – but with this difference, that whereas the ritual murders were the merest fictions, the vengeance exacted was real murder, indefinitely repeated.

Yet that is not the whole story. The deepest fear of all is that Jews are, collectively, poisoners or even themselves a sort of poison. This fantasy took shape at the same time as the fantasy of ritual murder; the first occasions when the disappearance of young boys was attributed to Jewish bloodlust were in 1144 and 1168, and the first time when Jews – 86 of them – were burnt for plotting to poison the Christian population was in 1161. By the fourteenth century such accusations were commonplace. In France in 1321 it was reported that the Jews were employing lepers to poison all the wells in Christendom. At the time of the Black Death in 1349 it was widely believed that the Jews had caused the plague by poisoning the wells with a mixture of Christian flesh, hearts and blood (obtained by ritual murder), and of spiders, frogs, and lizards. On that occasion some 300 Jewish communities in Germany, France, and Spain were exterminated; and similar accusations were made, with similar results, at innumerable local plagues down to the mid-sixteenth century. Not that the charges were limited to such emergencies – Martin Luther was expressing the general view when he wrote: 'If [the Jews] could kill us all, they would gladly do so, aye, and often do it, especially those who profess to be physicians. They know all that is known about medicine in Germany; they can give poison to a man of which he will die in an hour, or in ten or twenty years; they thoroughly understand this art.' As late as 1610 the medical faculty of the University of Vienna solemnly announced that Jewish physicians were obliged by their laws to poison every tenth Christian patient.

In the modern version of the myth of the Jewish world-conspiracy these accusations reappear in a pseudo-scientific form. The *Protocols* themselves talk not only of using drink and loose women to undermine the physique of the Gentiles but of actually inoculating the Gentiles with diseases; and in much *Protocols*-type literature, particularly in the United States, schemes for mass inoculation are interpreted as a Jewish plot to inject the population with syphilis. But here again it was Hitler who found the most effective and murderous formulation for an age-old obsession. By the peculiar interpretation which he gave to German racist theories he made sexual intercourse with a Jew appear as something which literally poisoned the blood. In Nazi propaganda the idea was carried to the point where the Jews were habitually called 'the world-poisoners' and were even themselves equated with bacteria.

Just as much as ritual murder, fantasies of this kind are rooted in the unconscious. Every psychoanalyst has had patients who are haunted by the illusion that they have taken in something bad, which is destroying them from within, or who live in perpetual dread of improbable infections; not to mention the true paranoiacs who are convinced that they are being poisoned by particular individuals. These are deep waters indeed, and this is not the place to speculate about etiologies on which specialists are by no means agreed. This much, however, can be safely said: that to imagine that the Jews have poisoned the water-supply or are corrupting people's blood is to ascribe to them truly uncanny powers. And it is likely that when antisemites kill not simply Jewish men but also Jewish women and children, when they see the extermination of all Jews as an indispensable cleansing or disinfection of the earth, they are moved by terrors stemming from the earliest stages of infancy.

There can be many kinds of unconscious negative projections, and it is a matter not merely of scientific interest but also of practical importance to appreciate just what projections have traditionally been attached to the Jews. It is often assumed that all ethnic prejudice is very much of a kind – that, for instance, hatred of Negroes must have precisely the same emotional roots as hatred of Jews; yet the assumption is certainly mistaken. It is of course true that the fanatical Negro-hater, say in the American South, is moved by unconscious as well as by conscious anxieties and that his view of Negroes is gravely distorted by projections. It is also true that much of the cruelty to which Negroes have been subjected has been dictated by these projections. Yet however whites may see Negroes, they can hardly see them as hidden, manipulating 'elders'. The fantasy of an infinitely powerful, world-dominating conspiracy does not in fact get projected on to Negroes, and that may well be why not even the most fanatical Negro-haters dream of genocide. It is a different matter with the Jews. In the most dangerous form of antisemitism Jews are seen above all as 'bad' parents, and this makes them seem so overwhelmingly powerful that the only way to cope with them is to destroy them utterly. That, it is suggested, is why from the twelfth to the twentieth century the truly fanatical antisemites – the kind who deal in tales of ritual murder and in the *Protocols* – have so frequently fomented vast massacres. For the ultimate ideal of such people is not a world where they can lord it over Jews, as the white supremacist likes to lord it over Negroes, but of a world where there are no Jews left at all.

The historical importance of the myth of the Jewish world-conspiracy lies in the fact that it has served as a warrant for many massacres, culminating in attempted genocide in the middle of the present century. Again and again over a period of some eight centuries, and over a wide range of countries, it has enabled organized groups to kill Jews. And it has done this in two ways, which seem to have remained pretty constant down the ages: by providing the organized groups with an ideology, and by bewildering the rest of the population.

Whether one considers the Black Hundreds of tsarist Russia, or those sections of the SS and SD which were directly concerned in the 'final solution', one finds very much the same combination of types; and so far as one can tell from the records, the same combination existed already in those earlier groups of Jew-killers which operated between the first crusade and the sixteenth century. It cannot be said that these groups consisted wholly of genuine fanatics. On the contrary, they contained plenty of purely destructive types, who wanted nothing but a chance to torture and murder, and also plenty of looters, whose main interest was in the property of the killed. To these one must add, for the modern period, the opportunists at all levels, for whom the organizing and carrying through of massacre was simply a means to a better income, more security, and more prestige than they could otherwise have hoped for. Yet it seems certain that however narrow, materialistic, or downright criminal their own motives may be, such men cannot operate without an ideology behind them. At least when operating collectively, they need an ideology to legitimate their behaviour, for without it they would have to see themselves and one another as what they really are – common thieves and murderers. And that apparently is something which even they cannot bear.[1]

The ideology which has proved most suitable for the purpose is the myth of the Jewish world-conspiracy, whether in the traditional form which centred on tales of ritual murder and well-poisoning or in the modern form which centres on the *Protocols*. And this is where the true fanatics have their place – as bearers and elaborators of that fantastic view of the world on which the whole murderous enterprise depends for its justification. Thanks to various empirical investigations carried out by psychologists and psychoanalysts, notably in the United States, a great deal is known about the typical personality-structure of such people.[2] What emerges when fanatical antisemites are subjected to psychological tests is a quite abnormal degree of fear and hatred of parental figures, who are seen now as menacing and now as mutilated and killed. This means that the unconscious fantasies of such people correspond with the unconscious content of the myth of the Jewish world-conspiracy. Fanatical antisemites are in fact people whose own deepest emotional needs compel them to see life as a struggle against just such a conspiracy as is portrayed in the *Protocols*. For them belief springs from an inner necessity; and this gives them an air of absolute con-

[1] Cf. Wanda von Baeyer-Katte, *Das Zerstörende in der Politik*, Heidelberg, 1958, pp. 211 seq.
[2] E.g. H. V. Dicks, 'Personality traits and National Socialist Ideology', in *Human Relations*, June 1950; and the works listed in the Bibliographical Note, under the psychology of antisemitism.

viction, which in turn gives the criminals and opportunists the reassurance and encouragement they need.

A group formed out of these elements is, sociologically speaking, a very special kind of group indeed. Reflecting in 1946 on the extreme forms of Nazi antisemitism, the psychoanalyst Ernst Simmel remarked that the process of group-formation itself, when occurring under pathological conditions, can bring about a mass delusion, in fact a mass psychosis. And he added: 'This clinical syndrome: unrestricted aggressive destructiveness under the spell of a delusion, in complete denial of reality, is well known to us as a psychosis; it is a paranoiac form of schizophrenia.'[1] The parallel is a suggestive one. For though the individuals who make up a group of Jew-killers are well within the bounds of reality, and most of them are not even fanatics, and even the fanatics are far from mad – yet it is perfectly true that the group as a whole behaves like a paranoiac in the grip of his delusion.[2]

There is another peculiarity of such groups that reminds one of paranoiac schizophrenics: their megalomaniac sense of mission. When it comes to describing their own role, not only the medieval Jew-killers but also the Black Hundreds and the Nazi leaders use apocalyptic imagery taken straight from the Book of Revelation. All alike see themselves as the angelic hosts overthrowing the powers of darkness, or a collective St Michael killing the dragon, even as a collective Christ overthrowing Antichrist. No army engaged in a real war against a real enemy has ever indulged in such self-exaltation as Jew-killers engaged in their one-sided struggle against an imaginary conspiracy. To hear them on the subject of themselves, one would think that killing unarmed and helpless people, including small children and old women, was a very brave and risky undertaking. It is a phenomenon which only begins to make sense when one recalls that a paranoiac murderer too can

[1] E. Simmel, 'Anti-Semitism and mass psychopathology', in *Anti-Semitism: a social disease* (ed. Simmel), New York, 1946, p. 39.

[2] Cf. G. M. Gilbert, *The Psychology of Dictatorship. Based on an examination of the leaders of Nazi Germany*, New York, 1950, pp. 270–3. Gilbert makes some useful observations about 'cultural pseudo-paranoia' and the way in which, when inflamed by fanatical ideologists, it can result in collective behaviour which resembles true paranoia.

feel terrified of his harmless victims. For what these people see as the enemy is in fact the destructiveness and cruelty in their own psyches, externalized. And the greater the un-conscious sense of guilt, the more fearsome the imaginary enemy.

For the sense of guilt is there, and unremittingly at work. Originally engendered by the murderous impulses felt by the small child towards its parents, it is enormously intensified by the real violence which the adult deploys against his victims. Yet it is not experienced as a sense of guilt, for it is completely denied and repressed into the unconscious. Instead it is experi-enced as a sense of danger, of threat, a blind terror lest the wronged ones, the parents killed in fantasy and the parent-surrogates killed in reality, arise and exact retribution. This alone can explain the extraordinary paradox about the Nazi massacres – that as the Jews became more and more helpless, as they were killed in ever vaster numbers, so they were felt to be more and more powerful, malignant, and dangerous. It also accounts for the fact that a man like Goebbels, for whom antisemitism was at first little more than a technique of vote-catching, ended his days raving about the omnipotent Jewish rulers of the world. It was his own guilt-ridden unconscious that made of the imaginary Elders of Zion a power more terrible than the Nazi régime itself.

It is when it has been adopted by groups of professional, organized Jew-killers that the myth of the Jewish world-conspiracy has revealed its true potentialities. For all the indications are that however widespread and intense anti-semitism may be, it does not result in killing unless and until such groups begin to operate. Pogroms as spontaneous out-breaks of popular fury seem to be a myth, and there is in fact no established case where the inhabitants of a town or village have simply fallen upon their Jewish neighbours and slaughtered them. This was true even in the Middle Ages – the great massacres which accompanied the people's crusades and the Black Death were all led by organized bands coming from outside. In modern times popular initiative has been still less in evidence, for the organized groups themselves have been effective only when they were carrying out the policy and enjoying the sponsorship of some kind of government – whether in tsarist Russia and under the 'White' régime during the Russian civil war or in Nazi Germany and Nazi-occupied Europe. Would-be *pogromshchiki* who lacked this kind of support and were resolutely opposed by the authorities – as in the United States – never managed to organize large-scale violence and soon lapsed, or were thrust, into obscurity.

Yet the myth of the Jewish world-conspiracy can have its effect on the mass of the population too, and this in turn has a bearing, even if an indirect one, on the fate of the Jews. Centuries of propaganda about sorcery and ritual murder and the secret Jewish government produced a general atmosphere of superstitious dread which was largely unconnected with specific economic conflicts. A certain suspicion that Jews constitute a united collectivity, devoted to sinister aims and endowed with mysterious powers, was still extremely widespread in the first half of the present century. No doubt fanatical believers in the conspiracy, the true adepts of the *Protocols*, were always a relatively small minority; but they were still numerous enough to make themselves heard, and there were vast numbers of half- and quarter-believers to pick up scraps of what they had to say. There is nothing strange about this, for only exceptionally mature personalities are wholly immune to the infantile fears and hatreds to which such a myth appeals. Particularly in periods of exceptional strain, anxiety, and disorientation, multitudes of people yielded to the temptation to blame all their troubles on the machinations of those uncanny beings – reacting to social and economic crises, for instance, very much as their ancestors had reacted to the plague.

What this meant in practice, whether in tsarist Russia or in Germany after the First World War or to some extent throughout the world in the fateful years 1933–45, was that people were unwilling to bestir themselves on behalf of the Jews. The very widespread indifference, the ease with which people dissociated themselves from the Jews and their fate, was certainly in part a result of a vague feeling that, even if there were no Elders of Zion, Jews were somehow uncanny and dangerous. And ironically enough this feeling grew stronger as the persecution of the Jews grew worse. The explanation is plain, if depressing: when people know even with half their minds that a great injustice is being done, and lack the generosity or the courage to protest, they automatically throw the blame on to the victims as the simplest way of easing their own consciences. Just as the organized killers needed the myth of the Jewish world-conspiracy if they were not to recognize themselves as common thieves and murderers, so very many ordinary people needed some smattering of it if they were not to see themselves as passive accomplices in the persecution and massacre of innocent people.

The story of the *Protocols* is the story of how in twentieth-century Europe a grossly delusional view of the world, based on infantile fears and hatreds, was able to find expression in murder and torture beyond all imagining. It is a case-history in collective psychopathology, and its deepest implications reach far beyond antisemitism and the fate of the Jews. Is it utopian to suggest that the more fully and widely these implications are faced, the better the chance of recognizing and limiting, perhaps even of forestalling, similar aberrations in future?

APPENDIX I

The Rabbi's Speech[1]

On this precursor of the *Protocols* see above, pp. 34–40.

Our fathers have bequeathed to the elect of Israel the duty of gathering together once each century around the tomb of the Grand Master Caleb, the holy rabbi Simeon ben Jehuda, whose knowledge gives the elect of each generation power over all the earth and authority over all the descendants of Israel.

For eighteen centuries Israel has been at war with that power which was first promised to Abraham but which was taken from him by the Cross. Trampled underfoot, humiliated by its enemies, living ceaselessly under the threat of death, of persecution, of rape, and of every kind of violation, the people of Israel has not succumbed; and if it is dispersed over the whole earth, that is because it is to inherit the whole earth.

For eighteen centuries our wise men have been fighting the Cross courageously and with a perseverance which nothing can discourage. Gradually our people is rising up and its power increases day by day. Ours is that God of today whom Aaron raised up for us in the desert, that Golden Calf, that universal deity of the age.

The day when we shall have made ourselves the sole possessors of all the gold in the world, the real power will be in our hands, and then the promises which were made to Abraham will be fulfilled.

Gold, the greatest power on earth . . . gold, which is the strength, the recompense, the instrument of every power . . . the sum of everything that man fears and craves . . . *there* is the only mystery, the deepest understanding of the spirit that rules the world. *There* is the future!

Eighteen centuries belonged to our enemies, the present century and future centuries must belong to us, the people of Israel, and they surely will belong to us.

---

[1] My translation from the French. N.C.

Now for the tenth time, in a thousand years of terrible and ceaseless war against our enemies, the elect of a given generation of the people of Israel are gathered in this cemetery, around the tomb of our Grand Master Caleb, the holy rabbi Simeon ben Jehuda, to take counsel as to how to turn to the advantage of our cause the great errors and sins which our enemies the Christians never cease to commit.

Each time the new Sanhedrin has proclaimed and preached a merciless struggle against our enemies; but in no earlier century were our ancestors able to concentrate in our hands so much gold, and therefore so much power, as the nineteenth century has bestowed on us. We can therefore expect, without any rash illusions, to achieve our aim soon, and we can look with confidence to our future.

Most fortunately, the persecution and the humiliations, those dark and painful days which the people of Israel endured with such heroic patience, are no more with us, thanks to the progress of civilization among the Christians, and that progress is the best shield for us to hide and act behind, so as to cross with firm and rapid strides the space that separates us from our supreme objective.

Let us just look at the material condition of Europe, let us analyse the resources which the Jews have got into their possession since the beginning of the present century simply by concentrating in their hands the huge amount of capital which they control at this moment. Thus, in Paris, London, Vienna, Berlin, Amsterdam, Hamburg, Rome, Naples, etc., and in all the Rothschild branches, everywhere the Jews are the financial masters, simply by possessing so many milliards; not to mention that in every town of second or third magnitude it is the Jews who control the currency in circulation, and that nowhere can any financial operation, any major undertaking be carried through without the direct influence of the children of Israel.

Today all reigning emperors, kings, and princes are burdened with debts contracted in keeping up large standing armies to support their toppling thrones. The stock exchange assesses and regulates those debts, and to a great extent we are masters of the stock exchange everywhere. We must therefore study how to encourage borrowing more and more, so as to make ourselves the regulators of all values and, as security for the capital we lend to countries, take the right to exploit their railways, their mines, their forests, their great ironworks and factories, and other kinds of real estate, even their taxes.

In every country agriculture will always be the greatest source of wealth. The possession of large landed property will always bring honours and much influence to the owners. From this it follows that we must concentrate on ensuring that our brothers in Israel acquire landed property on a large scale. So far as possible we must therefore encourage the splitting-up of large estates, so as to help us acquire it more quickly and more easily.

Under the pretext of helping the working classes, we must place the weight of taxation on the great landed proprietors, and when all properties have come into our hands, all the work of the Gentile proletarians will become a source of huge profits for us.

Since the Christian Church is one of our most dangerous enemies, we must work doggedly to diminish its influence; so far as possible, therefore, we must implant in the minds of those who profess the Christian religion the ideas of free thought, of scepticism, of schism, and provoke the religious disputes which are so naturally productive of divisions and sects within Christendom.

Logically, we must begin by disparaging the ministers of that religion. Let us declare open war on them, let us rouse suspicions about their piety, about their private conduct. So, by ridicule and malicious banter, we shall undermine the respect in which the profession and the cloth are held.

Each war, each revolution, each political or religious upheaval brings nearer the moment when we shall attain the supreme aim of our journey.

Trade and speculation, two branches so fertile in profits, must never leave Jewish hands, and once we have become proprietors we shall be able, thanks to the obsequiousness and the shrewdness of our agents, to penetrate to the first source of real influence and real power. It is understood that we are concerned only with those occupations which bring honours, power, or privileges, for those which demand knowledge, work, and inconvenience can and must be left to the Gentiles. The magistrature is for us an institution of the first importance. A career at the bar does most to develop the faculty of civilization and to initiate one into the affairs of our natural enemies, the Christians, and it is in this way that we can get them at our mercy. Why should Jews not become ministers of Education, when they have so often had the portfolio of Finance? Jews must also aspire to the rank of legislators, so that they can work to abrogate the laws which those sinners and infidels, the Goyim, have made against the children of Israel, who by their unvarying devotion to the laws of Abraham are the truly faithful ones.

Moreover, on this point our plan is on the brink of complete fulfilment, for almost everywhere progress has recognized and granted to us the same civil rights as are enjoyed by Christians.

But what must be obtained, what must be the object of our ceaseless efforts, is that the law against bankruptcy should be made less severe. Out of that we shall make ourselves a mine of gold which will be far richer than the mines of California ever were.

The people of Israel must direct its ambition towards that height of power which brings esteem and honours. The surest means of attaining it is to have supreme control over all industrial, financial, and commercial operations, while carefully avoiding every trap and temptation which might expose one to legal proceedings in the country's courts. In its choice of speculation the children of Israel will therefore display the prudence and tact which are the mark of its congenital talent for business.

We must be familiar with everything that earns one a distinguished position in society: philosophy, medicine, law, political economy. In a word all the branches of science, of art, of literature, are a vast field where our successes must give us a big part and show off our talent.

These vocations are inseparable from speculation. Thus the performance even of a very mediocre musical composition will give our people a plausible excuse to put the Jewish composer on a pedestal and surround him with a radiance of glory. As for the sciences, medicine and philosophy, they too must be incorporated into our intellectual domain.

A doctor is initiated into the most intimate secrets of the family. The health and life of our mortal enemies, the Christians, are in his hands.

We must encourage marriages between Jews and Christians, for the people of Israel loses nothing by the contact and can only gain from these marriages. Our race, chosen by God, cannot be corrupted by the introduction of a certain amount of impure blood, and by these marriages our daughters will secure alliances with Christian families of some influence and power. It is right that, in exchange for the money we give, we should obtain the equivalent in influence over everything around us. To be related to Gentiles does not imply a departure from the path we have chosen to follow; on the contrary, with a little skill it will make us the arbiters of their fate.

It is desirable that Jews should refrain from taking women of our holy religion as their mistresses and that they should choose Christian virgins for that role. It would be a great gain for us to replace the sacrament of marriage in church by a simple contract before some civil authority, for then Gentile women would stream into our camp!

If gold is the first power in this world, the second is undeniably the press. But what can the second achieve without the first? As the aims listed above cannot be attained without the help of the press, our people must become the editors of all daily newspapers in all countries. Our possession of gold, our skill in devising means of exploiting mercenary instincts, will make us the arbiters of public opinion and enable us to dominate the masses.

So, advancing step by step in this path, with that perseverance which is our great virtue, we will push the Gentiles back and undo their influence. We shall dictate to the world what it is to have faith in, what it is to honour, and what it is to curse. Perhaps some individuals will rise up against us and will hurl insults and anathemas against us, but the docile and ignorant masses will listen to us and take our side. Once we are absolute masters of the press we will be able to transform ideas about honour, about virtue, about uprightness of character, we will be able to deal a blow against that institution which so far has been sacrosanct, the family, and we will be able to achieve its disintegration. We shall extirpate all belief and faith in everything that our enemies the Christians have venerated up to the present and, using the allurements of the passions as our weapon, we shall declare open war on everything that people respect and venerate.

Let all this be understood and noted, let every child of Israel absorb these true principles! Then our might will grow like a gigantic tree whose branches will bear the fruits called wealth, enjoyment, power, as compensation for that hideous condition which for long centuries has been the only lot of the people of Israel. When one of our people takes a step forward, let another follow him closely; if his foot slips, let him be picked up and succoured by his co-religionists. If a Jew is summoned before the courts of the country where he lives, let his brothers in religion hasten to give him aid and assistance; but only if the accused has acted in accordance with the Law of Israel, so strictly observed and kept for so many centuries!

Our people is conservative, faithful to the religious ceremonies and the customs bequeathed to us by our ancestors.

It is in our interest that we should at least make a show of zeal for the social questions of the moment, especially for improving the lot of the workers, but in reality our efforts must be geared to getting control of this movement of public opinion and directing it.

The blindness of the masses, their readiness to surrender to that resounding but empty eloquence that fills the public squares, make them an easy prey and a double instrument, of popularity and of credit. We will have no difficulty in finding as much eloquence among our people for the expression of false sentiments as Christians find in their sincerity and enthusiasm.

So far as possible we must talk to the proletariat, bring it into subjection to those who have the handling of money. By this means we will be able to make the masses rise when we wish. We will drive them to upheavals, to revolutions; and each of these catastrophes marks a big step forward for our particular interests and brings us rapidly nearer to our sole aim – world-domination, as was promised to our father Abraham.

Some parallel passages in the *Protocols* and the *Dialogue aux Enfers*

For the story of how the forger of the *Protocols* plagiarized Maurice Joly's *Dialogue aux Enfers entre Montesquieu et Machiavel* see above, pp. 71–6. The following extracts are taken from the first (1920) British edition of the *Protocols*, which is a pretty free translation from the Russian. If one bears in mind that the Russian is itself a translation of the lost French text, it is remarkable that the parallelism with Joly's book, as exemplified in these extracts, should be as close as it is. But the similarity between Joly in French and Lambelin's French edition of the *Protocols* is much closer still.

In the first British edition the text is not divided into separate chapters or 'protocols'. The 'protocol'-numbers given below and in Appendix III refer to the Russian edition by Nilus and to most of its many translations.

Dialogue aux enfers[1]	*Protocols*
First dialogue	First 'protocol'

... The bad instinct is stronger in man than the good instinct.
... Fear and force have more power over him than reason.
... All men aim at domination, and there is none who would not be an oppressor if he only could; all or almost all are ready to sacrifice the rights of others to their own interests. Who restrains among themselves the beasts of prey we call men? In the beginnings of

... people with corrupt instincts are more numerous than those of noble instinct. Therefore in governing the world the best results are obtained by means of violence and intimidation, and not by academic discussions. Every man aims at power; everyone would like to become a dictator if he only could do so, and rare indeed are the men who would not be disposed to sacrifice the

[1] My translation. N.C.

society, it was brute, unbridled force; later it was law, that is to say force still, but regulated by certain forms. . . . Everywhere might appears before right. Political freedom is only a relative idea.

welfare of others in order to attain their own personal aims. What restrained the wild beasts of prey which we call men? What has ruled them up to now? In the first stages of social life they submitted to brute and blind force, then to law, which in reality is the same force, only masked. From this I am led to deduct [sic] that by the law of nature, right lies in might. Political freedom is not a fact, but an idea.

Seventh dialogue

. . . I would organize huge financial monopolies, reservoirs of public wealth, in which all private fortunes would be so closely involved that they would sink together with the credit of the state the day after any political disaster.

As head of the government, all my edicts would be constantly directed to the same aim: to develop the preponderance of the state, out of all proportion, to make it the sovereign protector, promoter and recompenser. . . . Nowadays the aristocracy, as a political force, is no more; but the landowning bourgeoisie still constitutes an element of dangerous opposition to governments, because it is itself independent. It may be necessary to impoverish it or even to ruin it altogether. To

Sixth 'protocol'

. . . Soon we will start organizing great monopolies – reservoirs of colossal wealth, in which even the large fortunes of the Gentiles will be involved to such an extent that they will sink together with the credit of their government the day after a political crisis takes place.
. . . We must use every possible kind of means to develop the popularity of our Supergovernment, holding it up as a protection and recompenser of all who willingly submit to us.

The aristocracy of the Gentiles, as a political power, is no more – therefore we need not consider it any more from that point of view. But as landowners they are still dangerous to us, because their independent existence is ensured through their resources. Therefore, it is essential for us, at all costs, to deprive the aristoachieve this it is only necessary to increase the rates and taxes on landed property, to keep agriculture in a state of relative inferiority, to give preferential treatment to trade and industry, and especially to speculation, for if industry prospers too much it can itself become dangerous, by creating too many independent fortunes.

cracy of their lands. To attain this purpose the best method is to force up rates and taxes. These methods will keep the landed interests at their lowest possible ebb. . . . At the same time we must give all possible protection to trade and commerce, and especially to speculation, the principal role of which is to act as a counterpoise to industry. Without speculation industry will enlarge private capitals. . . .

Twelfth dialogue

I foresee the possibility of neutralizing the press by means of the press itself. Since journalism is such a great force, my government will take to journalism. It will be journalism incarnate. . . .

I will count the number of newspapers that represent what you call the opposition. If there are ten for the opposition, I shall have twenty for the government; if there are 20 I shall have 40; if there are 40 I shall have 80. . . . But the mass of the public must have no suspicion of these tactics. . . .

Like the god Vishnu, my press will have a hundred arms, and these arms will give expression to all shades of opinion throughout the whole country. People will belong to my party without realizing it. Those who think they are talking their own language will be talking mine, those who think

Twelfth 'protocol'

Literature and journalism are the two most important educational powers; for this reason our government will buy up the greater number of periodicals. By these means we shall neutralize the bad influence of the private press and obtain an enormous influence over the human mind. If we were to allow ten private periodicals we should ourselves start thirty, and so forth.

But the public must not have the slightest suspicion of these measures, therefore all periodicals published by us will seem to be of contradictory views and opinions, thus inspiring confidence and presenting an attractive appearance to our unsuspecting enemies, who will thus fall into our trap and will be disarmed. . . . These newspapers, like the Indian god Vishnu, they are stirring up people on their side will be stirring up people on mine, those who think they are marching under their flag will be marching under mine. . . .

. . . You should know that journalism is a sort of free-masonry; those who live by it are all more or less bound to one another by the bonds of professional discretion; like the ancient augurs, they will not easily divulge the secret of their oracles. They would gain nothing by betraying one another, for they mostly have more or less shameful wounds. It is quite likely that at the heart of the capital, in certain circles, these things will be no mystery; but elsewhere people will know nothing of these things and the great majority of the nation will march with the utmost confidence in the footsteps of the guides I have given it.

will be possessed of hundreds of hands, each of which will be feeling the pulse of varying public opinion.

. . . If any chatterers are going to imagine that they are repeating the opinion of their party newspaper, they will in reality be repeating our own opinion, or the opinion which we desire. Thinking that they are following the organ of this party, they will in reality be following the flag which we will fly for them.

. . . Already there exists in French journalism a system of masonic understanding for giving countersigns. All organs of the press are tied by mutual professional secrets in the manner of the ancient oracles. Not one of its members will betray his knowledge of the secret, if such a secret has not been ordered to be made public. No single publisher will have the courage to betray the secret entrusted to him, the reason being that not one of them is admitted into the literary world without bearing the marks of some shady act in his past life. He would only have to show the least sign of disobedience and the mark would be immediately revealed. Whilst these marks remain known only to a few, the prestige of the journalist attracts public opinion throughout the country. The people follow and admire him.

My journalism will exercise its greatest influence in the provinces. . . . There I shall always arrange the climate of opinion which I need, and each of my blows will strike home. The provincial press will be entirely in my hands, for there no contradiction or discussion can be permitted. From the administrative centre where I preside, orders will be sent out to make the newspapers express such and such views, so that at a given moment a certain influence will be felt, a certain impulsion given, throughout the country, often before the capital has any idea. . . . When necessary, opinion in the capital will form more slowly than the external movement of opinion which will envelop it, if need be without its knowledge. . . . I do not wish the country to be disturbed by rumours . . . If some extraordinary suicide occurs, or some shady financial affair . . . I shall forbid the newspapers to mention it.

Our plans must extend chiefly to the provinces. It is essential for us to create such ideas and inspire such opinions there as we could at any time launch on the capital by producing them as the neutral views of the provinces.

Of course, the source and origin of the idea would not be altered: namely, it would be ours.

It is imperative for us that, before we assume power, cities should sometimes be under the influence of the opinion of the provinces – that is to say, that they should know the opinion of the majority, which will have been prearranged by us. It is necessary for us that the capitals, at the critical psychological moment, should not have time to discuss an accomplished fact, but should accept it simply because it has been passed by a majority in the provinces.

When we reach the period of the new régime – that is to say, during the transition stage to our sovereignty – we must not allow the press to publish any account of criminal cases; it will be essential that people should think that the new régime is so satisfactory that even crime has ceased.

Some passages in the *Protocols* not based on the *Dialogue aux Enfers*[1]

The following extracts give a fair idea of the mental world of Russian right-wingers in the 1890s. They reveal not only what these people believed about the Jews or tried to make others believe about them but also, in places, the social and political ideals which they themselves cherished. For paradoxically – and like the Nazis after them – these antisemites often attributed their own values and aspirations to the imaginary Jewish government.

First 'protocol'

. . . Alone an autocrat can conceive vast plans clearly assigning its proper part to everything in the mechanism of the machine of state. Hence we conclude that it is expedient for the welfare of the country that the government of the same should be in the hands of one responsible person. Without absolute despotism civilization cannot exist, for civilization is capable of being promoted only under the protection of the ruler, whoever he may be, and not at the hands of the masses.

The crowd is a barbarian, and acts as such on every occasion. As soon as the mob has secured freedom it speedily turns it into anarchy, which in itself is the height of barbarism.

Just look at these alcoholised animals stupefied by the drink, of which unlimited use is tolerated by freedom! Should we allow ourselves and our fellow creatures to do likewise? The people of the Christians, bewildered by alcohol, their youths turned crazy by classics and early debauchery, to which they have been instigated by our agents, tutors, servants, governesses in rich houses, clerks, and so forth, by our women in places of their amusement – to the latter I add the so-called 'society women' – their voluntary followers in corruption and luxury. . . .

[1] From the first (1920) British edition of the *Protocols*.

Third 'protocol'

Today I can assure you that we are only within a few strides of our goal. There remains only a short distance and the cycle of the Symbolic Serpent – that badge of our people – will be complete. When this circle is locked, all the States of Europe will be enclosed in it, as it were, by unbreakable chains.[1]

The existing constructional[2] scales will soon collapse because we are continually throwing them out of balance in order the more quickly to wear them out and destroy their efficiency. . . .

. . . Under our auspices the populace exterminated the aristocracy which had supported and guarded the people for its own benefit, which benefit is inseparable from the welfare of the populace. Nowadays, having destroyed the privileges of the aristocracy, the people fall under the yoke of cunning profiteers and upstarts.

We intend to appear as though we were the liberators of the labouring man, come to free him from this oppression, when we shall suggest to him to join the ranks of our armies of Socialists, Anarchists, and Communists. The latter we always patronize, pretending to help them out of fraternal principle and the general interest of humanity evoked by our socialistic masonry. The aristocracy, who by right shared the labour[3] of the working classes, were interested in the same being well-fed, healthy, and strong. We are interested in the opposite, i.e. in the degeneration of the Gentiles.[4] Our strength lies in keeping the working man in perpetual want and impotence; because, by so doing, we retain him subject to our will and, in his own surroundings, he will never find either power or energy to stand up against us. Hunger will confer upon Capital more powerful rights over the labourer than ever the lawful power of the sovereign could confer upon the aristocracy.

We govern the masses by making use of feelings of jealousy and hatred kindled by oppression and need. And by means of these feelings we brush aside those who impede us in our course.

When the time comes for our Worldly Ruler[5] to be crowned, we will see to it that by the same means – that is to say, by making use of the mob – we will destroy everything that may prove an obstacle in our way.

[1] Cf. the Epilogue to the *Protocols* below, and the map on Plate 4.
[2] *Sic*. An error for 'constitutional'.
[3] Should read 'shared the fruits of the labour'.
[4] In the standard British version this appears as 'the *killing out of the Goyim*', italicized.
[5] Should read 'Ruler of the World'.

The Gentiles are no longer capable of thinking without our aid in matters of science. That is why they do not realize the vital necessity of certain things, which we will make a point of keeping against the moment when our hour arrives – namely, that in schools the only true and the most important of all sciences must be taught, that is, the science of the life of man and social conditions, both of which require a division of labour and therefore the classification of people in castes and classes. . . .

The true science of social conditions, to the secrets of which we do not admit the Gentiles, would convince the world that occupations and labour should be kept in specified castes so as not to cause human suffering, arising from an education which does not correspond with the work which individuals are called upon to do. If they were to study this science, the people would of their own free will submit to the ruling powers and to the castes of government classified by them. Under the present conditions of science and the line which we have allowed it to follow, the populace, in its ignorance, blindly believes in printed words and in erroneous illusions which have been duly inspired by us, and it bears malice to all classes which it thinks higher than itself. For it does not understand the importance of each caste. This hatred will become still more acute where economical crises are concerned, for then it will stop the markets and production. We will create a universal economic crisis, by all possible underhand means and with the help of gold, which is all in our hands. Simultaneously we will throw on to the streets huge crowds of workmen throughout Europe. These masses will then gladly throw themselves upon and shed the blood of those of whom, in their ignorance, they have been jealous from childhood, and whose belongings they will then be able to plunder.

They will not harm us, because the moment of the attack will be known to us and we will take measures to protect our interests.

We persuaded the Gentiles that liberalism would bring them to a kingdom of reason. Our despotism will be of this nature, for it will be in a position to put down all rebellions and by just severity to exterminate every liberal idea from all institutions.

When the populace noticed that it was being given all sorts of rights in the name of liberty, it imagined itself to be the master, and tried to assume power. Of course, like every other blind man, the mass came up against innumerable obstacles. Then, as it did not wish to return to the former régime, it lay its power at our feet. Remember the French Revolution, which we call the 'great', the secrets of its preparatory organization are well known to us, being the work of our hands. From that time onwards we have led the nations from one disappointment to another, so that they should

even renounce us in favour of the King-Despot of the blood of
Zion, whom we are preparing for the world. . . .

Fifth 'protocol'

. . . In the days when the people looked on their sovereigns as on
the will of God, they quietly submitted to the despotism of their
monarchs. But from the day that we inspired the populace with
the idea of its own rights, they began to regard kings as ordinary
mortals. In the eye of the mob the holy anointment fell from the
head of monarchs, and, when we took away their religion, the
power was thrown into the streets like public property, and was
snatched up by us. Moreover, among our administrative gifts, we
count also that of ruling the masses and individuals by means of
cunningly constructed theories and phraseology, by rules of life
and every other kind of device. All these theories, which the
Gentiles do not at all understand, are based on analysis and
observation, combined with so skilful a reasoning as cannot be
equalled by our rivals, any more than these can compete with us
in the construction of plans for political actions and solidarity. The
only society known to us which would be capable of competing
with us in these arts, might be that of the Jesuits. But we have
managed to discredit these in the eyes of the stupid mob as being
a palpable organization, whereas we ourselves have kept in the
background, reserving our organization as a secret. . . .

We set at variance with one another all personal and national
interests of the Gentiles, by promulgating religious and tribal
prejudices among them, for nearly twenty centuries. To all this,
the fact is due that not one single government will find support
from its neighbours when it calls upon them for it, in opposing us,
because each one of them will think that action against us might be
disastrous for its individual existence. We are too powerful – the
world has to reckon with us. Governments cannot make even a
small treaty without our being secretly involved in it. . . .

Ninth 'protocol'
(See above, pp. 63, 102)

. . . It is contended that nations can rise in arms against us if our
plans are discovered prematurely; but in anticipation of this we
can rely upon throwing into action such a formidable force as will

make even the bravest of men shudder. By then metropolitan railways and underground passages will be constructed in all cities. From these subterranean places we will explode all the cities of the world, together with their institutions and documents.

Twenty-fourth 'protocol'

Now I will deal with the manner in which we will strengthen the dynasty of King David, in order that it may endure until the last day.

Our manner of securing the dynasty will consist chiefly of the same principles which have given to our wise men the management of the world's affairs, that is to say, the direction and education of the whole human race.

Several members of the seed of David will prepare Kings and their successors, who will be elected not by right of inheritance but by their own capabilities. These successors will be initiated in our secret political mysteries and plans of governing, taking great care that no one else should acquire them.

Such measures will be necessary in order that all should know that only those can rule who have been initiated in the mysteries of political art. Only such men will be taught how to apply our plans in practice by making use of the experience of many centuries. They will be initiated in the conclusions drawn from all observations of our political and economical system and in all social sciences. In a word, they will be told the true spirit of the laws that have been founded by nature herself in order to govern mankind.

Direct successors to the sovereign will be superseded in the event of their proving to be frivolous or soft-hearted during their education, or in case they show any other tendency likely to be detrimental to their power, and which render them incapable of ruling and even to be dangerous to the prestige of the crown.

Only such men as are capable of governing firmly, although perhaps cruelly, will be entrusted with the reins of government by our Elders.

In case of illness or loss of energy, our Sovereign will be obliged to hand over the reins of government to those of his family who have proved themselves more capable.

The King's immediate plans and, still more, his plans for the future will not even be known to those who will be called his nearest councillors. Only our Sovereign, and the Three who initiated him, will know the future.

In the person of the Sovereign, who will rule with an unshakable will and control himself as well as humanity, the people will recognize as it were fate itself and all its human paths. None will know the aims of the Sovereign when he issues his orders, therefore none will dare to obstruct his mysterious path.

Of course, the Sovereign must have a head capable of dealing with our plans. Therefore he will not ascend the throne before his brain-power has been ascertained by our wise men.

In order that all his subjects should love and venerate their Sovereign, he must often address them in public. Such measures will bring the two powers into harmony, namely, that of the populace and that of the ruler, which we have separated in the Gentile countries by holding the one in awe of the other.

We had to hold these two powers in awe one of another, in order that they, when once separated, should fall under our influence.

The King of Israel must not be under the influence of his own passions, especially that of sensuousness. He must not allow animal instincts to get the better of his brain. Sensuousness, more than any other passion, is certain to destroy mental and foreseeing powers; it distracts men's thoughts towards the worst side of human nature.

The Column of the Universe in the person of the World Ruler, sprung from the Holy seed of David, has to forgo all personal passions for the benefit of his people.

Our Sovereign must be irreproachable.

Signed by the representatives of
Zion, of the 33rd degree.

In many editions, including the early Russian editions of 1903–6 and also the first British edition of 1920, the text of the *Protocols* is followed by an epilogue on the Symbolic Serpent (see the extract from the third 'protocol' above, and the map on Plate 3). The key passage is as follows:

According to the records of secret Jewish Zionism, Solomon and other Jewish learned men already, in 929 B.C., thought out a scheme in theory for a peaceful conquest of the whole universe by Zion.

As history developed, this scheme was worked out in detail and completed by men, who were subsequently initiated in this question. These learned men decided by peaceful means to conquer the world for Zion with the slyness of the symbolic serpent, whose head was to represent the initiated into the plans of the Jewish administration, and the body of the serpent to represent the Jewish people – the administration was always kept secret, even from the Jewish nation itself. As this serpent penetrated into the hearts of the nations which it encountered, it got under and devoured all the non-Jewish power of these states. It is foretold that the snake has to finish its work, strictly adhering to the designed path, until the course which it has to run is closed by the return of its head to Zion and until by this means, the snake has completed its round of Europe and has encircled it – and until, by dint of enchaining Europe, it has encompassed the whole world. This it is to accomplish by using every endeavour to subdue the other countries by an economical conquest.

The return of the head of the serpent to Zion can only be accomplished after the power of all the Sovereigns of Europe has been laid low, that is to say, when by means of economic crises and wholesale destruction effected everywhere there shall have been brought about a spiritual demoralization and a moral corruption, chiefly with the assistance of Jewish women masquerading as French, Italians, etc.[1] These are the surest spreaders of licentiousness into the lives of the leading men at the heads of nations.

Women in the service of Zion act as a decoy for those who, thanks to them, are always in need of money, and therefore are always ready to barter their conscience for money. This money is in reality only lent by the Jews, for it quickly returns through the same women into the hands of bribing Jewry – but, through these transactions, slaves are bought for the cause of Zion.

It is natural for the success of such an undertaking that neither the public officials nor private individuals should suspect the part played by the women employed by Jewry. Therefore the directors of the cause of Zion formed, as it were, a religious caste – eager followers of the Mosaic law and of the statutes of the Talmud. All the world believed that the mask of the law of Moses is the real rule of life of the Jews. No one thought of investigating the effect of this rule of life, especially as all eyes were directed on the gold, which could be supplied by the caste, and which gave this caste absolute freedom for its economical and political intrigues.

A sketch of the symbolic serpent is shown as follows: Its first

---

[1] Some ladies were named at this point in the manuscript submitted by Nilus to the Censorship Committee in Moscow. The names, which were removed on the order of the committee, included not only the famous Jewish actress Sarah Bernhardt but also La Belle Otéro, who was a Spaniard with nothing Jewish about her. It is an extraordinary thought that La Belle Otéro lived for another sixty years. She died late in 1965, just as the present book was being completed.

stage in Europe was in 429 B.C. in Greece, where, in the time of Pericles, the serpent first started eating into the power of that country. The second stage was in Rome in the time of Augustus about 69 B.C.[1] The third in Madrid in the time of Charles V in A.D. 1552. The fourth in Paris about 1700, in the time of Louis XVI.[2] The fifth in London from 1814 onwards (after the downfall of Napoleon). The sixth in Berlin in 1871 after the Franco-Prussian war. The seventh in St Petersburg, over which is drawn the head of the serpent under the date of 1881.

All these states which the serpent traversed have had the foundations of their constitutions shaken, Germany, with its apparent power, forming no exception to the rule. In economic conditions England and Germany are spared, but only till the conquest of Russia is accomplished by the serpent, on which at present all its efforts are concentrated. The further course of the serpent is not shown on this map, but arrows indicate its next movement towards Moscow, Kieff, and Odessa.

It is now well known to us to what extent the latter cities form the centres of the militant Jewish race. Constantinople is shown as the last stage of the serpent's course before it reaches Jerusalem.

Only a short distance still remains before the serpent will be able to complete its course by uniting its head to its tail. . . .

[1] This is some forty years too early for Augustus.
[2] A mistake for Louis XIV.

APPENDIX IV

The *Protocols* and the Coming of Antichrist

(See above, pp. 43, 91–2, and Plate 6)

Though the *Protocols* were to form an important part of one of the major totalitarian creeds of the twentieth century, they grew out of an age-old apocalyptic tradition. The extent to which they were originally involved with the Antichrist legend emerges clearly from the note which Sergey Nilus appended to his edition of 1905[1]:

. . . There is no room left for doubt. With all the might and terror of Satan, the reign of the triumphant King of Israel is approaching our unregenerate world; the King born of the blood of Zion – the Antichrist – is near to the throne of universal power.

Events in the world are rushing with stupendous rapidity; dissensions, wars, rumours, famines, epidemics, and earthquakes[2] – what was but yesterday impossible, has today become an accomplished fact. Days rush past, as it were for the benefit of the chosen people. There is no time to minutely enter into the history of humanity from the point of view of the revealed 'mysteries of iniquity',[3] to historically prove the influence which the 'elders of Israel' have had on the misfortunes of humanity, to foretell the already approaching certain future of mankind or to disclose the final act of the world's tragedy.

The Light of Christ alone and that of His Holy Universal Church can penetrate into the Satanic depths and reveal the extent of their wickedness.

In my heart I feel that the hour has struck for summoning the Eighth Ecumenical Council to which, oblivious of the quarrels which have parted them for so many centuries, will congregate the pastors and representatives of the whole of Christianity, to meet the advent of the Antichrist.

---

[1] As translated in the first (1920) British edition of the Protocols.
[2] The traditional 'signs' of the last days of this world.
[3] The reference is to the prophecy of Antichrist in 2 Thessalonians II.

Bibliographical Note

IT would be impracticable to produce an exhaustive bibliography for the subjects touched on in this book, and the following survey is intended simply as an introduction to the field of study.

When it is completed by a further two volumes, Léon Poliakov's *Histoire de l'Antisémitisme* will be the fullest history of the anti-semitic tradition. At present (1966) it consists of Vol. I, *Du Christ aux Juifs de Cour* (Paris, 1955) (English translation, New York, 1965)[1], which deals with European antisemitism down to the eve of emancipation, and Vol. II, *De Mahomet aux Marranes* (Paris, 1961), which deals with the fate of the Jews under Islam and in Spain and Portugal. Meanwhile the essentials of the story have been skilfully compressed into a single volume by James Parkes: *Antisemitism*, London, 1963. Hugo Valentin's *Antisemitism Historically and Critically Examined*, London, 1936, can also be profitably consulted, and so can Salo W. Baron's great *Social and Religious History of the Jews*, 3 vols., New York, 1937, and 8 vols., New York, 1952–58.

Works dealing specially with the origins of antisemitism in early Christianity are James Parkes, *The Conflict of the Church and the Synagogue*, London, 1934; Marcel Simon, *Verus Israël*, Paris, 1948; and Jules Isaac, *Genèse de l'Antisémitisme*, Paris, 1956; while James Parkes, *The Jew in the Medieval Community*, London, 1938, and Joshua Trachtenberg, *The Devil and the Jews*, New Haven, 1943, deal with the period when the figure of the Jew was effectively demonized.

The revival of antisemitism in the past few generations is studied in: James Parkes, *The Emergence of the Jewish Problem, 1878–1939*, Oxford, 1946; K. S. Pinson (ed.), *Essays on Anti-Semitism*, New York, 1946; Howard M. Sachar, *The Course of Modern Jewish History*, Cleveland and New York, 1958; and Hannah Arendt, *The Origins of Totalitarianism* (second edition), London, 1958. Works on individual countries include R. F. Byrnes, *Antisemitism in Modern France*, New Brunswick, 1950 (which however stops short before the Dreyfus case); P. W. Massing, *Rehearsal for Destruction:*

---

[1] And London, 1966.

a study of political antisemitism in Imperial Germany, New York, 1949; P. G. J. Pulzer, *The Rise of Political Anti-semitism in Germany and Austria*, New York and London, 1964; and S. M. Dubnow, *History of the Jews in Russia and Poland*, 3 vols., Philadelphia, 1916–20.

Among works on the social preconditions of Nazi antisemitism Eva Reichmann, *Hostages of Civilisation*, London, 1950, and A. Leschnitzer, *The Magic Background of Modern Anti-semitism*, New York, 1956, remain very valuable, while on the ideological background George L. Mosse, *The Crisis of German Ideology*, New York, 1964, is now the standard work. The Nazi persecution of the Jews can be studied from documents in L. Poliakov and J. Wulf, *Le IIIe Reich et les Juifs*, Paris, 1959. The extermination itself is described in L. Poliakov, *Bréviaire de la Haine*, Paris, 1951 (translated as *Harvest of Hate*, Syracuse U.P. and London, 1954, 1956); Gerald Reitlinger, *The Final Solution*, London, 1953; and Raul Hilberg, *The Destruction of the European Jews*, Chicago, 1961; as well as in the many accounts of particular camps. Various German works illumine the psycho-social processes which made the extermination possible, notably K. Baschwitz, *Du und die Masse*, Amsterdam, 1938; M. Müller-Claudius, *Der Antisemitismus und das deutsche Verhängnis*, Frankfort/Main, 1948; Wanda von Baeyer-Katte, *Das Zerstörende in der Politik*, Heidelberg, 1958; and H. Buchheim, M. Broszat, H.-A. Jacobsen and H. Krausnick, *Anatomie des SS-Staates*, 2 vols., Olten und Freiburg in Breisgau, 1965. H. R. Trevor-Roper, *The Last Days of Hitler*, London and New York, 1947 (third edition 1962); J. R. Rees (ed.) *The Case of Rudolf Hess*, London, 1947; G. M. Gilbert, *The Psychology of Dictatorship. Based on an examination of the leaders of Nazi Germany*, New York, 1950; R. Hoess, *Commandant of Auschwitz*, London, 1953; and Hannah Arendt, *Eichmann in Jerusalem, a report on the banality of evil*, New York, 1963, provide valuable and varied insights into Nazi mentality. For the history of the Nazi movement Alan Bullock, *Hitler, a Study in Tyranny*, 5th edition, London, 1964, is indispensable.

For the psychology and sociology of antisemitic prejudice the series of pioneering volumes sponsored by the American Jewish Committee and entitled *Studies in Prejudice* is of fundamental importance: *The Authoritarian Personality*, by T. W. Adorno, Else Frenkel-Brunswik, D. J. Levinson and R. N. Sanford, New York, 1950; *Dynamics of Prejudice*, by R. Bettelheim and M. Janowitz, Chicago, 1950, and its expanded version, *Social Change and Prejudice*, Glencoe, 1964; and *Antisemitism and Emotional Disorder*, by N. W. Ackerman and Marie Jahoda. A comparable British study is J. H. Robb, *Working-class Anti-semite, a psychological study in a London borough*, London, 1954. All these works are primarily concerned with the personality-structure and social situation of typical present-day antisemites. As a psychoanalytical interpretation of the antisemitic tradition as a historical phenomenon R. M. Loewenstein, *Christians and Jews*, New York, 1951 (translation of *Psychoanalyse de l'antisémitisme*, Paris, 1951) is still unrivalled.

The story of the *Protocols* has been told many times, with varying degrees of accuracy, in newspaper articles and in books dealing with famous impostures. But between the two world wars there also appeared more than a dozen works solely devoted to the historical and critical study of the *Protocols*. Early studies, which by now have themselves acquired historical interest, include: for Britain: L. Wolf, *The Jewish Bogey*, London, 1920; P. Graves, *The Truth about the Protocols* (*The Times* articles reprinted), London, 1921; for the United States: H. Bernstein, *The History of a Lie*, New York, 1921; John Spargo, *The Jew and American Ideals*, New York and London, 1921; for Germany: O. Friedrich, *Die Weisen von Zion. Das Buch der Fälschungen*, Lübeck, 1920; H. L. Strack, *Jüdische Geheimgesetze?*, Berlin, 1921; B. Segel, *Die Protokolle der Weisen von Zion, kritisch beleuchtet*, Berlin, 1924, and a more popular version of the same: *Welt-Krieg, Welt-Revolution, Welt-Verschwörung, Welt-Oberregierung*, Berlin, 1926 (translated as *The Protocols of the Elders of Zion, the greatest lie in history*, New York, 1934); and a Russian work, Yu. Delevsky, *Protokoly Sionskikh Mudretsov*, Berlin, 1923, which contains little-known documentary material. The Nazi period saw a fresh spate of studies: H. Rollin, *L'Apocalypse de notre temps: les dessous de la propagande allemande d'après des documents inédits*, Paris, 1939, which is an important work of original scholarship; P. Charles, S.J., *Les Protocoles des Sages de Sion*, Paris, 1938 (reprinted from the *Nouvelle Revue Théologique*); another and fuller study by Bernstein, *The Truth about the Protocols of Zion*, New York, 1935; J. Gwyer's witty *Portraits of mean men: a short history of the Protocols of the Elders of Zion*, London, 1938; two works directly inspired by the Berne trial: V. Burtsev, *'Protokoly Sionskikh Mudretsov' Dokazanny Podlog* (*'The Protocols of the Elders of Zion' a proven forgery*), Paris, 1938, and E. Raas and G. Brunschvig, *Vernichtung einer Fälschung: der Prozess um die erfundenen 'Weisen von Zion'* Zurich, 1938; and three works devoted to showing Hitler as a pupil of the Elders: A. Stein, *Adolf Hitler, Schüler der 'Weisen von Zion'*, Karlsbad, 1936; I. Heilbut, *Die öffentlichen Verleumder. Die Protokolle der Weisen von Zion und ihre Anwendung in der heutigen Weltpolitik*, Zurich, 1937; and R. Blank, *Adolf Hitler, ses aspirations, sa politique, sa propagande et les Protocols des Sages de Sion,* Paris, 1938. A valuable study of the various editions of the *Protocols* was produced by E. Cherikover, probably in 1934: *Les Protocoles, leur origine et leur diffusion.* It seems never to have been printed, but it was known to Rollin and is available in mimeograph at the Wiener Library. The latest study, J. S. Curtiss, *An appraisal of the Protocols of Zion,* New York, 1942, is a meticulous survey of the facts of the forgery as generally known, but without the benefit of Rollin's researches. Writing a generation later Walter Laqueur, in *Russia and Germany, a century of conflict,* London, 1965, has thrown fresh light on the Russian and German propagators of the forgery and the links between them. A chapter by J. M. Machover in *Dix ans après la chute de Hitler (1945–1955),* published by the Centre de Documentation Juive Contemporaine in Paris in 1957, deals with the *Protocols* in the years immediately following the war.

The books, pamphlets, and articles defending and elaborating the *Protocols* are believed to number more than a thousand. The following list of some of the editions of the *Protocols* themselves will give some idea of the dissemination of the forgery:

Russian:

Shortened version in Krushevan's newspaper *Znamya,* St Petersburg, from 26 August to 7 September 1903.

Complete text in Chapter XII, second edition of S. A. Nilus, *Velikoe v Malom i Antikhrist . . .,* Tsarskoe Selo, 1905.

In G. Butmi, *Vragi Roda Chelovecheskago,* St Petersburg, 1906; second edition 1907.

In new edition of Nilus's book, renamed *Bliz Gryadushchy Antikhrist,* Moscow, 1911.

In further edition of Nilus's book, renamed *Bliz Est, Pri Dverekh,* Moscow, 1917.

Sionskiye Protokoly, Novocherkask, 1918. Nilus text, printed by printing office of Don Cossack Army, and known to have been edited by A. Rodionov.

Russian emigration:

Luch Sveta, Vol. III, dated May 1920, contains complete text of Nilus's book, 1911 edition. Berlin.

Vsemirny tayny zagovor. Protokoly sionskikh mudretsov (po Nilusu), New York, 1921.

Protokoly sionskikh mudretsov (po tekstu S. A. Nilusa). Vsemirny tayny zagovor, Berlin, 1922.

M. K. Gorchakov, *Sionskiye Protokoly. 'Doloy Zlo!',* Paris, 1927.

German and Austrian:

Gottfried zur Beek (pseudonym of Ludwig Müller, also called Müller von Hausen), *Die Geheimnisse der Weisen von Zion*, Charlottenburg, 1919 (really 1920). Six editions in 1920. The Nazi Party acquired rights in this edition in 1929. A shortened version had run to fifteen editions by 1933 and twenty-two editions by 1938.

T. Fritsch, *Die zionistischen Protokolle*, Leipzig, 1920. This version had reached its 13th edition by 1933.

E. von Engelhardt, *Jüdische Weltmachtpläne*, Leipzig, 1936.

Die Protokolle der Weisen von Zion. Das Welteroberungsprogram der Juden, published by Erste Wiener Vereins-Buchdruckerei, Vienna, 1940.

British:

The Jewish Peril: Protocols of the Learned Elders of Zion, London, 1920.

Protocols of the Learned Elders of Zion. Translated by V. E. Marsden and published by The Britons Publishing Society, London, 1921. Since reissued under various titles. Currently called *World Conquest through World Government. The Protocols of the Learned Elders of Zion*. Marsden's translation was also published in various parts of the British Empire; in 1934, for instance, a New Zealand edition was published.

In Lesley Fry's *Waters Flowing Eastwards*, Paris, 1921 and 1933. Marsden's translation. The book was published by the *Revue internationale des sociétés secrètes*.

American:

The Protocols and World Revolution; including a translation and analysis of the 'Protocols of the Meetings of the Zionist Men of Wisdom', Boston, 1920. A 'White' Russian production.

'Praemonitus Praemunitus', The Protocols of the Wise Men of Zion, New York, 1920.

The Protocols of the Meetings of the Learned Elders of Zion, Chicago, 1934. The Patriotic Publishing Co. Marsden's translation.

The Protocols of the Learned Elders of Zion, Chicago, 1935. Right Cause Publishing Co.

French:

'Protocols'. Procès-verbaux de réunions secrètes des Sages d'Israël, Paris, 1920. Published by La Vieille France.

Jouin, Mgr E. *Le Péril judéo-maçonnique*, Vol. I, *Les 'Protocols' des Sages de Sion*, Paris, 1920. The Nilus version, though not translated directly from the Russian. Vol. IV, *Les 'Protocols' de 1901 de G. Butmi*, Paris, 1922. Cheap editions of both these volumes were published by the *Revue internationale des sociétés secrètes*, including a new edition of the Nilus version in 1934.

R. Lambelin, *'Protocols des Sages de Sion*, Paris, 1921. Translated from Nilus. Frequently reissued down to 1939.

U. Gohier, *Les Protocoles des Sages d'Israël*, Paris, 1924, 1925.

In Lesley Fry's *Le Retour des flots vers l'Orient. Le Juif notre maître*, Paris, 1931. Published by the *Revue internationale des sociétés secrètes*.

W. Creutz, *Les Protocoles des Sages de Sion*, Paris, 1934.

Le Complot Juif. Les Protocoles des Sages de Sion, Paris, n.d. Published by the Rassemblement Anti-Juif de France (Darquier de Pellepoix), *c.* 1938.

Polish:

Baczność!! Przeczytaj i daj innym. Rok 1897–1920 (Protokóły posiedzeń Mędrców Sjonu), Warsaw, *c.* 1920.

Protokóły Mędrców Sjonu, Warsaw, 1923. Published by the organization Rozwój.

'Wróg przed bramą!', Bydgoszcz, 1930.

Protokóły Mędrców Sjonu, Warsaw, etc., 1934.

Polish emigration:

'Mane, Tekel, Upharsin!' . . . *Księga Straszliwa Protokóły Obrad Mędrców Sjonu*, New York, 1920.

Rumanian:

Ion I. Moţa, *Protocoalele Înţeleptilor Şionului*, Orăştie, 1923.

Politica Secretă a Ovreilor Pentu Cucerirea Lumii Creştine, Bucharest, 1934.

Hungarian:

Sion Bölcseinek Jegyzökönyvei. A Bolsevikiek Bibliája, Budapest, 1922.

Czech:

Ze Shromažděni Sionských Mudrců, Prague, 1927.

Yugoslav:

M. Tomič, *Prave Osnove ili Protokoli Sionskih Mudraca*, Split-Šibernik, 1929.

Patrioticus, *Ko potkopava čovečanstvo*, Belgrade, 1934.

Protokoli skupova sionskih mudraca, Belgrade, 1939.

Jedan vazan dokument, a Croatian translation published in Berlin, 1936.

Greek:

A Greek translation of the *Protocols* was published by 'Drasis' in 1928 and reprinted several times, for instance in 1934 and 1940.

Italian:

L'Internazionale Ebraica. Protocoli dei 'Savi Anziani' di Sion, Rome, 1921. Published by *La Vita Italiana* (G. Preziosi). New editions, 1937 and 1938.

Spanish:

Los Protocols. Los Sabios de Sion. El Gobierno Mundial Invisible. El Programa Judío para Subyugar al Mundo. Published by Fritsch's 'Hammer' publishing house, Leipzig, 1930.

Alfonso Jaraix (trans), *Los Poderes ocultos de España*, Barcelona, 1932.

Protocols de los Jefes de Israel, Madrid, 1932.

Duke de la Victoria (trans), *Los Protocolos de los Sabios de Sion*, (5th edition), Madrid, 1935. Translated from Lambelin.

L'Internationale Hebraica: Los 'Protocolos' de los Sabios Ancianos de Sion, Rome, 1938. Translated from the Italian edition of 1937–38.

Portuguese:

F. P. de Sequeira (ed.), *Os Planos da Autocracia Judaica*, Porto, n.d.

Dutch:

J. Nijsse, *De Protocollen van de Wijzen van Sion*, with introduction by P. Molenbroek, Amsterdam, n.d. The same version, with Molenbroek's introduction, appeared over the names of other editors. The 7th edition was published in Amsterdam in 1943.

Flemish:

L. Welter, *Het Jodendom ontmaskerd als de Aartsvijand*, Courtrai–Brussels–Paris, 1937.

Walloon:

A. Robert, *Les Protocols des Sages de Sion*, Brussels, 1935.

Swedish:

Förlåten Faller . . . Det Tillkommende Världssjälvhärskardömet Enligt 'Sions Vises Hemliga Protokoll', Helsingfors, 1919.

Israels Vises Hemliga Protokoll. Judarnas Strategiska Plan att Med Lögn och List Erövra Världsherraväldet, Stockholm, 1934.

Norwegian:

Den nye verdenskeiser; en sensasjonell avsløring av de hemmelige trådtrekkere bak verdens-politikkens kulisser, Oslo, 1944.

Latvian:

Zianas protokoli . . . No kreewu walodas tulkojis un isdewis J.O., Riga, 1923.

Brazilian:

G. Barroso, *Os Protocolos dos Sábios de Sião,* São Paulo, 1936–37.
T. Moreiro, *Os Protocolos dos Sábios de Sião. O Dominio do Mundo pelos Judeus,* Rio de Janeiro, n.d.

The above list covers only the period to 1945, and is not complete even for that period. For instance, the Arabic editions, of which there were several already in the 1920s and 1930s, are not included; and there were certainly more South American editions than the two Brazilian ones listed here.

Index